THE PERFORMANCE APPARATUS

The Performance Apparatus

ON IDEOLOGICAL PRODUCTION OF BEHAVIORS

Branislav Jakovljević

UNIVERSITY OF MICHIGAN PRESS

Ann Arbor

For questions or permissions, please contact um.press.perms@umich.edu
Published in the United States of America by the
University of Michigan Press
First published April 2025

A CIP catalog record for this book is available from the British Library.

Library of Congress Cataloging-in-Publication Data

Names: Jakovljević, Branislav, author.
Title: The performance apparatus : on ideological production of behaviors / Branislav Jakovljević.
Description: Ann Arbor : University of Michigan Press, [2025] | Includes bibliographical references and index.
Identifiers: LCCN 2024054849 (print) | LCCN 2024054850 (ebook) | ISBN 9780472077335 (hardcover) | ISBN 9780472057337 (paperback) | ISBN 9780472904945 (ebook other)
Subjects: LCSH: Performance art—Philosophy. | Ideology.
Classification: LCC NX456.5.P38 J345 2025 (print) | LCC NX456.5.P38 (ebook) | DDC 702.81—dc23/eng/20241230
LC record available at https://lccn.loc.gov/2024054849
LC ebook record available at https://lccn.loc.gov/2024054850

DOI: https://doi.org/10.3998/mpub.12877381

The University of Michigan Press's open access publishing program is made possible thanks to additional funding from the University of Michigan Office of the Provost and the generous support of contributing libraries.

Authorized Representative: Easy Access System Europe, Mustamäe tee 50, 10621 Tallinn, Estonia, gpsr.requests@easproject.com

In loving memory of my mother,
Branislava

Contents

Digital materials related to this title can be found on the Fulcrum platform via the following citable URL: https://doi.org/10.3998/mpub.12877381

Figures

Acknowledgments

Coming of age in the waning days of Yugoslavia, the mystery of ideology was front and center of innumerable ruminations, conversations, and debates I had with myself and others. It informed much of my writing before and after I moved to the United States. In 2016, at the time when *Alienation Effects* was published, I included a unit on the performance apparatus in my graduate seminar on Dramaturgy at Stanford. I am grateful to my students for bearing with my half-baked thoughts on that subject. In 2018, Christopher Fynsk and Nemanja Mitrović invited me to offer a seminar at European Graduate School the following summer, and I suggested the performance apparatus as my topic. Even though the seminar did not pan out, the preparation for it and visit to Saas-Fee were pleasurable and productive. I am grateful to Fynsk and Mitrović, who invited me to revisit that idea in a Zoom lecture I gave at EGS in the summer of 2020. The previous fall, at the invitation of Dejan Sretenović, I gave a talk at the Museum of Contemporary Art in Belgrade on the same topic. That marked the formal beginning of the process of writing this book. My thanks go to Dejan for his invitation and hospitality. While not much carried over from those lectures into the final version of the book, they provided necessary impetus for my work on *The Performance Apparatus*. I am very grateful to scholars and artists who shared their work with me and who gave me permission to reproduce their creations in this book: Richard Schechner, Matthew Goulish, Nicholas Lowe, Carole Condé, Clive Robertson, and especially Michael Corris and Cassils. Marita Loosen-Fox, thank you for the permission to reproduce Terry Fox's work, and Claire Burrus, thank you for your help with the images related to the inimitable Philippe Thomas. I offer my special thanks to Joe "Jio" Williams and Joe Caposella, formerly of the Advanced Workers, for their time, help, and information about Amiri Baraka's band, and to Komozi Woodard for information and comradery. I am especially grateful to Ljubiša Matić for his careful reading and indexing the book. I first approached Routledge with the idea for this book, and I appreciate Laura Hussey's understanding when I decided to go back to my old publisher, the University of Michigan Press. While that delayed the process of publication, it was a great privilege and pleasure to work, one last time, with the irreplaceable LeAnn Fields, who retired after seeing this project through. I made final revisions of the full manuscript in the summer of 2023, as I was taking care of my ailing mother Branislava, to whose loving memory I dedicate this book.

Preface to Post-ideology

When it comes to ideology, a preface always already seems to be an epilogue. That is, at least, the place that the prominent conservative sociologist Daniel Bell assigned to it in his influential book *The End of Ideology* (1960). This 474-page volume concludes with a brief chapter, "The End of Ideology in the West: An Epilogue," in which Bell offers his vision of ideology and explains the causes of its demise. According to him, what was "exhausted" by the end of the 1950s was total, or rather "totalitarian," ideology, which he identifies with the other side in the Cold War. He argues that in the USSR, this ideology was defeated, on the one hand, by the disasters of Stalinism (the Moscow trials 1936–1938, the Gulag, systems of oppression in Eastern Europe) and, on the other, by the "modifications of capitalism" and "the rise of the Welfare State" in the West as a viable alternative to the workers' state ([1960] 1962:402). Therefore, totalitarian ideology did not end in a total explosion—say, nuclear warfare—but in a total meltdown: "Ideology, which by its nature is an all-or-none affair . . . is intellectually devitalized, and few issues can be formulated any more, intellectually, in ideological terms" (404). Bell adopted the idea of "total ideology" from Hungarian-German sociologist Karl Mannheim's 1929 book *Ideology and Utopia*.

Mannheim's suggestion that the radical right and left "total ideologies" of fascism and communism marked the first half of the twentieth century also comes very conveniently to Bell. He builds on Mannheim's idea by asserting that only one of them survived the Second World War: while the left "total ideology" triumphed in the Soviet-dominated bloc, in the liberal West ideology has been reduced to the level of particularism, which easily becomes transmuted into a personal caprice of sorts. Bell's ideological triumphalism sets the paradigm for cultural, economic, and finally military triumphalism of Western liberalism over its communist rivals. While borrowing freely from Mannheim, only by scrupulously avoiding one of his key insights could Bell make his case for the end of ideology. Said insight is the paradox so prominent that it was named after Mannheim. In Paul Ricoeur's pithy summary, this paradox concerns the "nonapplicability of ideology to itself" (1986:8). He puts it succinctly and plainly: "If everything that we say is bias, if everything that we say represents interests that we don't know, how can we have a theory of ideology which is not itself ideological?" (8). However, there is more to proclaiming the end of ideology than betraying the lack of awareness of one's own ideological position. Why rush to issue a death sentence to ideology? And why is it important to go back to that question now, in the first decades of the twenty-first century?

In his explanation of the concept of ideology, Bell starts from the basics, suggesting that in its "popular usage," this "vague term . . . seems to denote a world-view or belief-system or creeds held by a social group about social arrangements in society, which is morally justified as being right" (399). He clarifies this convoluted explanation by means of examples: one can use this poignant term to refer to the "ideology of the small businessman," but also to "liberalism" or "fascism" (399). With an evident understanding that it would be too simplistic to define it as a system of beliefs, or a generalized idea of sorts, Bell ventures his concise definition of ideology as "the conversion of ideas into social levers" (400). He came to this understanding by resorting to Marx's notion of false consciousness, or "false ideas," which, according to him, "mask particular interests" (396). Bell explains that "what people say they believe cannot always be taken at face value, and one must search for the structure of interests beneath the ideas; one looks not at the *content* of ideas, but their *function*" (397). All of this takes Bell's investigation to its central insight about "particular" and "total" conceptions of ideology. The first conception pertains to values and convictions that "individuals" will "link" with their interests (economic, ethnic, political, etc.). In short, here ideology seems to be a question of personal choice and convenience. The second conception is an "all-inclusive system of comprehensive reality" or "a set of beliefs, infused with passion," that "seeks to transform the whole of a way of life" (400). Clearly, for Bell the most important aspect of ideology is its emotional content: it is not only a set of beliefs but a conviction that is, as he repeatedly points out, held passionately. "Particular" ideologies don't ask anyone to die for them; the "total" ones do. In order to discredit the other side in the sharply escalating Cold War, which culminated in the Cuban Revolution as Bell was working on articles collected in his book, he doesn't hesitate to reach for the most sensationalistic examples of ideologically inspired political violence. His coup de grâce is a turn-of-the-twentieth-century anarchist bombing of a packed café in Paris, followed by its stylish and rather nihilistic defense from the pen of the poet and literary critic Laurent Tailhade: "What do a few human lives matter; it was a *beau geste*" (406). Bell explains that what he means by "the end of ideology" is that the days of this kind of impassioned violence are over.

The End of Ideology was not the earliest, and certainly not the last, verdict of that kind. If ideology appears capable of surviving a thousand deaths, that is because it is most effective when it is playing dead. An ideology that allows cracks to appear on its surface is already finished and done for. Slavoj Žižek was able to formulate his signal insights about ideology already in his first book published in English, *The Sublime Object of Ideology* (1989), in part because he was writing from the firsthand experience of observing the ideological crisis that had been gripping Yugoslavia for over a decade. Here is a particularly effective elaboration of the Mannheim paradox:

> Ideology is not simply a "false consciousness," an illusory representation of reality, it is rather this reality itself which is already to be conceived as "ideological"—*"ideological" is a social reality whose very existence implies the non-knowledge of its participants as to its essence*—that is, the social effectivity, the very reproduction of which implies that the individuals "do not know what they are doing." (1989:21)

One of the most reliable ways of discerning the trajectory of ideology through its circuitous game of hide-and-seek, at least in the last century, is by focusing on its critiques. The interest in ideology on the European left was spurred by the publication, in 1932, of *The German Ideology*, a manuscript that Karl Marx and Friedrich Engels completed in 1846. Mannheim's *Ideology and Utopia* and the writings of Walter Benjamin and Bertolt Brecht, both of whom found an effective way of addressing ideology by looking at it askance, came during that period. In one of telling ironies that surround Bell's book, the decade and a half that followed his declaration of its end saw some of the most incisive critiques of ideology to date.[1] The most productive period came toward the end of the 1960s. While Theodor Adorno, Max Horkheimer, and Herbert Marcuse engaged in a sustained critique of ideology throughout the 1960s, their younger colleague from the Frankfurt school, Jürgen Habermas, published in the fateful year 1968 the essay "Technology and Science as 'Ideology,'" which became one of the most enduring statements of *Ideologiekritik*. It was followed two years later by Louis Althusser's landmark article "Ideology and Ideological State Apparatuses (Notes towards an Investigation)."

Throughout the 1970s, fresh theoretical insights from the Frankfurt school critique of ideology and from French Marxist structuralism, as well as the practice of liberation movements in what is today referred to as the Global South, generated vigorous inquiries into the nature of ideology, its strategies and operations. This flurry of activity seemed to abate in the following decade, only to stage a big comeback around the end of the Cold War. This resurgence of theoretical activity concerning ideology is probably best exemplified by the almost simultaneous appearance in print of two scholarly trilogies: in 1990, British literary scholar Terry Eagleton published his *The Ideology of the Aesthetic*, followed by *Ideology: An Introduction* (1991) and the edited volume *Ideology* (1994). In a strikingly similar pattern, Žižek's above-mentioned *Sublime Object of Ideology* (1989) preceded his *Tarrying with the Negative: Kant, Hegel, and the Critique of Ideology* (1993) and the book he edited titled *Mapping Ideology* (1994). While in the 1990s these critical engagements with ideology informed many of the film and literary studies in American academia, this wave started to recede in the first decades of the twentieth-first century. Recently, ideology came into focus again in unexpected places, such as the work of one of the most renowned economists of our time, Thomas Piketty, who in his book *Capital and Ideology* (2019) explores ideological justifications of the regimes of extreme inequality under which most of the humanity lives today. This ebb and flow in scholarly interest in ideology is ideological in its own right. While taking Althusser as my point of departure, in this book I am not calling for a revival and (yet another) reassessment of his theory of ideological state apparatuses, but for a renewed and sustained critical attention to ideology from the point of view of performance.

Performance is, of course, a vague term, and it can refer to many different kinds of activity. Slightly paraphrasing Thomas Elsaesser's quip about cinema, we can say that performance comes in many live practices, only some of which belong to the theater.[2] Within the realm of aesthetic performance (differentiated from managerial, labor, sports, religious, civic, etc. performances) performance art aspired to remove bodily practices from mediating frameworks used in traditional performing arts in the West, such as theater, opera, and ballet. In this book, I am focusing on new live art practices that emerged in the late 1960s and 1970s, only to enter the art industry's mainstream in the 2010s. This broad range of practices has been summarily classified as "performance art." It is not by sheer chance that its rise overlapped with the emergence of the theory of ideological apparatuses. The basic premise of this book is that, while structuralist Marxism engaged ideology discursively, performance art did that through its practices. A certain visceral awareness of ideology and its operations has informed the praxis of performance artists from the moment of its inception until the present. In that sense, this book explores a particular trajectory within the history of performance art. Still, *The Performance Apparatus* is not a survey of the critiques of ideology in performance art, nor is it an "and" book: performance and ideology, apparatus and performance, et cetera. Rather, in it I explore a number of instances in which performance art offered its own contributions to critique of ideology. My work on this book has also been motivated by the recognition that the engagement of performance art with ideology has remained insufficiently theorized. Performance and other new live art practices called for new methodologies and theoretical frameworks, which coalesced in the new scholarly field of performance studies. Unlike in film studies, in which apparatus theory was one of the driving forces in the 1970s and beyond, it never became the part of the theoretical arsenal of performance studies. The initial impulse behind this book was a simple question: How did that come to pass? Does performance, as distinct from traditional theater, have its apparatus? If so, what constitutes it? What are its basic properties and operations? If not, how can it sustain itself as an art form?

The End of Ideology, or more precisely, the conditions of its production, can offer insights that help us start answering these questions. What Bell's hyperbolic estimation of ideological affect conceals is the material existence of ideology that undergirds the production of that very assessment as purportedly *un*ideological. Upon closer inspection, it becomes abundantly clear that his argument is steeped in hypocrisies and contradictions that were not only of an intellectual, but primarily of a material, nature. These contradictions can be glimpsed from the information consigned to the margins of the book, such as the brief "Acknowledgment" placed at its very end, right before the endnotes. Here we learn that Bell wrote most of the articles collected in the book while he was the labor editor for *Fortune*, a magazine that caters to and promotes big business. While that was how he supported himself, most of the articles compiled in the book were first published in the journals *Commentary* and *Encounter*, edited by the scion of neoconservatives, Irving Kristol. Some essays in which he happened to discuss ideology were presented at conferences sponsored by the Congress for Cultural Freedom, which Bell describes as "an international organization of intellectuals opposed to totalitarianism" (408). This fine organization, which was, as it turned out, funded by the CIA, also supported Bell's research year in Paris, where he had elucidating conversations about ideology with the likes of Michael Polanyi, one of the earliest theoretical advocates of capitalism's neoliberal turn (408).[3] All of this is to say that, from the historical perspective, *The End of Ideology* was a clear indication that "in the West" ideology was never doing better.

Clearly, Bell's eulogy to ideology was supported by business magazines, neocon journals, conferences, research trips, government agencies . . . All of the producers and instruments of non-knowledge that Bell *acknowledges* as his funding sources are what, by the end of the decade in which *The End of Ideology* was published, Althusser would define as ideological state apparatuses. If ideology's material existence is lodged in social apparatuses, then to deny ideology is to deny these very apparatuses. This denial, that is to say, this non-knowledge, is not specific to Bell and his generation of neocons. It affects, to a larger or smaller degree, all areas of society at all times. Importantly, apparatus is not only a machinery, a tool, a piece of equipment, a device, an institution (a film projector and screen, theatrical stage, the internet, prison, hospital) but a coherent set of social formations and practices. Since the mid-twentieth century, recognition of these formations and practices at the very center of Western industrialized societies has been, paradoxically, much more consistent than the engagement with ideology. In other words, while the apparatus (*appareil*) is central to Althusser's theorization of ideology, in the final phase of his work Michel Foucault seems intent to excise the apparatus (*dispositif*) from the domain of ideology and locate it in the power-knowledge nexus. And it goes from there: Pierre Bourdieu substitutes habitus for ideology, and Gilles Deleuze and Félix Guattari deny its existence altogether. My contention is that, while theoretically possible, the removal of the apparatus from its proper ideological environment makes it vulnerable to seemingly ideology-neutral speculations (consider, for example, Luc Boltanski and Ève Chiapello's idea of the "artistic critique" in *The New Spirit of Capitalism*). If the apparatus is always already ideological, then the task of this book is to discern which aspect of ideological apparatuses performance art was able to expose more effectively than any other aesthetic (and non-aesthetic) live practice. In other words, the main question of this book concerns the fabric of the performance apparatus. What is it? How is it different from other ideological state apparatuses, including those it borders and with which it is often conflated, such as theater and cinema?

I will return one last time to Daniel Bell, whose interests and activities in, as it were, the aftermath of ideology can provide some clues about possible responses to these questions. For example, he begins the "Acknowledgment" note by disclosing that he worked on *The End of Ideology* while he was a fellow at the Center for Advanced Study in the Behavioral Sciences at Stanford University. That seems to have been a strategic choice. By mid-decade, he was appointed the chair of the American Academy's Commission on the Year 2000. Only two years later, in 1967, the reports from this commission were published in the Academy's journal *Daedalus*, followed by the book *Toward the Year 2000: Work in Progress*, which Bell also edited. In this substantial volume, there is almost no mention of ideology. Clearly, the scientists, sociologists, and political strategists who participated in the commission did not think it would play a significant role in Western societies at the beginning of the twenty-first century. Instead, in their forecasting of the future, they deem much more important technology, informatics, urbanism, education, biology, communication, and even religion and mysticism. It is consistent with the commission chairman's interests from the beginning of the decade that behavior and behaviorism appear as a consistent theme that weaves its way through papers and reports assembled in this volume. For example, to the implicit question about the possibility of "deliberate efforts to control human behavior and modify personality," the neuroscientist Gardner C. Quarton responded with a resounding and well-substantiated yes. Even more significantly, behavior figures prominently in Herman Kahn and Anthony J. Wiener's report "The Next Thirty-Three Years: A Framework for Speculation," positioned immediately after Chairman Bell's introduction and the transcript of the commission's first working session. Kahn and Wiener open their report with the list "One Hundred Innovations Likely in the Next Thirty-Three Years" ([1967] 1969:79–84). It's a mishmash of speculative predictions: some surprisingly accurate (from "more reliable and longer range weather forecasting" to "widespread use of computers" and "personal 'pagers'" and even "two-way pocket phones"), others the fruit of fanciful imagination ("programmed dreams," "artificial moons and other methods of lighting large areas at night"). Significantly, almost twenty, or a full one-fifth, of their predictions concern modifications and control of human behavior. In this extrapolation of the present into the future, behavior appears as a material akin to "super-performance fabrics" and "new improved plants and animals." This "material" is what the performance apparatus is made of.

ONE | Performance (Art) Apparatus

PERILS OF THE PERFORMATIVE

During a relatively short time span, from the time I started working on this book in the fall of 2019, and its final revisions, which I am completing in early 2024, one of the key terms in the field of performance studies went through a dramatic semantic change. The case in point is, of course, "performative." Prior to the summer of 2020 and the uprisings that followed the brutal police murder of Black American George Floyd, it was a relatively obscure academic term used primarily in philosophy, performance, literary, and gender studies. In these fields, performativity has been used largely in the sense that the English philosopher J. L. Austin recognized in those utterances that can acquire the social significance of an act. Over the summer of 2020, this word went viral, and at the same time changed its meaning to designate the complete opposite: an empty statement devoid of any commitment to action. This new notion of performativity was used on the internet and social media to condemn those false and hollow statements by individuals and companies declaring their support for the Black Lives Matter movement, while doing nothing to help its efforts.

The wide usage of the adjective "performative" came hand in hand with the complete reversal of its meaning. The rate and depth of this change was remarkable. According to the internet portal Mashable, the social media usage of this word went from some 15,000 daily mentions prior to the murder of George Floyd on 25 May 2020, to 550,000 mentions during the height of the protests that summer (Levine Beckman 2020). This change registered on Merriam-Webster online dictionary, where searches of the word "performative" went up 1,240 percent in June of that year to rise to top 4 percent of looked-up terms (Levine Beckman 2020). By the end of 2020, the dictionary did its due diligence and added another section to its definition of "performative." While the first two referred to uses that came from the Austinian linguistics ("being or relating to an expression that serves to effect a transaction or that constitutes the performance of the specified act by virtue of its utterance") and theater studies ("relating to or marked by public, often artistic performance"), the third one, marked as "disapproving," recorded its new, colloquial, usage: "made or done for show (as to bolster one's own image or make a positive impression on others)". Even if popularity comes at a cost, this seems too steep.

The field responded to this sea change in the usage of one of its key concepts quickly and comprehensively. By the spring of 2021 (light speed in the world of academic publishing), the *Journal of Dramatic Theory and Criticism* had published a special section, "#PerformativeX," that explored this transformation. Michelle Liu Carriger, the editor of the special section, captured the prevalent sentiment in the field: "For the performance and dramatic theory community, inculcated with Austinian and Butlerian notions of 'performativity' and 'performative' utterance (or action) *that actually accomplishes something,* the social media performative's negative valence of 'merely for show' or empty narcissism still delivers a shock" (2021:9). The special section, consisting of full-length articles and forum-like selection of short contributions, offered measured and inclusive redress to this shock. "#PerformativeX" provided a number of important clarifications. One of them is that the field had been dealing, both in practice and in scholarship, with the breach between felicitous acts and empty statements for some time, and that this rupture has been the site of intense interrogation, (self-)criticism, and even soul-searching. Another, no less important, is that the fields of theater and performance studies never settled for one and definitive meaning of the word "performative." In his helpful survey of its usages in these fields, Aaron C. Thomas shows that, since the late 1960s, scholars have been using this term to designate both statements and actions that imply certain social efficacy and events that are akin to theater performance. A number of contributors to "#PerformativeX" show how these two senses of the word have been used interchangeably, and that there have been very few efforts to establish rigorous boundaries between them. Indeed, performance studies is not formal logic, and its creative effusion comes, in great part, from ideas and practices that are ambiguous, debatable, and open to interpretation. Still, there is a sense that this lack of rigor contributed to the undermining of one sense of performative by another, and that the deployment of this term to serve different research agendas contributed to its all too easy conflation with "theatrical," which was often seen as its exact opposite.

Before it went viral on social media, performativity appears to have been the victim of its own success on a much smaller scale, within the fields of theater and performance studies. While it emerged from the narrow confines of the philosophy of ordinary language, the theory of performativity became an interdisciplinary concept, and it gained in complexity and richness from its passage through different schools of thought. As a quick reminder, in his Harvard lectures (1955), Austin set out to "isolate" and analyze specific speech forms, utterances he described as "performatives," explaining that this name is derived from "perform" to indicate "that the issuing of the utterance is the performing of an action" (1962:6). What distinguished these from other, descriptive, statements he called "constatives" is their self-referentiality: they don't describe anything and cannot be submitted to the test of truth and falsity. Instead, the evaluative measure that applies to them is not their aesthetic form, but their success in accomplishing actions. Here, beauty or form is not relevant: words either work or not. Because of all of this, the aesthetic uses of language fall outside the sphere of Austin's considerations. Infamously, in his lectures he asserted that "a performative utterance will, for example, be *in a peculiar way* hollow or void if said by an actor on the stage, or if introduced in a poem, or spoken in a soliloquy" (22). It is not surprising, then, that much of the scholarship on Austin's performative speech act theory came from literary studies and was engaged in exploring the ambiguities surrounding those performative utterances he deems "*parasitic*" upon their "normal use," which puts them into category of "*etiolations* of language" (22).[1] "Etiolated" is, in a way, even more disparaging than "parasitic": even a parasite can flourish, while an etiolated plant, grown away from the sun, sprouts weak stems and pale leaves. Kept out of the light of institutional efficiency, language does not so much die as fade and wither.[2]

Initially, Judith Butler approached performativity not from the perspective of literature, but of psychoanalysis. This allowed her to explore the relationship between language and bodily acts in a way that is mutually constitutive. So in *Gender Trouble* (1990) she writes that, if gender is the "disciplinary production of the figures of fantasy through the play of presence and absence on the body's surface," then its "acts, gestures, enactments, generally construed, are *performative* in the sense that the essence of identity that they otherwise purport to express are *fabrications* manufactured and sustained through corporeal signs and other discursive means" ([1990] 2006:185). If gender is constituted linguistically, then the forms of speech that Butler explores are taking place not only in the field of literature but also in the broader arena of ideological formations such as law, politics, the military, et cetera. It was perhaps Butler's signal contribution to bring into considerations of performativity the work of French Marxist philosopher Louis Althusser, who in his landmark essay "Ideology and

Ideological State Apparatuses" (1970) argued that the subject is constituted through the process of interpellation. His example, like Austin's, is as simple as it is effective: when hailed (interpellated) by a policeman in the street, an individual will recognize him- or herself by responding to that call of authority. Butler observes that this call and response does not denote a relation of repression or control of the individual by state power. Instead, the call is "a crucial part of the juridical and social *formation* of the subject. The call is formative, if not *per*formative, precisely because it initiates the individual into the subjected status of the subject" (1993:122). As evidenced in Liu Carriger's almost routine mention of her name next to Austin's, Butler's elaboration in *Bodies That Matter* of performative acts as constitutive of gender identity had a transformative impact on understanding and uses of performativity in theater and performance studies scholarship.

Both the complexity of the term and its geographic expansion have been closely tied to the disciplinary history of performance studies. It is not necessary to rehearse that history in great detail here. Having emerged in the 1970s, the institutionalization of this nascent discipline began with the formation of the first performance studies departments at New York University and Northwestern University in the early 1980s. As evidenced in the research that Jon McKenzie, Heike Roms, and C.J. Wan-ling Wee did in the early 2000s, barely twenty years later performance studies was on its way toward global proliferation. If in 2006 McKenzie raised a pointed question, "Is performance studies imperialist?," the book *Contesting Performance: Global Sites of Research* that came a few years later as a result of the research project McKenzie, Roms, and Wee undertook offers an affirmative answer, with the provision that in its march across cultures, performance studies went through a number of transformations. While McKenzie's question implies that, together with some of its research methods, performance studies took over from anthropology the burden of its complicity in the imperialist project, the edited volume seems to suggest that in the process of its global expansion, the concept of performance has been exposed to a series of vigorous contestations. The editors' central research question is clear and pointed: "How . . . have scholars around the world variously incorporated, appropriated, decentered, and challenged a 'Western' or 'US' model of performance research for their own ends, anti-imperialist and otherwise?" (2010:3). One of the most influential appropriations of performativity belongs to that latter rubric of "otherwise."

In her 2004 book *Ästhetik des Performativen* (translated four years later as *The Transformative Power of Performance: A New Aesthetics*), German theater scholar Erika Fischer-Lichte took performativity as the starting point of an entirely new aesthetics. Having in her previous work on theater semiotics and German theater history written extensively on theatricality, Fischer-Lichte argued that performativity is a critical concept capable of addressing new and increasingly globalized performance practices. Whereas other scholars who engaged with this subject maintained a distinction between performance and performativity, Fischer-Lichte seemed intent to set up a certain correspondence between the two. Having established that in the mid-twentieth century Western art went through a "performative turn," which ultimately resulted in the emergence of the new genre of performance art, Fischer-Lichte posits performativity as a theoretical counterpart to performance. It turns out that this operation requires a great deal of distortion and revision of some of the foundational premises of performativity associated with speech act theory.

For example, Fischer-Lichte flattens the distinctions that Austin established between constative and performative utterances, making them almost interchangeable. She suggests that, in his Harvard lectures, the philosopher "collapsed the binary opposition between constantives and performatives," replacing them with categories of locutionary, illocutionary and perlocutionary utterances ([2004] 2008:25). Further, she maintains that, in doing so, "he demonstrated that speaking always involves acting, which in turn makes it possible for statements to actually succeed or fail and for performative utterances to be true or false" (25). This turns out to be not just a benign mistake but a massive distortion. It was necessary for Fischer-Lichte to turn Austin against himself in order to be able to aestheticize that which, in his speech act theory, resists aesthetization in the first place: the performative utterance. Similarly, she bends Butler's ideas to unrecognizability in order to force them into her schema of an "aesthetic of the performative." This is her laconic summation of Butler's idea of gender performativity:

> Individuals alone do not control the conditions for the process of embodiment; they are not free to choose what possibilities to embody, or which identity to adopt. Neither are they wholly determined by society. While society might attempt to enforce the embodiment of certain possibilities by punishing deviation, it cannot generally prevent individuals from pursuing them. Evidently, Butler's concept of performative acts reaffirms their capacity to collapse dichotomies, already recognized by Austin. (27)

According to Fischer-Lichte, the "crucial difference" between Austin and Butler is in the latter's attention to "phenomenal conditions of embodiment" evidenced in her references to Maurice Merleau-Ponty (27). What about the other philosophers she engages with in her work, from Plato to Luce Irigaray and, especially, Louis Althusser?

Flatly ignoring Butler's warning that "theatricality need not be conflated with self-display or self-creation," Fischer-Lichte suggests that the feminist philosopher "likens the conditions for embodiment to those of theatrical performance" (1993:232; 2008:28). In her project of aestheticizing the performative, Fischer-Lichte approaches her sources like Play-Doh to be molded to her needs. So she decides that, in order to meet her standards for performativity as a theoretical foil to performance art, "Butler's definition requires further modification" (28). Hence, she subjects the citational nature of performatives as an instance of discursive formation of identity to another laconic dismissal: "We are not dealing with the repetition that is central to Butler's argument since every act occurred only once in the course of Abramović's performance"—that is, *Lips of Thomas*, which Fischer-Lichte uses as the key example in the project of "developing an aesthetics of the performative out of the notion of performance" (28, 36). Fischer-Lichte effectively "modifies" Butler's idea of performativity into nonexistence, brushing aside her explicit warnings, such as this one in the concluding pages of *Bodies That Matter*:

> In no sense can it be concluded that the part of gender that is performed is therefore the "truth" of gender; performance as a bounded "act" is distinguished from performativity insofar as the latter consists in a reiteration of norms which precede, constrain, and exceed the performer and in that sense cannot be taken as the fabrication of the performer's "will" or "choice"; further, what is "performed" works to conceal, if not disavow, what remains opaque, unconscious, unperformable. The reduction of performativity to performance would be a mistake. (234)

Fischer-Lichte does exactly that, and turns the notion of *performativity* into *performability*, an idea that is clearly outside of Butler's sphere of theoretical concerns. What was at its center was the role of performativity in the constitution of relations of power, and, specifically, those power relations at play in the instance of ideological interpellation. Butler's final say on that matter builds on Althusser's idea of the "bad subject," the one who does not respond to the interpellation of power in a way prescribed by convention:

> Performativity describes this relation of being implicated in that which one opposes, this turning of power against itself to produce alternative modalities of power, to establish a kind of political contestation that is not a "pure" opposition, a "transcendence" of contemporary relations of power, but a difficult labor of forging future from resources inevitably impure. (241)

This and many other of Butler's assertions about performativity owe much to Althusser's idea of ideological interpellation. In *Excitable Speech: A Politics of the Performative* (1997), she directly addresses the relation between Austin and Althusser. There, she acknowledges that, "at first," it seems that Austin's idea of performative speech act is "incompatible" with Althusserian interpellation. Here the key difference is in the position of the subject: whereas for the former, the subject precedes the performative utterance, for the latter, interpellation as the performative call "brings the subject into existence" (1997a:24). What brings these two theories together is their shared recognition of the situation of performative utterance as ritual and ceremonial in nature. Butler notes that "Austin's view that the illocutionary speech act is conditioned by its conventional, that is 'ritual' or 'ceremonial' dimension, finds a counterpart in Althusser's insistence that ideology has a 'ritual' form, and that ritual constitutes 'the material existence of an ideological apparatus'" (25). In her essay on Althusser in *The Psychic Life of Power*, she elaborates on the relationship of the ideological ritual and performance understood in the sense of the constitution of the self: "The notion of the ritual suggests that it is performed, and that in the repetition of performance a belief is spawned, which is then incorporated into the performance in its subsequent operations" (1997b:119). Butler's theorization of performativity has been significant for performance studies, and for reasons that Fischer-Lichte clearly did not fathom.[3]

One of those reasons, which went largely unacknowledged, was that through Butler's work, performance theory experienced a belated encounter with the theory of ideological apparatuses. Fischer-Lichte's excision of Althusser from Butler's theory of performativity, which was the central operation in her project of the aestheticization of the performative, might have been the first step in reducing this form of performativity to mere show. This removal amounts to stripping performance of its apparatus, that dynamo which endows it with its specific force. This dynamism calls for a closer consideration of the relationship between Althusser's idea of ideological apparatus and aesthetic performances in theater and, especially, outside of it.

IDEOLOGICAL APPARATUS

First published in the June 1970 issue of the journal *La pensée*, Louis Althusser's essay "Ideology and Ideological State Apparatuses (Notes towards an Investigation)" was arguably the most notable contribution to the critique of ideology since the publication of Marx and Engels's *The German Ideology*, which they wrote in 1846, but which remained unpublished until 1932. The first work that deploys the method of historical materialism and places front and center some of the major themes of classical Marxism—the division of labor, world proletariat, communist revolution, et cetera—*The German Ideology* offers a sharp critique of Ludwig Feuerbach and the young Hegelians. Here Marx takes explicit aim at the idea of "consciousness" that the Hegelian left adopted uncritically from the classical German idealism.[4] He makes a pointed argument that consciousness is not an autonomous agent in history. Instead, it is a "social product" made by "real living individuals" ([1932] 1998:50, 41). Marx's argument that "the material production of life" constitutes "the real basis of ideology" offers the outline of the topological schema of the bourgeois society he made in his later writings, which became most recognizable in the sharp division between "infrastructure" and "superstructure" (67). Ideology is not a Hegelian world spirit, but a "representation" of real conditions of production. This representation is not, and can never be, accurate: it always distorts the real material conditions of the society. This distortion is all but random, as it is the ruling class that imposes its ideas on the rest of the society. The "means of mental production" are contingent on the "means of material production" (64). In one densely packed paragraph of the first part of *The German Ideology*, Marx offers a series of assertions that deeply influenced the analyses on ideology in orthodox Marxist circles in the first decades after its publication.

First, the hierarchical relation between material existence and consciousness is the obverse of the order presented by idealist philosophy: "The production of ideas, of conceptions, of consciousness, is at first directly interwoven with the material activity and the material intercourse of men, the language of real life. Conceiving, thinking, the mental intercourse of men, appear at this stage as the direct efflux of their material behaviour" (42). Further, the subject of consciousness is not the absolute spirit or any other superhuman entity, but "real living individuals": "Men are the producers of their conceptions, ideas, etc.—real, active men, as they are conditioned by a definite development of their productive forces and of the intercourse corresponding to these, up to its furthest forms. Consciousness can never be anything else than conscious existence, and the existence of men is their actual life-process" (42). Finally, we get to the heart of the matter: "If in all ideology men and their circumstances appear upside-down as in a *camera obscura*, this phenomenon arises just as much from their historical life-process as the inversion of objects on the retina does from their physical life-process" (42). Insofar as ideology is representation of real material conditions of existence that is not only distorted but inverse and essentially false, the *camera obscura* stands out as the most primitive model of ideological apparatus. It is a mechanism that stands between, and keeps apart, the real basis of material production and its portrayal by the dominant classes, and in accordance with their specific interests. Althusser's key intervention is not, as some hold, to present "science" as the opposite of ideology, but to show the functioning of the topology of infra- and superstructure of bourgeois society.[5] Ideological apparatuses are zones of powerful feedback loops between these seemingly discrete zones of capitalist state.

There is a clear path in Althusser's writings from the ideological "regions" he spoke about in the 1960s to the "apparatuses" of the 1970s. In a number of texts he published early in the intervening decade, he presented ideology as a social "bond" connecting unreflected activities in which individuals participate in a "passive and mechanical manner, through reflexes, judgements, attitudes" ([1965] 1990:24). Ideology seen as a bond that provides social cohesion is consistent with the foundational ideas of structuralism, such as Ferdinand de Saussure's language (*langue*) in linguistics and Claude Lévi-Strauss's system of kinship in anthropology: it is a general and abstract structure that regulates, but is not reducible to, its specific manifestations (speech/parole in the former, or various forms of families and societies in the latter). Althusser's early theorization of ideology resonates with Barthes's analysis of myth as "a second-order semiological system" ([1957] 1972). In this complex system of reflections and transfers, the sign in the "first-order" system becomes "a mere signifier" in the second (114). Echoing Marx's notion of ideology, Barthes wrote that "*myth hides nothing*: its function is to distort, not to make disappear" (121). Furthermore, through language, the myth actively engages in the constitution of the subject. For Barthes, "mythical speech" has a "buttonholing character": "It is *I* whom it has come to seek" (124). It is easy to recognize in Althusser's writings of the early 1970s the resonances with Barthes's "interpellant speech" with which the ideology "hails" the subject: "At the moment of reaching me, it suspends itself, turns away and assumes the look of generality" (125). This "frozen speech" leaves the subject in the state of "*arrest*, in both the psychical and the legal sense of the term" (125). Barthes goes on to describe the situation of hailing in the military, which Althusser adapts in his example of ideological interpellation.

If there is a significant change in Althusser's conceptualization of ideology between his early and later work, it is in the increased specificity of his thinking about the coexistence of abstract structures and their material manifestations. This transformation came as a result of vigorous debates within the French Left, initiated in part by the ascendance of structuralism and by the activities of social movements that culminated in the student protests in May 1968 and the general strike of French workers the following month. Henri Lefebvre, one of the most perceptive Marxist critics of structuralism, approached the discrepancy between the expansiveness of structure and vagueness of its concrete manifestations in his article "Althusser's Paradoxes" ("Les paradoxes d'Althusser"), published in July 1969, in which he suggested that the "lived" always exceeds any kind of "system." He argued that the function and purpose of ideology is not only to "hold the significance of social relations in the unthought and the unspoken, that is in the 'unconscious,' but also and above all to create that kind of non-understanding" ([1969] 1971:386). It is precisely in this shift away from the systemic that Lefebvre opens up an area that would be of signal importance for Althusser's sharpening of his analytical rigor in dealing with the material workings of ideology. Namely, Lefebvre points out that

> social space is not mental space only; it is also a space of behavior. Ideologies have that conscious or unconscious goal: to induce a certain behavior, to "motivate" it, to arouse and perpetuate certain behaviors. They are invested in a certain practice. By becoming attitudes and behaviors, the temporality of thought becomes a social space. If there is a "system" and systematization, effective coherence and cohesion, they can be sooner recognized and analyzed on the level of (practical) behaviors than on the level of representations. (386)[6]

Human behaviors constitute a social field that is far too important to be allowed to self-regulate, and at the same time too expansive to be managed by any one "thinking individual," or even a class, or the state (387). Lefebvre proposes that only an apparatus (*appareil*) can possess the "traits and qualities" requisite for this task. So, here it is: "the apparatus" as "an *institution* that is hard to analyze because it has a certain capacity to deny and even penetrate analysis" (387). It is only the apparatus that can take possession of, master, and manage on a day-to-day basis that vast social space which consists of behaviors. When Althusser turned from his 1960s writings about "ideological regions" and "ideological tendencies" to apparatuses in the 1970s, he, unlike Lefebvre, didn't conceive of them as discrete entities removed from the state but as its constitutive parts.

In his essay, Althusser concisely and rather laconically defines ideological state apparatuses, or ISAs, as "a certain number of realities which present themselves to the immediate observer in the form of distinct and specialized institutions," such as religion, education, family, law, and, last but not least, culture (137). They stand in addition to, and not as a replacement for, the repressive state apparatus (RSA)—the army, the police, the courts, and the prison system (136). He uses the same term as Lefebvre, *appareil,* which in French has a range of meanings: from that of a device or a mechanism, to those that appear in similar form in English, such as "appliance," or identical, as "apparel." In addition to technological gears such as equipment for recording (camera) and fishing, in this context it is important to recognize that in French this word is used to depict more abstract mechanisms in law and politics: *appareil de la justice* and *l'appareil stalinien* (judicial apparatus and Stalinist party apparatus, respectively). Only on a couple of occasions in the course of the essay does Althusser use *dispositif,* a word that holds a similar meaning as *appareil* but has a narrower palette of uses, limited to those related to mechanism or device. In his *Lectures on Ideology and Utopia,* delivered in English at the University of Chicago, Paul Ricoeur notes that "in French *dispositive* expresses the idea of something which functions by itself, something that shapes behavior" ([1975] 1986:146). In the mid-1970s, Michel Foucault started his elaboration of the idea of the *dispositif* in his analytics of power, which was distinct from Althusser's use of *appareil* in his critique of ideology.[7]

In his analysis of ISAs, Althusser advances two theses, both of which appear simple and to the point. The first reads: "Ideology represents the imaginary relationship of individuals to their real conditions of existence" (153). The second is even more concise: "Ideology has a material existence" (155). Ideology is irreducible to Marx's metaphor of the contraption that simply reverses images, and ISAs are there to confirm that position: "Ideology always exists in an apparatus, and its practice, or practices. Its existence is material" (156). Curiously, Althusser repeats the first thesis twice: first as the title of a section in his essay, and then as a thesis within that same section. In the title, he places the word "representation" in inverted commas. If he doesn't explain his reasons for doing that, it is most likely because he had already addressed this textual strategy in his essay "On the Materialistic Dialectic," published in his 1965 book, *For Marx*. Here he addresses specifically his use of inverted commas and capitalization in an attempt to assign different shades of meaning to the word "theory," explaining that "'theory' (in inverted commas)" designates "the determinate *theoretical system* of a real science" such as "the theory of universal attraction, wave mechanics" or "the '*theory*' of historical materialism" (1969:168).[8] If we follow Althusser, we can read the inverted commas as a way of removing ambiguity from the word *représentation*, which in French can denote both a mental image and a visual display (such as theatrical performance). Here the representation is not just a mental image, as that inverted picture in the camera obscura, but primarily the "real" and "determinate" system of representation, which is to say the apparatus itself.

Althusser suggests that "reality" and "determination" in a concrete representation, such as we find in theater, don't stop at the proscenium, wings, or even auditorium, but extend to social relations enacted in any performances, anywhere. He refers to these instances, significantly, as his "little theoretical theater" and even describes them as "mise-en-scène." He famously cites everyday situations of call and response, such as a our reaction when, upon hearing a knock on our door, we ask the visitor to identify himself and are satisfied with a simple response, "It's me" (161);[9] or when an individual gets stopped in his tracks upon hearing a police officer's voice calling, "Hey, you there" (163). These scenarios are marked by a certain asymmetry, which can be social in the case of police officer hailing a passerby, or entirely situational, as in the case of the door knock. However ordinary they may appear, these scenes belong to an unusual theater. They are deprived of any drama or uncertainty: the emphasis is on the response rather than on the call, on the self-identification of the individual as the addressee of the call. As Althusser points out, this self-recognition is almost unmistakable, and it works "nine of ten times" (163). Not only is there no suspense, but the duration is reduced to such a degree that this "drama" almost completely abolishes chronology and brings about a breakdown of temporal order. That is because "the existence of ideology and the hailing or interpellation of individuals as subjects are one and the same thing" (163). The subject is a constitutive category of ideology only insofar as it is itself constituted by ideology. It is hard to find a human action that is not integrated into ideological apparatuses.[10]

There is nothing extraordinary about the everyday workings of ideology. Its effectiveness comes precisely from its ordinariness, or, as Althusser puts it, "primary obviousness" (161): a greeting, a call in the street, "a small mass in a small church, a funeral, a minor match at a sports' club, a school day, a political party meeting, etc." (158). There they are, the ISAs: religion, culture, sports, education, politics. These apparatuses don't reside in pews and altars, bleachers and goalposts, desks and chalkboards, daises and auditoriums, but in actions necessary for their enactment. These actions are repeatable and routinized: "They are rituals of ideological recognition" and in order to become so, they are "practical" (161). The effectiveness of ideological apparatuses comes from their integration into the fabric of everyday life, not from their technological or organizational complexity. Althusser therefore puts lived and embodied materiality front and center:

> The ideology of ideology thus recognizes, despite its imaginary distortion, that the "ideas" of a human subject exist in his actions, and if that is not the case, it lends him other ideas corresponding to the actions (however perverse) that he does perform. This ideology talks of actions: I shall talk of actions inserted into *practices. And* I shall point out that these practices are governed by the *rituals* in which these practices are inscribed, within the *material existence of an ideological apparatus*. (158)

Althusser presents a vision of ideology in which ideas don't precede or follow actions, but are lodged within them. The subject exists in her actions: this coincidence of actor and action precludes any idea of a noninterpellated subject, or a subject who is not ideologically constituted. At the same time, it removes the possibility of a position outside of ideology and its apparatuses. In Warren Montag's apt formulation, "Ideology is immanent in its apparatuses and their practices" and "has no existence apart from these apparatuses and is entirely coincident with them" (1995:63). While ideology is lodged in the commonplace, in run-of-the-mill actions that every individual performs without giving them much thought, there are instances when the smooth operation of ideological apparatuses skips a beat, even for a brief moment.

Untenability of a subject position outside of ideology was observed already in the 1930s by Hungarian-German sociologist Karl Mannheim, who lent his name to the paradox of ideology. According to Paul Ricoeur, at the center of this paradox is the question, "Are not in fact all theoretical claims in some sense ideological?" And further, "If everything is ideological, then how is it possible to have other than an ideological discourse on ideology?" (1986:157). As a result, Mannheim enlarges "the Marxist concept of ideology to the point where it becomes a perplexing concept, because it includes the one who asserts it" (159). Althusser extends this paradox to ideological apparatuses. In the absence of an outside that would provide a critical vantage point, he suggests that only a theory that is at the same time a political practice can offer a critique of ideology from within the ideology itself. In his ISA essay he expressed his deep conviction that it is from "within the ideology [that] we have to outline a discourse which tries to break with ideology" (1971 162). He started searching for an answer to the question of the method of fulfilling this impossible task in his writings of the early 1960s. In his essay "On the Materialist Dialectic," Althusser argued that dialectical materialism constitutes a science that, as such, can provide a perspective on ideology. According to this argument, dialectical materialism is not only a science but also a method. A practice has to have an object, or a "raw material." It always exists in relation to that object, and Althusser speaks of it in terms of labor: it is "any process of *transformation* of a determinate given raw material into a determinate *product*, a transformation effected by a determinate human labour, using determinate means (of 'production')" ([1965] 1969:166). "Production" in inverted commas, which designate its nonmetaphorical material status, pertains to theatrical performance no less than to industrial manufacturing.

PICCOLO TEATRO TEORICO

Althusser's work on ideological apparatuses was shaped not only by his reading of Marx's *Capital* and his analysis of Lenin's philosophy but also by his viewing experiences in theater and by his high regard for certain theater practitioners, most notably for Bertolt Brecht. In an unfinished text from the late 1960s, he went as far as to say that "Marx's philosophical revolution is in every respect similar to Brecht's theatrical revolution—it is a revolution in philosophical *practice*" (2003:139). There seems no doubt for Althusser that, if there is a theoretical practice in theater, it is exemplified by Brecht.[11]

As early as 1930, the German playwright and director opened his "Notes on the Opera *Rise and Fall of the City of Mahagonny*" with a critique of theater as one of the "apparatuses" operative in the bourgeois state that "as it were," "perpetuate their views incognito" (2015:61). The anonymity of apparatuses such as the opera, the theater, and the press comes from the naturalization and normalization of these media within the bourgeois society. The position and impact of these apparatuses as the pillars of a modern capitalist state is beyond question. By presenting its views "incognito," an apparatus wants to say that its presentation of social reality is indistinguishable from that reality. So, by concealing their socially produced nature, apparatuses are perpetuating the social relations that made them possible in the first place. "Society uses such apparatuses to assimilate whatever it needs to reproduce itself. And so the only 'innovations' that can get through are those that lead to the renovation—but not the transformation—of existing society, no matter whether this form of society is good or bad" (62). It is analyses such as this one that motivated Althusser to place Brecht high on the list of thinkers and artists who developed a rigorous understanding of the workings of apparatuses and their function in modern capitalist societies.[12]

Althusser's investment in Brecht and more broadly in theater received the attention it deserves only recently. In his essay "Althusser's Dramaturgy and the Critique of Ideology," which leads off an entire issue of the journal *differences* dedicated to Althusser and theater, Étienne Balibar suggests that the French philosopher used theater as one of his "theoretical *dispositifs* or *machines*" in order to resolve "theoretical problems and identify the objects of theory" (2015:2). Balibar notes the prominence of theater not only in Althusser's discussions of Brecht but also in some of his major works, such as "Ideology and Ideological State Apparatuses" (1970). Specifically, he invites Althusser's readers to take "entirely seriously" his "seemingly marginal remark" about seeing the police calling out to a passerby as his "little theoretical theater" and pursue it "as an investigation of its structure and prerequisites" (2015:12). According to Balibar, that "structure" has a "machinic" nature, a view suggested by his focus on its spatial properties, which routinely upstage and minimize performances that take place within that very arena. According to Balibar, for Althusser theater is a philosophical metaphor, or a pure "analyzer" (2). He suggests that in Brecht's theory of *Verfremdungseffekt* as well as in his practice, Althusser finds the much-needed "machinery . . . that has the power to *attract* the spectator's consciousness into its fictitious 'world' only to *eject* her *into the real world* after it has been dislocated by the machine itself" (7); or, in the same vein, "The machine that makes the ideological fabric visible is also the one that forces a subject called a spectator to break with its conformism, if only momentarily or instantaneously" (8). This emphasis on the theatrical machine (*appareil*) persists in other essays in this volume, which brings together a number of philosophers and social critics while notably omitting scholars of theater and performance.[13] What gets lost in these discussions of Althusser's "theatrical machines" is the proper acknowledgment of the attention he paid to performance in his writings on theater, specifically in his essay "The 'Piccolo Teatro': Bertolazzi and Brecht: Notes on a Materialist Theater," which, as Balibar observed, stands at the "geometrical and theoretical center" of his book *For Marx* (3).

In this chapter, Althusser engages in a detailed analysis of Giorgio Strehler's production of a late nineteenth-century melodrama by Italian playwright Carlo Bertolazzi, *El nost Milan* (Our Milan). It was performed in Paris in 1962 under the auspices of the Théâtre des Nations, the same festival that showcased Brecht's productions from the Berliner Ensemble in the 1950s. Strehler was widely considered one of the great transmitters of Brecht's legacy, a view espoused by Brecht himself.[14] What sets Althusser's analysis of this production apart from other theoretical interpretations of the "new" theater coming from Central and Eastern Europe was that, rather than focusing on narrative, semiotic, or visual aspects of theatrical productions, as did Roland Barthes and Bernard Dort, he engaged in a temporal analysis of Strehler's production.[15] According to him, it was not the scenic machinery that made this theater "materialist," but its organization and utilization of scenic time.

Althusser recognizes two temporal orders in this melodrama set at the fringes of the industrial city of Milan, where poor families, members of the lumpen-proletariat, workers, and criminals cross each other's paths: on the one hand, there is a "long, slowly passing, empty time" that belongs to the mass of the unemployed, who seem frozen in a state of perpetual waiting; and a "lightning-short, full time" of the four main characters of the play (1969:134). The former is a "wretched time . . . in which nothing happens, a time without hope or future, a time in which even the past is fixed in repetition, . . . a stationary time in which nothing resembling History can yet happen, an empty time" (136). The latter temporal order, animated by rapid outbursts of conflict between the main characters, is "an articulated time, a 'dramatic' time, . . . a time moved from within by an irresistible force, producing its own content . . . : a dialectical time *par excellence*" (137). Althusser observes that the "empty time" becomes perceptible through the gradual uncluttering of stage space. The first act, crowded by the imagery of a busy street, gives way in the second act to a cheap soup kitchen, which he describes as an "empty, closed cube" (136). The mise-en-scène in the second act seems aimed to enlarge the physical proportions of the stage: "The bareness of this immense field created by the parallel tables against the interminable background of the wall . . . constitutes an unbearably austere and yawning location" (136). The clearing up of stage space unleashes a propulsive force in performance. Action bursts out to shatter the slow pace of "chronological time" and creates a "dialectical time" that "is acted marginally, so to speak, in the wings, somewhere in one corner of the stage and at the ends of acts" (138). The materialism of this theater is not constituted through the deployment of stage machinery, but conversely, by its gradual removal to the point where the onus of action is solely resting on actors. The dialectical time explodes from the corners of the stage, and it is the actors, not props and furniture, lights and pulleys, that ignite that explosion.

Both here and in his unfinished essay on Brecht, Althusser emphasizes to the highest possible degree the importance of "displacement" as both a staging and an acting technique: "It is in relation to himself that the actor has to keep a 'distance': the actor has to displace himself in relation to the ideology of the actor" (2003:144). He argues that Brecht's theatrical practice involved an expansive understanding of the mise-en-scène, "which itself depends on a certain conception of the subject, which depends on a certain relation of stage to public, of actors to public, which depends on a certain conception of the relation of theater to history, which depends on a certain philosophical conception" (139). So, when in another of his "seemingly marginal remarks" Althusser brings up "'actors' in [the] *mise en scène* of interpellation," it is the reference to the actor that should stand out, and not the idea of theatrical machine (1971:165).[16] That makes it all the more astonishing how little impact his writings on Brecht, Strehler, and ideological apparatuses had on the theater practice and the theory of theater and performance in the 1970s. Despite his vigorous and explicit engagement with theatrical performance, Althusser's idea of the apparatus reached performance studies in a belated and derivative way.

THEATRICAL MACHINE

The simultaneous emergence of the theory of ideological apparatuses and performance art in the transition between the 1960s and the 1970s was not a mere coincidence. As I hope to demonstrate in this book, Marxist theory and performance art were two avenues of registering a massive shift in attitudes toward human behavior in advanced industrial societies. If Althusser's "science" of historical materialism critiqued ideological apparatuses discursively, performance art did it practically. Its practice amounts to a powerful theorization of behavior. Paradoxically, apparatus theory occupies a fleeting and marginal place in the history of performance art's theorizations. The reason for that may be in performance art's excessive confidence in its critical engagement with ideological sources of behavior, which carried over to scholarship of performance. Still, it is important to recognize those rare scholars who recognized the common objectives of apparatus theory and performance art.

Feminist performance scholar Jill Dolan's first book, *The Feminist Spectator as Critic* (1988), was, to the best of my knowledge, the earliest and most prominent attempt to introduce the discussion of ideological apparatuses into performance studies. In the final chapter of her book, entitled "Materialist Feminism: Apparatus-Based Theory and Practice," Dolan argues that "materialist feminist," as opposed to cultural feminist, "theory and practice" develops "strategies of intervention that trace the subject positions *sculpted by the lights of the theatrical apparatus*" (101; emphasis added). She takes as the main representatives of this new performance and theater practice writers and directors such as Hélène Cixous and Simone Benmussa, as well as Theodora Skipitares, whose "performance work with puppets and sculpture also foregrounds the apparatus by absenting the live bodies from representation" (101). The "apparatus theory" that Dolan puts to work in this chapter does not refer directly to Althusser's writings on ideological apparatuses or Brecht's theater. In her book, Dolan demonstrated that feminist performance criticism is a critical intervention that can offer a powerful analysis both of the Western realist cannon and of some major figures in experimental theater and performance of the 1970s, such as director Richard Foreman. In her critique of Foreman's theater, she relies on the feminist film theorist Teresa de Lauretis, who in her influential works *Alice Doesn't: Feminism, Semiotics, Cinema* (1984) and *Technologies of Gender: Essays on Theory, Film, and Fiction* (1987) takes the cinematic apparatus as the operative model for the workings of the "technology" of gender. Althusser's ISA essay was one of the foundational texts in the formation of the "apparatus theory" in film studies, which in the course of the 1970s became one of the cornerstones for theoretical consideration of the very nature of the film medium. This kind of rigorous engagement with the idea of the apparatus has been absent from performance studies.[17] So, when the apparatus entered, briefly, American theater and performance scholarship, it came as a critical term developed in relation to a medium that is defined by its dependence on technology.

The "apparatus theory" Dolan invokes in her essay has its sources in Jean Louis Baudry's article "Ideological Effects of the Basic Cinematographic Apparatus" (1970), in which he establishes a direct link between techniques of seeing in Renaissance perspective painting and those in film. Of course, film is not reducible to trompe l'oeil, and Baudry calls attention to the "cinematic specificity" of the film apparatus. What brings together cinema and single-point perspective is the strict alignment of the subject with the field of frontal representation. While the psychic process of identification and projection is not technological in its own right, the cinematic apparatus provides a mechanism that epitomizes and generalizes that process. Cinema is not only a technological assemblage consisting of a camera, a projector, and a screen: it is a "special technical arrangement" of these elements that enables it to effectively play the role of "an ideological machine" ([1970] 1980:32). The cinema "constitutes the 'subject' by the illusory delimitation of a central location—whether this be that of a god or of any other substitute. It is an apparatus destined to obtain a precise ideological effect, necessary for the dominant ideology: creating a fantasmatization of the subject, it collaborates with a marked efficacy in the maintenance of idealism" (34). Baudry clearly followed Althusser when in his article he used *appareil* in his discussion of the cinematic apparatus.[18] In a follow-up to his first apparatus article published five years later, he used French *dispositif,* which can be seen as an attempt to restrict the meaning of the central concept of his inquiry to cinematic mechanism.[19] Still, it is important for this discussion that both *appareil* and *dispositif* fit into a larger representational schema that Baudry first addressed in his rarely discussed article "Writing, Fiction, Ideology" ("Écriture, fiction, idéologie"), published in *Tel Quel* in the fall of 1967.[20] The schema of the "metaphysical model of knowledge" he outlines here is strikingly similar to the cinematic apparatus: it resembles "a cone whose base, being a limited surface, is the only visible part. All points of the base are linked to a single, invisible dot, the summit, located at infinity. Infinity is exterior to the surface, beyond it. Each point of the limited surface is the projection of the vertex onto this base" (1967:21). So, if the filmic apparatus is prefigured by perspective painting in the Renaissance and Plato's allegory of the cave in ancient Greece, that is because all of them are operational within a transcendental form of knowledge, which is ideological in its nature. From its initial elaboration to the debates it initiated, including critiques from feminist and psychoanalytic perspectives, the cinematic apparatus theory has been one of the main animating forces of cinema studies.[21] Some of these debates entered theater studies and touched the (then) emergent performance studies, most significantly in instances in which it aligned with psychoanalytic and feminist approaches to performance art.

The apparatus theory that developed in film studies focuses on the specific effects of cinema in the formation of modern subjectivity. *The Cinematic Apparatus,* which de Lauretis and Stephen Heath coedited, offers a veritable summary of the film apparatus theory at the end of the 1970s. This collection opens with Heath's view of the cinematic apparatus as "a relation between the technical and the social," and closes with de Lauretis's affirmation of cinema as a "social technology" that is "at once a material apparatus and a signifying practice in which the subject is implicated, constructed, but not exhausted" (1980:6, 188).[22] In her subsequent publications, she located the possibility of a feminist critique of apparatuses, in this case the apparatus of cinema, precisely in this non-coincidence between the social technology and the subject. Taking cinema, narrative, and theory as primary sites for her examination of the workings of the social technology of gender, de Lauretis argues that even the most advanced theoretical propositions, such as Althusser's critique of ideology and Jacques Lacan's psychoanalytic theory, cannot overcome their position within the culture of patriarchy. The clear case in point is their construction of femininity as "purely a representation, a positionality within the phallic model of desire and signification," and not a "quality or a property of women. Which all amounts to saying that woman, *as* subject of desire or of signification, is unrepresentable; or, better, that in the phallic order of patriarchal culture and in its theory, woman is unrepresentable except as representation" (1987:20). (As we have seen, Dolan extends this analysis to what she calls "cultural feminist performance.") In his return to the apparatus theory, Elsaesser observed that "for feminists, the materialism claimed for the dispositif was itself a cover-up, a disavowal of an even more fundamental lack, an absence, which the invocation of the apparatus . . . was designed to disguise or to compensate" (2016:111). Peggy Phelan's critique of this aspect of the apparatus as it operates in performance art helped performance studies enter, so to speak, its theoretical maturity.[23]

A certain tendency toward identification of the performance apparatus with theatrical machinery was predominant in performance studies of the 1980s. Herbert Blau offers an excellent example of this approach in his 1983 essay "Ideology and Performance." His detailed elaboration of this kind of the ideological apparatus of theatrical performance merits extensive citation:

> Everything in the structural reality of theatre practice is ideological: not only the price of a ticket, but the conditions of the gathering, the attitude of the ushers, the advertising or want of it in the playbill, program notes or their absence (on the grounds, as they say, that a play ought to speak for itself, which it never does because it ideologically can't), air conditioning in the theatre, the size of the candy bar, one's distance from the stage, the thickness of the makeup or its absence, whether or not you can see the actors sweat, the division of

> the audience from the stage (a figure of almost all ideological controversy, up to religious wars) or the opening of the stage into a thrust or its displacement into an "environment" which, however scattered, may be ideologically the same old frame, since ideology is a *mental* set; the weight of the platforms that a specific quantity of labor has to move, even with two boards and a passion (in educational theatre often more than two boards, an ideological ripoff on false educational grounds), the use and exposure of lights, and the weird phenomenon of the curtain (emblematic fabric of an irreparable division, *now you see it now you don't*, even when the curtain is not there), the teasers and tormentors which conceal and seduce and suggest an invisible truth in their very names; the casting of a play, the number and gender of the actors, the very presence of an actor who, before he disrupted the ideological unity of the Chorus, once *was not* there, nor the second actor, nor the third, with their agonistic voices and competing claims, the space of desire in which a performance occurs, from the brightness of the landscape on a wine-dark sea to the motes in around a single lightbulb on a stanchion when the rehearsal ends, signifying as it were the forlorn economy of the theatre we commonly know, with its producers and agents and reviewers and, with more or less paranoia, the authority of the director who sets the rehearsal schedule within that mental set in ideologically determined time; and of course the choice of the text to be performed, and to which we once thought we could be faithful, and so on through the habits and reflexes of our theatre, its ideological consciousness, or absence, *in* the interpretation which, as we're told, is ideological to its core, by the nature of interpretation itself, even if there is no text—to which we *could* be faithful if the text, unlike the teasers, were *transparent* and not concealing *something else*. (1983:447)

Placing on the same footing a candy bar, a ticket stub, and a performer's body, which would be otherwise scandalous, is here justified by a certain leveling that takes place with the technological and social apparatus of presentational theater.[24] Once it emerged as an art form in its own right, performance art chipped away, blow by blow, technological layers from the apparatus that has been considered indispensable for the live arts in the West. It seemed to achieve that "equipment free" access to "immediate reality" which represented, in Walter Benjamin memorable phrase, "the Blue Flower in the land of technology" ([1935] 2002:115).[25] So much so that it appeared that it dispensed with the apparatus altogether.

A NONOBJECTIVE PROPERTY

It appears that in his essay on Strehler's production of *El nost Milan*, Althusser does not so much recollect but rather restages the production he had witnessed. Luciano Damiani's stage designs for the second act of Bertolazzi's play show a stage crowded with tables and benches that leave very little free space.[26] It is as if Althusser needed to create that "empty cube" in order to expose the limits of the theatrical apparatus and, at the same time, focus our attention on the actors' performances. In doing this, he was very much in step with the experimental theater tendencies of the mid-twentieth century. The progression from an illusionistic stage cluttered with objects toward a clear stage space outlines a trajectory of theater in Europe and the United States over several decades after the Second World War. And furthermore, this arc of escalating reduction is applicable not only to theater but to visual arts as well.

The publication of "Ideology and Ideological State Apparatuses" came at the moment of an unprecedented convergence of theater and visual arts. The point of their intersection was the body. This focus on the corporeal does not imply an automatic equivalence of these two kinds of performance. Nor does it mean that they construed the body in the same way, or that they were, for that matter, dealing with the same notion of the body. In his discussion of performance and ideology in modern dance, Andrew Hewitt flags a "critical tendency to fetishize the body as the bearer of 'the real'" and its "implicit identification with . . . materiality per se" (2005:7). As he correctly points out, the body is neither a "brute soma" nor a "purely discursive construct" (14). Every cultural practice, or to use Althusser's locution, every ideological apparatus, produces a different idea of the body, and that becomes particularly visible at this intersection of two different trajectories of performance. In a short essay entitled, simply, "Performance" Noël Carroll offers a brief summary of these histories seen in tandem. Carroll uses the term "art performance" to designate live activities that emerged within the framework of fine arts, starting from action painting and moving to Allan Kaprow's Happenings, Jim Dine's "para-paintings," Robert Morris's experiments at Judson Dance Theater to body art of Vito Acconci and Chris Burden, and Adrian Piper's "concept performance" (1986:69). He juxtaposes this sequence with a similar tendency in experimental theater, which he labels "performance art," starting from The Living Theatre's activist and participatory performances, to Joseph Chaikin's "emphasis on craft" in The Open Theater, to The Performance Group's exploration of ritual techniques (73). The bareness of mid-century Brechtian (or for that matter, Beckett's) stage turned out to be not the end, but the starting point, of a tendency to minimize the expressive means based on technology, perhaps best epitomized in Jerzy Grotowski's poor theater and Germano Celant's *arte povera*.

Theater's uncoupling of the actor's body from the theatrical machine can be seen as an expression of a modernist aspiration to undo the layers of history in order to return to an imagined "pure" beginning, to its origin, whether it is the ritual, or the Greeks, or Shakespeare, or one of the many non-Western performance cultures. This essentialist stripping of cultural deposit from the theatrical apparatus creates a space that remains at the disposal of a virtuosic actor. The body conceived in this kind of performance is probably best exemplified in Grotowski's call for an ascetic performer stripped of all trimmings of the spectacle, and at the same time capable of overcoming his own bodily limitations: "The actor is a man who works in public with his own body, offering it publicly. If this body restricts itself to demonstrating what it is—something that an average person can do—then it is not an obedient instrument capable of performing a spiritual act" (1968:33). Obedient to the point of self-renunciation: the body of the actor striving to achieve this aesthetic spirituality of theater "must be freed from all resistance. It must virtually cease to exist" (36). The development of a virtuosic technique that helps the actor overcome herself is inseparable from the mimetic logic of theater. Even when it does away with the conventional dramatic text, conventional seating, light, costumes, et cetera, a theatrical performance preserves some of its basic representational conventions, such the roles that actors play. That is certainly not the case with performance that comes from visual arts.

Casting away the object, the spectacle, and everything that comes with them (starting, in art, from seemingly innocuous things such as the picture frame, then the gallery walls, and then museums, gallerists, and art market; and in theater the auditorium with its hierarchy of seats, then stage scenery, costumes, lights, makeup, etc.), performance seemed to set itself free from its material and institutional constraints. In 1968, the same year in which Althusser started his project of outlining the "general theory" of ideology, Peter Brook published his influential book *The Empty Space*, in which he argued for a theater that finds its meaning in the "moment of performance," leaving "fancy dress" "far behind" (1968:94). The same year, Lucy Lippard and John Chandler observed in "The Dematerialization of Art" that "performance media are becoming a no man's or everyman's land in which visual artists whose styles may be completely at variance can meet and even agree" (2000 [1968]:204). The emergence of body art in the early 1970s brought with it an intense focus on the artist's body as the artistic material.

In a series of articles from the early 1980s, in which she looked back at her performance work from the previous decade, Adrian Piper indicated that this positioning of the body in place of the object constitutes only half of performance practice. In "Performance and the Fetishism of the Art Object" (1982) she called attention to a potential split of live art along the lines of its "dual character" determined by the artist's paradoxical status as a reproducible and commodifiable "object" and a "unique human being" (1996:48, 60). It is precisely in relation to this positioning of the artist as both the producer and the object of production that she addressed the deployment of the body in performance art. Even when she uses her body as performance material, the artist is not reducing herself to a mere object. If "the performer is not merely an instrumental medium through which metaphysical inclusiveness is achieved," that is because she is also a "human subject" (1996:102). Writing almost at the same time, and also looking at his performance work from the 1970s, one of the pioneers of performance art in Yugoslavia and Serbia, Raša Todosijević, used a similar insight to address mimetic and non-mimetic performance. He suggested that, unlike in theater, music, or traditional dance, in performance art, "the artist, using his body and other props, engages in a speech presented in first person. . . . In performance, the artist is the subject; he expresses his own will, his ideas, and spiritual attitudes which are results of his experiences and viewpoints" (1983:60).[27] If in theatrical performance the virtuosic body of the actor aspires toward self-erasure, in performance art the non-virtuosic body of the artist strives toward self-assertion; and if in the former that body is spiritual, in the latter it is confrontational. That provocative nature of performance art is inscribed even in its spatial organization. Todosijević observed that the practitioners of performance art rejected eclecticism of Happenings and their effusiveness, which was reflected in its assimilation of audience into artistic action (57, 60). Instead, they opted for the austere artistic means, presented frontally. This "little theater," theater of a few means, is also theoretical in its attentiveness to the artist as subject and object of performance.

In performance art, the body is positioned at the intersection between the subject and the object of art. This is the body that rejects not only the external elements of the spectacle but also technique as the last vestige of the theatrical apparatus. What emerges from these multiple renunciations is a self-governing body that stands both as the minimal condition of performance art and as the artist's declaration of independence from what are commonly understood as material aspects of social apparatuses and their ideological constrains. The removal of the object from the work of art and its replacement with the body of the subject collapses the "material," the "product," and the "means" of production. The hallmark of performance art is this coincidence of subject and object. It marks the collapse of the ideology of the "theological stage" defined by the relationship of the author's, that is to say creator's, simultaneous absence from and command over the work of art.[28] Performance art doesn't offer a critique of ideology by occupying an imaginary and impossible position outside of it. In the very act of establishing the relation of immanence between the artist and the artwork, performance art engages the defining characteristic of ideological apparatuses. And this is where it powerfully intersects with Althusser's idea of ideological apparatuses.

Althusser was perfectly clear that "the material existence of the ideology in an apparatus and its practices does not have the same modality as the material existence of a paving stone or a rifle" (1971:156). With behavior, it's not just a question of propriety, but quite literally of property. Within a certain ideological framework, to be is to have. Behavior is a special form of property that is inseparable from the body. It is as if the history of the capitalist form of property is inscribed in the history of the English word "behaviour." Its etymological roots are in the half-forgotten word "haviour," originally "aver," which comes from Old French *aveir* and *avoir*, in the sense of "having," "possession," affiliated with English verb "have."[29] By stipulating and standardizing behaviors, ideological apparatuses take possession of bodies through their actions, practices, and gestures. Paradoxically, individuals come into subjecthood at the price of that which is inalienable: the actions and gestures that are inseparable from their bodies. The dis-possession of the subjects' bodies is one of the major effects of ideological apparatuses. If repressive state apparatuses take possession of bodies—those of slaves, soldiers, and inmates—most bluntly and brutally, thus often provoking insubordination, ISAs accomplish that task more efficiently by creating the least amount of resistance.

The labor of performance art, its practice, consists of forging bodily actions consisting of specific movements, gestures, attitudes, sounds, actions, et cetera, and inserting them into behaviors that the society doesn't invite and rarely approves. Importantly, this labor ends up transforming not only the apparatus but also the artist herself. Performance art is an artistic practice based on the premise that, as Piper recognized, the artist is both the subject and the object of representation:

> The performer offers a double enticement not only of insight, realization, grasping the work conceptually, understanding it, getting it

> right, and so on, but also of confirmation by participation, of having the object actively confirm our realization through the conceptually charged pattern of physical responses and interactions by which we mutually chart our relationship. Think of this as transformation qua self-transcendence. (1996:103)

Performance art forged its distinct medium through renunciation of theatrical apparatuses: unlike traditional theater, it doesn't need stage, lights, props, costumes, or any of the elements of the spectacle; unlike classical and modern dance, its practitioners don't need to go through gruesome formal training; and unlike Happenings, it gave up on the eclecticism of means, profusion of effects, and illusion of audience's agency. Setting aside all technological properties of live arts, performance art takes the process of subjectivation as its central and distinguishing feature. If embodiment is to performance art what technology is to cinema, then the relation between the behaved and the social is its defining quality. While never losing their materiality, performances circulate through bodies. This circulation is the condition of possibility of any process of socialization. One of the main insights of performance art is that ideological apparatuses are constituted by, and in turn constitute, behaviors that have the durability of the matter and at the same time the malleability of a socially produced configuration. It would be too reductive to consider performance in terms of the dematerialization of art. Instead, what it does is to rematerialize art, or materialize it differently: the matter of this art does not consist of objects and mechanisms, but of behaviors and actions. This is the matter of the performance apparatus.

On the other hand, the emerging field of performance studies responded to this reliance of artists on their own bodies in creating performance works by fully endorsing it as intrinsically subversive and resistant, even impervious, to the art and culture industries. As a result, the "dematerial" nature of performance art has often led to a certain exceptionalism in its theorizations. Drawing on anthropological theories of Victor Turner, early performance studies scholarship insisted on the liminal (in-between, threshold) position of performance, which was perceived to almost automatically challenge not only the cultural mores, but also the very political economy of capitalist societies. By the early 2000s, Jon McKenzie recognized this (over)valuation of performance as a "liminal norm": "we have come to define the efficacy of performance and of our own research, if not exclusively, then very inclusively, in terms of liminality—that is, a mode of activity whose spatial, temporal, and symbolic 'in-betweenness' allows for social norms to be suspended, challenged, played with, and perhaps even transformed" (2001:50). Only a few years later, Sven Lütticken placed this self-exceptionalism of performance theory in its proper ideological framework. In his article "Progressive Striptease: Performance Ideology Past and Present" he argues that the "new 'progressive' ideologization of performance" combines "the old leftist slogans on dematerialization" and more recent discourses, such as "experience" and "creative" economies and what came to be known as "greenwashing" of corporate practices. In the end, he suggests, performance offers a way of rescuing "capitalism from its own destructive tendencies. Only if it relinquishes producing things can capitalism have a future. Performance art can prepare and instigate this relinquishment." The uncritical assessments of the political potential of performance "turns it into a hypocritical fable—an ideological magic mirror held up to the existing order" (2005:170). In short, according to Lütticken, the ideology of performance consists in its self-perception of being immune to capitalist ideology. His article came in response to the "relational art" of the 1990s, the first successful attempt by the art industry to fully absorb and commodify this art form. Accordingly, he proclaims Tino Sehgal the chief "performance ideologist," and does not spare other prominent artists of the 1990s such as Rirkrit Tiravanija, and theorists of performance such as Kristine Stiles and Peggy Phelan, whose scholarly work has been often used by the art industry to justify its wholesale commodification of this art form.

Little did he know what was coming. In chapter 7, I am addressing the massive integration of performance into the art industry that started only a couple of years later. In the second chapter, I look closely at the relation between behaviorism and art during the 1970s, and the relevance of these performance histories for the critique of the twenty-first-century logic of capitalist production based on the financialization of behavioral surplus. In chapter 3, I engage the political work of Amiri Baraka to explore the seemingly paradoxical idea of an apparatus in search of an ideology. The fourth chapter looks at practices and theories of situation as a way of moving beyond Althusserian idea of the apparatus. Chapters 5 and 6 focus on subjectivation as the central operation of the performance apparatus: in the former, I take the moment of the implosion of the New York branch of Art & Language as one of the rare instances of an attempt to formulate and practice a consistent critique of the apparatus, and in the latter I take the work of the French artist Philippe Thomas as a case study for the transformation of the apparatus under neo-liberal conditions. What all of these stories show, without exception, are the enormous stakes in deploying performance to engage critically ideological apparatuses, including its own, the apparatus of performance.

TWO | The Social Science of Performance

THE ARTIST AS A BEHAVIORIST

In March 1971, a small group of young people dressed in silver space suits with helmets was going door-to-door in two quiet neighborhoods of Nottingham, England. They would jump out of a "silver time machine," ring the doorbell and introduce themselves in this way: "I am the Man From The Twenty-First Century who has come down to earth in 1971 to ascertain your attitudes and perceptions about the Environments you live in" (Willats [1973] 2010:88). The visitors from the twenty-first century made rounds in two carefully selected "environments": a working-class area Hyson Green and a middle-class suburb of Bramcote. This was one of the earliest examples of "behavioral art" projects that the artist Stephen Willats worked on during the 1970s and 1980s. In a brief note about *Man from the Twenty-First Century* he discloses that initially the canvassers did not use any costumes, but that Nottingham residents tended to respond poorly to "art student" types when they showed up at their doorsteps. The number of positive responses to canvassers' visits rose from only 29 percent to 95 percent after they changed into space suits. Willats attributes this significant uptick to the shift in the technique of canvassing, which "wasn't far removed from certain advertising campaigns" that the inhabitants of these neighborhoods "had already encountered" ([1973] 2010:89). Willats dropped the silver space suits and time travel machine (whatever that might have been) from the *Social Resource Project for Tennis Clubs* he conducted the following year, also in Nottingham. He used this project to further develop and refine certain core techniques, such as carefully devised questionnaires, engagement with the "audience" through interviews and handouts, and focus on urban areas with marked social differences. Like Happenings and early performance art, Willats' social science projects relied on liveness and participation. And yet, they never made it into histories of new live art forms of that period, which calls for their closer investigation.

The experiences from Nottingham informed Willats' first fully complete project of this kind, *West London Social Resource Project*, which he and his team of collaborators completed in 1972. The goal of this project was to study social behaviors in several west London neighborhoods, with the goal of offering the residents suggestions for potential changes and improvements. It unfolded in a series of complex and carefully planned phases. First, Willats selected four neighborhoods suitable for the hierarchical "decision role model" he devised for this project. Rather than by wealth, he differentiated between social groups by their decision-making power, giving his schema a distinctly arboreal form: from "Upper Middle Class," which he placed at the top of his "Decision Tree," to "Middle Class," to "Lower Middle Class," and finally to the "Working Class" at the "Machine Base of the Decision Model," which had "limited or non-decision-making" role in society ([1973] 2010:43). Next, he put together a group of "Project Operators" consisting of a photographer, a sociologist, a cybernetician, and a group of three young women he called "West London Super Girls" instrumental in the operative phase of the project, which involved canvassing the residents of communities selected for this project.[1] The third step in the process involved "participant-gathering interviews" in which the canvassers went door-to-door explaining the project and distributing "publicity leaflets," customized for each neighborhood. The residents who agreed to partake in this project were invited to display the leaflets in their street-facing windows, thus communicating their decision to their neighbors and creating a sense of community of participants. This was followed by the second round of door-to-door visits, during which the canvassers distributed "West London Manual," a booklet containing information sheets, maps and diagrams of specific neighborhoods, and questionnaires "designed to extract the mental models participants held about their Environment" (48). The most important was the questionnaire with incomplete cues, which were left for participants to fill out. According to Willats, unlike conventional social surveys "aimed at retrieving information" from residents, this art project was asking them to contribute their ideas about possible alterations to their social environment (48). In the booklet, there was a sheet of carbon paper inserted behind the page containing the questionnaire followed by a blank copy of the same questionnaire, which the canvassers collected in yet another round of visits to project participants. Willats and his team arranged these carbon copies on vertical panels he named "Public Register Boards," which were placed in local libraries. Using the findings form this first round of canvassing, the Panel of Experts wrote its summaries for each neighborhood. Together with statistics from the survey, the summaries were included in another publication, the "Rule Book," which Willats's team distributed to the residents who participated in the project.

This is not where this elaborate procedure ended. There was another publication titled "West London Re-Modelling Book," which included a set of suggestions culled from participants, and another questionnaire, and another carbon copy, and another collection of responses. For this phase in the process, Willats set up four "supervisory organizations" charged with distributing the booklet, collecting completed questionnaires, and putting together Public Register Boards No. 2. Unlike the first set of boards, these panels had ballot boxes attached to them. Participants were invited to fill out "Public Decision Slips" in which they could vote "for their model of preference" and "to adapt, alter or comment on the model they had voted for" (59). Finally, these were collected and published together with the experts' syntheses, and sent back to the participants. It was Willats's hope that this complex set of operations would prompt the participants to reflect on their social behavior and alter both their daily routines and their physical and social surroundings. In his summary of the project, he concluded that, based on the empirical evidence from surveys and questionnaires, it did manage to modify, "considerably in some cases, the participants' perception and understanding of themselves, their Environment and other participants' social groups, perhaps causing restructuring of aspects of their social relationships with one another" (61). The *West London Social Resource Project* was the most elaborate of Willats's social works to date, topped next year with his *Edinburgh Social Model Construction Project*.

Willats presented the documentation from his west London project at an exhibit he organized at the Centre for Behavioral Art (CBA), which he founded and ran in London's Gallery House from May 1972 until July of the following year. He conceived of CBA as a "think tank" dedicated to fostering a dialogue between artists and social scientists working in the fields of cybernetics and behaviorism. He stated as much in the CBA mission statement published in the Gallery House *Newsheet*, where he declared that "its fundamental concern" is "the furtherance of the growing interests in establishing relationships between Art and the Behavioural Sciences" (in Hudek 2018:42). The following spring, he published in *Leonardo*, a journal dedicated to promoting exchanges between art, science, and technology, a short notice that summarizes CBA's purpose and mode of operations:

> The main aim of The Centre for Behavioural Art, London, is the furtherance of the growing interest amongst artists in establishing relationships between art and cybernetics and the behavioural or social sciences. Lectures and seminars are held regularly at the Centre by both artists and scientists. There is an exhibition space to display or document projects developed by members. Papers are published

> and distributed to whole membership free of charge. The annual subscription is 1 pound and cheques should be made payable to S. Willats. (1973:166)

Over sixteen months of its existence, CBA hosted lectures and presentations by artists such as Victor Burgin and scientists such as the computer programmer Stuart Pound, as well as a regular Thursday evening seminars (Irish 2020:203). In 1973, Willats organized the exhibit *The Artist as an Instigator of Changes in Social Cognition and Behaviour,* in which, in addition to the records form *West London Social Resource Project,* he included his project *Visual Meta Language Simulation* (1971–72), a "complex electronic game for two players" he constructed in collaboration with the Motorola Semiconductor Company and the electrical engineer Derek Aulton (Irish 2020:27).

By the time he produced his large-scale "social resource projects" and organized the CBA exhibit, Willats had been engaged in the exploration of behaviorism for a full decade. He encountered cybernetics in a lecture by British polymath and cybernetics pioneer Gordon Pask, who entered this new science through a chance meeting with one of its founders, Norbert Wiener (Pickering 2010:324). Willats's work on cybernetics in the 1960s bears a deep stamp of Pask's approach to this discipline: his interest in its social aspects, the building of machines that train and guide their users, the uses of cybernetics in pedagogy, and the application of cybernetics in arts.[2] In her book *Concerning Stephen Willats and the Social Function of Art,* Sharon Irish writes that Pask belonged to "second-order cybernetics" (2020:3). His cybernetic ideas were idiosyncratic, but he hardly belonged to this school, which went a step further than the first-order cybernetics: if the first generation of cyberneticians, starting in the 1940s, explored behavior of autonomous systems, from organisms to machines, the second generation focused on the ways in which autonomous systems interact with one another (Heylighen and Joslyn 2001:3). By the late 1960s and early 1970s, when the second-order cybernetics emerged with its distinct set of questions and methodologies, Pask's, and by and large Willats's, ideas about cybernetics were well formulated.

In the United States, neo-behaviorism went through its formative period in the 1920s, and during the Second World War it went through a transformative period, together with other social sciences such as anthropology and sociology. The war effort accelerated technological advancements, which depended on breakthroughs in natural sciences and engineering. The dominance of scientism and its emphasis on objective, verifiable, and applicable knowledge was transformative for research that was focusing on social instead of natural phenomena. These new attitudes, as well as the abundant funding from federal agencies and private foundations, led in the 1940s and 1950s to a revolution in behaviorism and the emergence of the new science of cybernetics. In his historical exploration of the early days of cybernetics, Steve Heims suggests that "according to behaviorist tenets, psychology was to resemble physics in methodology" (1991:10). While emotions and other mental events are not readily observable and measurable, behaviors are: "Behaviorism focuses on the relation of an organism's actions to the environment and pays scant attention to internal events" (10). The status of performance in Willats's behavioral art, as in behaviorism in general, is that of a data unit defined by a quantifiable relationship between input to a system and its output. In order to be measurable, these data units have to be discrete and detectable. "Behavior, Purpose, and Teleology," one of the central statements of neo-behavioral revolution, which was at the same time one of the foundational texts of cybernetics, coauthored by Arturo Rosenblueth, Norbert Wiener, and Julian Bigelow, is clear on this point: "The behavioristic approach consists in the examination of the output of the object and of the relations of this output to the input"; therefore it intentionally "omits the specific structure and the intrinsic organization of the object" (1943:1). Together with purposiveness and negative feedback loop, this exclusion of the internal organization of the object of study that came to be known as the "black box" approach was one of the central principles of both neo-behaviorism and cybernetics. As Edward Shanken points out in his long essay about the work of Roy Ascott, an artist and educator engaged in the exploration of the use of cybernetics in art, the methodology of these social sciences functions "by bracketing out or, in cybernetic terms, 'black-boxing' the internal mechanism operating in the organism. In this way, difficult problems (in psychology or engineering) could be simplified by allowing the complex internal mechanism inside the 'box' to remain unexplained" (2003:45). Problem-solving and black-boxing are the two central features of Willats's behavioral art. They define not only his approach to the "social resources" he is exploring but his positioning of art in relation to these resources.

Willats belonged to the generation of British artists who resolutely turned away from object and gallery art in order to explore media previously considered adjacent to art proper, such as art publications, new media, and artistic events placed outside of traditional art institutions. In the early 1960s, he attended Ealing College of Art, where he explored the relationship between visual perception and cognition in his work on expanded sculpture, such as *Variable Shift Machine* (1963), *Shift Boxes Nos 1 and 2* (1964) and the *Visual Automatics* series (1964–65). Toward the end of his stay in Ealing he met Ascott, who later invited him to teach at Ipswich Civic College's School of Art. Ascott was a regular contributor to *Control*, Willats's art magazine he first published in 1965, and has been its publisher and editor ever since. His choice of an art publication as one of his main modes of artistic engagement and his adoption of theoretical sources that come outside of art history are reminiscent of practice and strategies of the British conceptual art collective Art & Language. Since he abandoned painting in 1963, Willats has been looking for an appropriate designation for the artist under new social conditions. Initially, he called himself a "conceptual designer," a title appropriate for the range of activities he undertook in the mid-1960s, such as magazine publication and design of innovative clothing and furniture. He subsequently settled just for "artist."

In the same manner in which Terry Atkinson, Michael Baldwin, and others associated with Art & Language found in the philosophy of Ludwig Wittgenstein and A. J. Ayer ways to transform the relationship between language and art, Willats found in the cybernetics of Wiener and Pask a method of repositioning art, as an autonomous system, within society. His choice of cybernetics as his main theoretical source deeply informed his art practice and his understanding of art's position in modern industrial societies. Willats saw each artwork as a summa of a series of behaviors, from the creative behavior of the artist to the behavior of reception on the part of the audience. Traditional art, or as he puts it, art of the "machine age," segregates these behaviors into a series of discrete units: creative behavior of the artist is confined to the studio, and the outcome of that behavior is contained in an art objects; these objects are enclosed in art galleries and museums, which, on their part, stipulate the passive behavior of the audience. If, as Shanken points out, cybernetics "offered an explanation of phenomena in terms of the exchange of information in systems," then it could help reorient the decision flow in the "systems" of art. One of the most significant ideas that Willats adopted from cybernetics was that of "homeostasis" as a model of "adaptive control" that enables postulating of "self-organising decision-making systems" (2010:23). Homeostasis offers to replace linear, discrete, and hierarchical systems into networked, connected, and collaborative processes. In Willats's social resource projects, art becomes a device for the accomplishing of "social homeostats" by altering the behavior of participants. It leaves the gallery and the studio and becomes engaged in discovering and altering social structures.

Willats's art is behavioral insofar as it affects the conduct of the audience he tries to engage. He writes that the very fact that "artists seek to obtain an audience" suggest that they are "concerned with the affecting of behaviour, if not structuring it" (1969:n.p.). For Willats, any possibility of creation or alteration of behavior is inherently tied to the structure that precedes it. In order to "instigate" change, the artist has to alter the structure of behavior. Even while he talks about the "decay" of "gallery art," Willats takes as his starting point the relationship between artists and their audiences. In his article "The Artist as a Structurist of Behavior," published in the fifth issue of *Control* (1969), Willats asserts that as soon as they confront an audience, artists become concerned with affecting, and structuring their behavior. Encountering art, then, is not about having an aesthetic, affective, or cognitive experience, but about behavioral response to the artwork. By removing the art object from this relationship, the artist directly engages individual and collective behaviors of audience members. These sets of behaviors are the material of artistic production. However, unlike with conventional materials, the artist is not imposing form on them, but discovering their inherent structures in order to shape and transform them. As Willats sees it, the basic problem that the artist encounters "is the structuring of the acquisitional behaviour that the audience would have to undergo in order to obtain the necessary conditions to operate within the restricted behavioural conditions that have been designated for the points of threshold" (1969:n.p.). Here, the "point of threshold" stands for the fundamental relationship between the two "systems," the artist and the recipient of art. In positing this minimal communication unit, Willats comes surprisingly close to Althusser. To be clear, Willats's idea of "social art" was far removed from the New Left of the late 1960s and early 1970s, and as far as I know, in his works he never engages the political ideas of Althusser or of other Marxists, classical or contemporary. Still, his understanding of behavior can help us clarify this concept that is, as we have seen, of central importance for Althusser's theory of ideological apparatuses. At the same time, it shows clearly the distance between artistic projects centered on behavior and Althusser's contemporaneous critique of ideology and its mechanisms for the production of behaviors.

FIGURING IDEOLOGY: THE TOWER AND THE FIELD

Having organized a series of social resource projects, in a text he wrote for the catalog of his exhibition *Life Codes and Behaviour Parameters* in Nottingham's Midland Group Gallery (7–28 February 1976), Willats invokes the very same situation that Althusser placed at the center of his "little theoretical theater." Here, instead of the "point of threshold," Willats talks about a social "parameter" as the "fundamental nodal construct that underlies the behaviour of a system" (1976:3). That "nodal construct" between different members of the system, or individuals, could be a simple everyday occurrence such as a "greeting behavior" (3). The "greeting behavior" is the basic model of any kind of encounter, including the one that takes place between the artist and the audience. Just like the greeting, the work of art is a social model that regulates relationships between individuals: it mediates between the basic "underlying rules" of the society and concrete social situations. Willats suggests that "it is in the form of coded structures of behavior conventions that a social model will be manifest as an operational prescription, different ideologies resulting in distinct coding patterns. The establishment of formal relationships between persons is fundamental to coherency in the fabric of any social organization, regardless of ideology" (6). Here Willats is not invoking Althusser's or even generally the Marxist notion of ideology. In the mid-1970s, his work on social resource projects brought him to a point where he reformulated his theoretical framework, augmenting the notion of "environment" (an urban unit, a neighborhood) with references to ideology.

Willats's social resource projects appear close to Althusser's thesis about materialization of ideology through apparatuses integrated into everyday behaviors of individuals. His practice seems to engage the very same apparatuses Althusser talks about in his landmark essay. Furthermore, the way in which he conceives of "social resources," those basic units of his research, seem to expand the scope of Althusser's ideological state apparatuses. In *The Artist as an Instigator of Changes in Social Cognition and Behaviour*, Willats discusses a range of social resources, "from gentleman's clubs, dance halls, British Legion, football on a Saturday afternoon, tea break at work, political group meetings, to boy scouts, Sunday morning church, etc." ([1973] 2010:36). In one of his earliest social research projects, which he organized in 1972, Willats examined one of those apparatuses that, unlike schools, police, or political parties, have no obvious ties with the state and its institutions: a neighborhood fitness club. In his *Social Resource Project for Tennis Clubs* he aimed to "establish the environmental conditions that would enable members of tennis clubs in Nottingham to vary their perception of their Physical and Social environment, so that they could remodel the game of tennis around what they considered to be their club needs" (89). Following his large-scale social resource projects in London and Edinburgh, in the mid-1970s he turned to high-rise residential buildings that since the 1950s have become the staple of urban living in London (and across the industrialized world). In 1977, he organized two projects in the housing estate Skeffington Court, *Vertical Living* and *Living with Practical Realities*. Using the methods he developed in his social resource projects from the early 1970s, in these projects he focused on a single tower block instead of several different neighborhoods.

This was a change of orientation, and in more than one way. First, this architectural structure forced Willats to shift from horizontal localities to a vertical "street." Second, and more importantly, instead of a range of neighborhoods with representatives of different social classes, the tower block was a single and discrete social unit, in which all residents belonged to the same social class.[3] The same year he worked on Skeffington Court projects, Willats produced the diagram *The Ideological Tower* (1977), in which he took the residential high-rise as the basic structure of a social model. The diagram consists of nine squares stacked vertically.[4] In the upper left corner of the drawing, he inserted a caption explaining that "each floor in the tower represents one concept frame" (in Munder 2019:109). The lower left corner features the diagram of the concept frame, that is to say, a single floor of the tower. It is a simple square with four cardinal points marked as (starting from upper right corner and going clockwise) (A) identity, (D) behavior, (B) code, and (C) values. Two diagonal lines connect these corners to form pairings identity-code (A-B) and values-behavior (C-D). In another caption underneath this diagram, Willats explains that "each concept frame views a social problem via four axioms" (109). On the right side in relation to the tower diagram, there is a vertical arrow, with captions "particular structures" on the top, "models of relationships" in the middle, and "general structures" at the bottom. The diagram seems to present ideology as a set of "social problems" organized around four cardinal axioms of conceptual frames, which are stacked along a vertical axis, indicating a hierarchical structure.[5]

In *Vertical Living*, Willats presents a documentation of "concept frames" within the tower. Unlike in the West London project, where the team members asked participants to fill out questionnaires and offer suggestions, here they entered the living quarters of Skeffington Court residents equipped with a camera. The panel marked as "First problem display" features two black-and-white photographs of a middle-aged woman in her living room, engaged in everyday behaviors such as reading the newspaper. The captions beneath the photographs read, "How can I reduce the amount of external noise that is disturbing my thoughts in here" and

"What do you think people like me can do to stop the feeling of isolation from others around them while being on their own" (in Casser and Ziegler 2010:87). In the lower part of the panel are two sets of photographs arranged in "concept frames." One of the frames has a photograph of a television set and caption "Single" in the upper left quadrant marked as "Identity," and a picture of the exterior of the building with the caption "Quiet" in the quadrant next to it marked as "Motivation"; in the lower left, marked with "Behavior," there is a picture of a parked car with the caption "Restlessness" and a picture of a bed marked as "Privacy" in the "Code" quadrant. This and other panels were displayed in the lift lobbies of the tower block, the idea being that they would prompt residents to offer solutions to problems documented among their neighbors, thus "instigating" new behaviors.

By the time he produced his "ideological tower" diagrams, Willats already had in his conceptual repertoire a model that much more accurately describes the operations of ideology. The case in point is the idea of homeostasis, which he took over from cybernetics. In 1969, he produced two diagrammatic drawings, *Homeostat Drawing No. 1* and *Homeostat Drawing No. 2*, that represent complex structures of mutually interconnected units (squares).[6] A few years later, in *The Artist as an Instigator of Changes in Social Cognition and Behaviour* he explained that homeostasis is a cybernetic "model of adaptive control" that has "enabled self-organising decision-making systems to be postulated" ([1973] 2010:23). He added that "systems that exhibit homeostasis generally have a channel structure between their various parts, resembling a net. In a net structure that is essentially single-layer, each node is connected to other nodes by channels" (23). He presented the homeostatic structure in two diagrams in this booklet, which appear as variations of his earlier homeostat drawings. He further elaborated on this idea in the section "A Model of Social Organization," which serves as a theoretical introduction to the discussion of *West London Social Resource Project*. Here Willats notes that "in complex organisms that exhibit homeostasis, a state of equilibrium between the fabrication and organization and its external environment is sought after as the best position for its survival" (35). The internal self-regulation of the homeostat resonates strongly with one of key features of ideology that Althusser highlighted in his ISA essay: "Ideology *has no outside*" and at the same time, "*It is nothing but outside*" (1971:164). Any imaginary position outside of ideology is ideological in its own right. Althusser rephrases Mannheim's paradox in striking, almost blunt, terms: "One of the effects of ideology is the practical *denegation* of the ideological character of ideology by ideology: ideology never says, 'I am ideological'" (164). If there is a resonance between cybernetics and the critique of ideology, it is in the recognition that it is only from within the system that one can observe and critique that system. One does not step outside of ideology by departing from one of its apparatuses, for that departure is only a passage from one apparatus to another. Science offers no neutral ground free from ideology. In his essay "Technology and Science as 'Ideology'" (1968), another landmark piece of *Ideologiekritik* from the period under consideration, the Frankfurt school philosopher Jürgen Habermas argues that in industrialized Western societies, "Technology and science *also* take on the role of an ideology" (1970:104). According to Habermas, "it is a singular achievement" of technocratic ideology "to detach society's self-understanding from the frame of reference of communicative action and from the concepts of symbolic interaction and replace it with scientific model" (105). By adopting uncritically the goals and procedures of cybernetics, Willats effectively inserts this technocratic ideology into art practice. In doing so, he posits the artist as a disinterested agent in relation to the social homeostat.

In his comments on the *Edinburgh Social Model Construction Project*, Willats expressed his conviction that "the artist can develop art methodologies that enable him to function meaningfully outside existing art institutions, and determine himself what social, physical context he works within, and the criteria with which it is seen by its audience" (1974a:9). To bring back the model of the "greeting behavior" discussed earlier, the artist is not less of a "black box" than her audience is. This is precisely where Willats's "fundamental nodal construct" differs from Althusser's "theoretical theater" of interpellation. In Willats's model, the social structure precedes the moment of the encounter, while for Althusser, ideology is always co-constitutive with the subject, who is called into existence in the very act of greeting. It is from this understanding of the emergent nature of the system, which comes from cybernetics, that Willats draws the potential for its structural transformation. In behavioral art projects, the performer, that is to say the artist, is supposed to leave the performance unchanged. There is an assumption in Willats that taking art out of art institutions would turn it into a pure mediator freed from its apparatic nature. Furthermore, in its reentry into art institutions (museums, galleries, art publications, etc.) behavioral art (or its documentation) is supposed to retain that extra-apparatic disinterestedness. In Willats's "problem displays," the art appears neutral. The art and the artist are never part of the problem under examination. It is worth recalling that in *The Artist as an Instigator of Changes in Social Cognition and Behaviour*, he refers to the personnel involved in these complex performances not as performers, actors, activists, or, simply, artists, but as "project operators" ([1973] 2010:44). In a sharp distinction from Althusserian ISAs, the individuals ensnared in "ideological towers" never rise to the status of the subject; instead, Willats refers to them as "residents," "persons," "tenants," et cetera. While placing front and center behaviors that Althusser is talking about, behavioral art manages to "blackbox" them away from ideology, even when it tries to address ideology in the most direct way. The problem of the "ideological tower" is that ideology is not vertical, and that it informs behaviors of the "tenants" as much as "project operators."

THE IDEOLOGY-APPARATUS BRAID

While they differed widely, the artistic, curatorial, and scholarly projects that explored behavior in the early 1970s shared their engagement with performance. In curatorship, this turn to behavior registered already in the Italian Pavilion at the 1972 Venice Biennial, for which the art critic Renato Barilli curated the exhibition *Opera o comportamento* (Work or Behavior). In his 1976 book *Situazioni dell' arte contemporanea,* he disclosed that he started using the term "behavior" in artistic contexts in 1969. He explained that he believes that conceptual art is, generally, "behavioral," and declares that he considers some conceptual artists more narrowly to be "behaviorists" (*comportamentisti*).[7] In *Opera o comportamento,* the title he picked for his Venice Biennial exhibition, the first word does not refer to "work" or "labor" in general, but specifically to artworks. In the exhibition catalog, Barilli pointed out that while "the aim of *opera* has in fact meant (and not only in art) a commitment to sacrifice so many of one's existential reasons, to hide them and 'sublimate' them" in an art object, behavior (*comportamento*) "veers towards the programmatic liberation of all of its faculties, of all types of intervention in the world, starting with the most elusive and precarious, in the conviction that the time has come (in social, economic and technological terms) to rediscover immediate pleasure in living, and in being, and to let go of the momentous sacrifices of self-annihilation in a detached product" ([1972] 2017:48). Accordingly, Barilli's selection of artists and works featured in the Italian pavilion at Venice Biennial was eclectic. It ranged from an installation by *arte povera* pioneer Mario Merz, to participatory work by Franco Vaccari, to the highly controversial proto-delegated performance by the conceptual artist Gino de Dominicis, who for his piece enlisted the participation of a child and an adult with Down syndrome.[8]

If *comportamentismo* was but a phase in Barilli's curatorial work, in other, bordering, disciplines the turn to behavior and to the social sciences in general had much broader and field-altering proportions. Specifically, it played a pivotal role in the formation of the new academic discipline of performance studies.[9] One of the foundational moments in the emergence of this new discipline was the special issue of *TDR* "Performance & the Social Sciences," published in the winter of 1973. In the introduction to this issue, which he guest-edited, having left the post of *TDR* editor four years earlier, Richard Schechner proposed the creation of a whole new scholarly discipline of "performance theory" based on "the convergence of the social sciences and the performing arts" (1973b:4). Unlike Willats, Schechner did not focus on cybernetics, but on anthropology and its exploration of ritual phenomena. As he explained in his brief introduction, performance theory and social sciences have a "shared basic assumption" that the ritualization of behavior is the hallmark of social situations (3). He went on to outline seven key areas of overlap between performance theory and the social sciences. The list included performance of everyday life, sports and other forms of public behaviors, semiotics of communication, ethology, psychotherapy, and ethnography. If the first six areas were based on the object of study, the last one was methodological. It called for the "construction of unified theories of performance, which are, in fact, theories of behavior" (3).[10] Allowing that this special issue is a "far from perfect and less than panoramic start of an effort to establish in a systematic way a continuum between the social science and performance," Schechner indicated that it is only the first step in that process (3). The special issue featured contributions from prominent theater- and dance-makers such as Peter Brook and Anna Halprin; the dancer-choreographer Valentina Litvinoff had a piece about the Yaqui Easter; and the psychoanalyst Daniel Stern discussed kinetic analysis. The head article was Schechner's "Drama, Script, Theatre, and Performance," which could be seen as the volume editor's exemplary contribution to the unified theory of performance.

In its range of examples and academic disciplines on which it is drawing, this article appears, on the one hand, as a showcase of the seven areas of intersection between performance and social sciences, and on the other, as a demonstration of what Schechner would name the "broad spectrum approach" to study of performance (1988:4). Almost unwieldly in its breadth, the article brings together classical Western drama, tribal ceremonies in Papua New Guinea, the production of Sam Shepard's play *The Tooth of Crime* that Schechner had directed only a few months earlier in the Performing Garage in New York's SoHo, Paleolithic cave paintings, and ethology of chimpanzees in central Africa. Adhering to his project of integration of aesthetic performance (primarily theater and dance) and social sciences, in this early exploration of ritual Schechner referenced the Austrian ethologist Konrad Lorenz, who in 1973 received the Nobel Prize in Physiology or Medicine for his work on animal behavior. Following Lorenz, Schechner adopts the idea of ritualized behavior that cuts across the variety of social events he cited in his article. While a range of behaviors, such as play and combat, are shared among several species, specific ritualizations are characteristic for humans, somewhat less for chimpanzees, "and so on down the primate ladder" (1973a:29). What distinguishes performance from other forms of primate behavior is its mode of socialization. Following this line of reasoning, Schechner comes to one of his earliest, "tentative" as he put it, definitions of performance: "*Ritualized behavior conditioned/permeated by play*" (29). Defined in terms of behavior, performance would became the cornerstone of the integration of live arts and social sciences.

Three years after the publication of the special issue of *TDR*, the project of exploring the convergence between performance and the social sciences received a more elaborate and "panoramic" continuation with the publication of *Ritual, Play, and Performance: Readings in the Social Sciences / Theater* (1976), the volume that Schechner edited together with Mady Schuman. So there it was, the broad-spectrum approach, in its embryonic form. The book is divided into five sections that generally adhere to the areas of overlap between performance theory and the social sciences Schechner outlined earlier: "Ethology," "Play," "Ritual and Performance in Everyday Life," "Shamanism, Trance, Meditation," and "Rites, Ceremonies, Performances." The authors featured in the volume ranged from the classics such as Konrad Lorenz, Claude Lévi-Strauss, and Johan Huizinga, to more recent research of Jane Goodall, Gregory Bateson, Erving Goffmann, and Victor Turner; and from Ray Birdwhistell's work on communication theory to Jerzy Grotowski's writing on experiments in his Theatre Laboratory. The book concludes with Schechner's essay "From Ritual to Theater and Back," in which he first presented his thesis about the efficacy-entertainment braid as the defining characteristic of performance, considered interdisciplinarily, across the broad spectrum of subjects in the arts and the social sciences.[11] This essay, together with a revised and expanded version of "Drama, Script, Theater, and Performance," was included in Schechner's book *Essays on Performance Theory* published the following year (1977), thus concluding the first phase in the formation of a "movement" that would be, as he announced in the special issue of *TDR*, "more iconographic than icon-

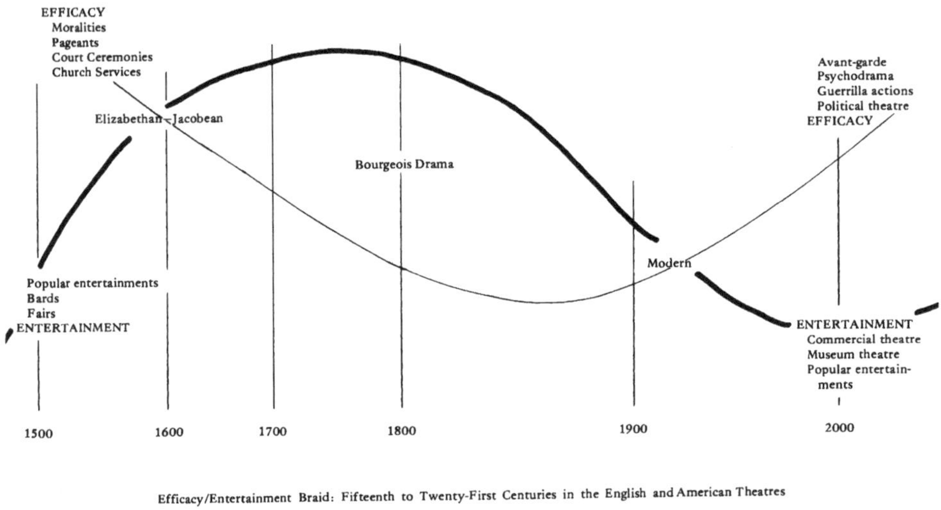

Figure 1. Richard Schechner: Efficacy-Entertainment Braid, 1974

oclastic; more conservative than prodigal; and more based on sheer observation and analysis than intuition and feeling" (1973b:4). Or put simply, more scholarly than artistic.

The efficacy-entertainment braid not only presents a broader and more complex idea of performance than the one that was operative in theater studies but also demonstrates the introduction of the social science methodologies (observation, analysis, diagrammatization) to the study of aesthetic performance. In this essay, Schechner argues that performance exists on a continuum that ranges from efficacy to entertainment, which he associates with ritual and theater, respectively. "These oppositions, and others generated by them," he suggests, "comprise performance: an active situation, a continuous turbulent process of transformation" ([1977] 1988:142). This continuous oscillation between efficacy and entertainment is cultural as well as historical, and it gives the entire history of theater in the West the structure of a braid, in which the opposed sides come close to each other, get apart, only to again twist and intersect. According to Schechner, "efficacy is the ideological heart" of the post–Second World War theatrical avant-garde, and its recent expansion "to include direct political action, performance in everyday life . . . , psychotherapy and other manifestly efficacious kinds of performance," is the outcome of that ideological blueprint (124). Jon McKenzie takes the "challenge of efficacy" as the distinguishing feature of this new understanding of performance and the emerging academic field that was built on and around it: "At the heart of its movement of generalization, Performance Studies scholars have constructed cultural performance as an engagement of social norms, as an ensemble of activities with the potential to uphold societal arrangements or, alternatively, to change people and societies" (2001:30).[12] The adoption of methods, procedures, and goals from the social sciences was instrumental for the separation of performance as a theoretical model from aesthetic representation. McKenzie notes that "performance is not a passive mirror of these social changes but a part of a complex feedback process that brings about change. At all times a dialectical tension exists between efficacious and entertainment tendencies" (31). In this integration of cultural studies and social sciences, ritual emerged as the social phenomenon capable of sustaining these two powerful tendencies.

Anthropology was as central for performance studies as behaviorism was for cybernetic art of Willats and Ascott. While both of these tendencies attempted to integrate the arts and social sciences, their attitudes toward the latter differed significantly. The key difference between Willats's behavioral art and the art of behavior at the center of performance studies is the attention the latter gives to the body and the phenomena of embodiment. The study of performance in the arts or in society can't afford to "blackbox" behaviors of participants into value-neutral performances. On the contrary, it is invested in the exploration of that which Wiener explicitly excluded from his brand of behaviorism: the functional analysis of organisms and, more specifically, their bodily actions. Much more productive for the study of performance than behaviorism was the approach to the corporeal that the anthropologist Marcel Mauss identified as "techniques of the body"; and similarly, "habitus" as the field constituted by these techniques is much closer to performance than the idea of homeostasis ([1935] 2006:80, 83). Building and expanding on Mauss's ideas, the French sociologist Pierre Bourdieu argued for the importance of the bodily placement of the observer in relation to and within the observed social phenomena. In doing that, he references Victor Turner, one of the key figures in the movement of integration of performance theory and the social science ([1980] 1990:36). In his elaboration of the "theory of practice" Bourdieu relied on his research on ritual practices in northern Africa, and on the same anthropological scholarship that was formative for performance studies. In that sense, his work comes across as independent from the field that emerged on the other side of the Atlantic, while at the same time complementing it. Significantly, he takes the embodied performance in theater or music to make his point about representation as an object of knowledge that is "constructed, not passively recorded" and asserts that "the principle of this construction is the system of structuring, structured dispositions, the *habitus*" (52). More specifically:

> The conditionings associated with a particular class of conditions of existence produces *habitus,* systems of durable, transposable dispositions, structured structures predisposed to function as structuring structures, that is, as principles which generate and organize practices and representations that can be objectively adapted to their outcomes without presupposing a conscious aiming at ends or an express mastery of the operations necessary in order to attain them. Objectively "regulated" and "regular" without being in any way the product of obedience to rules, they can be collectively orchestrated without being the product of the organizing action of a conductor. (53)

Because of its attention to bodies and their social arrangements, the habitus offers a figure of ideology that is far more nuanced than the homeostat. The relation of institutions to the habitus adds a necessary detail to the description of the relationship between ideology and its apparatuses:

> [The] *habitus* is what enables the institution to attain full realization: it is through the capacity for incorporation, which exploits the body's readiness to take seriously the performative magic of the social, that the king, the banker or the priest are hereditary monarchy, financial capitalism or the Church made flesh. Property appropriates its owner, embodying itself in the form of a structure generating practices perfectly conforming with its logic and its demands. (57)

And behavior is that kind of non-objective property which is constituted through social circulation and that endures only insofar as it participates in a system of exchanges. According to Bourdieu, the habitus is the central operating mechanism for regulation of behaviors. It makes sure that "the most improbable practices are excluded, as unthinkable," or put differently, "It tends to exclude all 'extravagances' ('not for the likes of us'), that is, all the behaviours that would be negatively sanctioned because they are incompatible with the objective conditions" (54, 56). Through the process of institutionalization, performance studies absorbed the ideological operations inherent in the habitus. If the ideological function of performance studies as an academic discipline is to regulate some "improbable" and "extravagant" practices that emerged in the area of live art, it accomplished that not through exclusion, but instead through their incorporation into the realm of the "thinkable" within the existing structure of the arts in the capitalist West.

One such "unthinkable" and "extravagant" moment took place in the first decades after the Second World War, with the uncoupling of aesthetic performance from the mimetic paradigm that had dominated live arts in the West since Aristotle. The emergence of pointedly anti-mimetic live art practices such as Happenings, Fluxus events, and the new dance removed from aesthetic performances the hallmark of naturalness that Aristotelian theory of mimesis imprinted on them. These new forms of nonnarrative, nonrepresentational, immersive, and often non-iterative events signaled the emancipation of aesthetic performance from the mimetic imperative that defined live arts in the West for centuries. As humble as Allan Kaprow's *18 Happenings in 6 Parts* was, it was one of the pivotal moments that called into question any easy identification of performance with the theater apparatus. One of the key operations in the separation of this new form of aesthetic performance from theater was its refusal of what Althusser called the "reproduction of skills of labor power" (1971:127). The "extravagance" of this new form of performance was in its status as a free labor power: free in the sense that it did not depend on or promote the acquisition of skills, and also free from any kind of use, from commercial entertainment to social activism.

Probably one of the earliest decisive gestures toward the new academic field centered on performance was the inclusion of these free-floating forms of live art into the corpus of theater. It happened in another special issue of *TDR*, which came out in the winter of 1965. Still published under the moniker *Tulane Drama Review*, the "New Theater" issue edited by Michael Kirby included an extensive catalog of representatives of these new performance forms, from the visual artists Allan Kaprow, Robert Whitman, and Claes Oldenburg, to the poets Dick Higgins and Jackson Mac Low, to the founder of Fluxus George Maciunas and the composer La Monte Young, to the choreographers and dancers Anna Halprin, Yvonne Rainer, and Robert Morris. Kirby and Schechner's interview with John Cage can be seen as a gesture of co-opting the very initial gesture of this movement to the repertoire of the New Theater. With this annexation of live art that explicitly rejected craft and theater research that emphasized technique (Grotowski, Brook, Chaikin), the emerging discipline of performance studies entered the process in post–Second World War arts that John Roberts described as "the dialectic between deskilling and reskilling in art" (2007:87). New live art forms that emerged in the second half of the twentieth century can be seen as a part of a general tendency toward deskilling in art, which is, as Roberts points out, epitomized in the phenomenon of the readymade. Indeed, just like Duchamp, the early happeners made use of industrially produced, disposable objects. The key difference from Duchamp was that they matched these objects with inexpert behaviors of untrained bodies. Roberts writes that "reskilling is emergent from deskilling precisely because as nonheteronomous labor the deskilling of art is open to autonomous forms of transformation, and these forms of transformation will of necessity find their expression in other skills than craft-based skills: namely, immaterial skills" (87–88). If the performance paradigm overturned the rejection of adept acting in new forms of live art, it did not do it by transforming Happenings into a new performance technique, but by taking it as one of the foundational elements of performance theory.

The new performance practices that emerged in the late 1950s and the early 1960s called for a radical change in the approach to the study of performance from an internal experience of performers toward their external, observable, and analyzable behaviors. This reorientation of theater studies toward the social sciences came as a rejection of flimsy psychologism that gradually invaded the dominant modernist theory of acting first systematized by the Russian theatrical reformer Konstantin Stanislavski and embraced by several generations of American actors and directors. The revisionist approach to the theory of acting is perhaps best exemplified in the work of Kirby, who in one of his most enduring essays, "On Acting and Not-Acting," discusses theatrical performance in terms of quantity (instead of "quality"), which he places on a "continuum of behavior" ([1972] 1987:3). Where Stanislavski and his American adherents would talk about experience, affective memory, and recollection, in "Restoration of Behavior," the next major step in forging a ritual-based theory of performance, Schechner talks about "strips of behavior" that have "a life of their own" ([1981] 1985:35).[13] Progressing, in a scientific manner, toward a simplification of basic concepts of performance theory, he refined his previous "tentative" definition to state that performance is "*a twice behaved behavior*" (36, emphasis added). While placing theoretical weight on the ideas of repetition, "twiceness," and "secondness," behavior that is observable and reproducible remains the basic component of his theoretical intervention. Keeping in line with a "broad spectrum approach" and drawing examples from theater, ritual, sports, and popular entertainment, he writes that the practitioners of these disciplines "assume that some behaviors—organized sequences of events, scripted actions, known texts, scored movements—exist separate from the performers who 'do' these behaviors" (36). And, further, to the point: "Restored behavior is 'out there,' distant from 'me.' It is separate and therefore can be 'worked on,' changed, even though it has 'already happened'" (36). Of all of the new live art forms that flourished in the 1960s, Happenings were especially useful for the theoretical and practical reformulation of performance and its shift away from purely aesthetic ("entertainment") toward the social science ("efficacy") side of the continuum. The turn from deskilling as one of the defining characteristics of Happenings toward repetition and (re)production of skills represents one of key ideological operations of performance theory.

In the early 1970s, Schechner's theoretical writings were resonating with the terminology of the social sciences. One of the catchwords was certainly "behavior," and another was "environment." However, as he himself acknowledged, he didn't borrow the latter from cybernetics (as Willats did), but from the artistic practice of Allan Kaprow. In "Six Axioms of Environmental Theater," the article that stands at the intersection between his performance practice and the emerging performance theory, Schechner credits Kaprow as one of the key sources for his new approach to theater. Specifically, he emphasizes Kaprow's "doing away altogether with the frame" in performance ([1968] 1994:xix). Like Happenings, in which the audience was often surrounded by action and immersed in it, the new spatial organization of theater is "multi-focus": "Each independent event competes with the other for the audience's attention. The space is organized so that no spectator can see everything." And: "In multi-focus, events happen behind, above, below, around, as well as in front of the spectator" (xxxvii). First published in *TDR* in 1968 and then reprinted five years later in Schechner's book *Environmental Theater* ([1973] 1994), this text is contemporaneous with Jean-Louis Baudry's "Ideological Effects of the Basic Cinematographic Apparatus" (1970), and yet it is completely at odds with its main premises. Thomas Elsaesser offers a useful summary of the basic tenets of Baudry's film apparatus: "the enforcement of the laws of Renaissance perspective; the Cartesian mind-body split; the fixed geometrical arrangement of the three main elements: screen, projector, spectator; and, finally, the metaphoric association of this arrangement with Freud's (or Lacan's) concept of mis-recognition, a founding moment of psychic identity, and philosophical analogy with Plato's parable of the cave, a founding moment of Western idealism" (2011:34). Experimental theater of the late 1960s, from Judith Malina's Living Theatre, to Jerzy Grotowski's Theatre Laboratory, to Peter Brook, Luca Ronconi, and many others expressly rejected this kind of apparatus and the perceptual and psychic arrangements that it imposed on the spectator.

Environmental theater appears as a complete opposite of this mise-en-scène structured by the frontality and flatness of the picture frame. In order to achieve multisensory, multidirectional, and enveloping experience of the environment, "The whole space is needed." Schechner is adamant that "the kind of work I am talking about can't happen if one territory belongs to the audience and another to the performers. The bifurcation of space must stop." Environmental theater stages the abolition of the perspectival illusion: "The final exchange between performers and audience is the exchange of space, spectators as scene makers as well as scene watchers" (xxvi). It is this abolition of the separation between spectators and the field of representation that gives this form of theater its "blue flower" appearance of an apparatus-free art form. Theater that is immersive, participatory, and flexible is bound to acquire a ritual-like quality of efficaciousness. However, here the ritual is not the theoretical model but the strategic means of appropriating "extravagant" and "unthinkable" performance to the habitus of contemporary capitalist culture. Bourdieu writes that "as an acquired system of generative schemes, the habitus makes possible the free production of all the thoughts, perceptions and actions inherent in the particular conditions of its production—and only those" (1990:55). At the same time, it has the ability to absorb heterogeneous behaviors, to harmonize them with its overall purpose, adapt them to its structure, and incorporate them into its repertoire of practices: "In new situations, [it] can invent new ways of fulfilling the old functions" (291). In its limiting function and adaptive nature, ritual, as described by Schechner and Turner, repeats on a smaller scale the key characteristics of the habitus. Through the rigorous removal of technological mechanisms, environmental theater is not relieving itself of the apparatus, but conversely, it exposes the deeper relation of the apparatus to ideology. Recapitulating the general properties of ideology on a small, concrete, and material scale, the apparatus appears in its true light, as a specific folding of ideology, or to use the figure that Jacques Derrida favored, an instance of its invagination. Like a twist in a braid, it forms a distinct enclosure in the weaving of the ideological field, yet it remains continuous with it. While it has a different appearance, it is an extension and instantiation of its operations. What is enfolded in the apparatus is the process of subjectivation, which is no less central to the seemingly apparatus-free environmental theater space than to the apparatus-heavy film projection room. If anything, it is more effective in the former because it is harder to pinpoint.

To invoke Erwin Piscator's assessment of naturalist theater, with which environmental theater has deep and unobvious ties, "it never got past stating the problem" ([1963] 1978:33). And further, like naturalism some hundred years earlier, it for a time reveled in its subversive relation to mainstream theater and the ideological formation it represents. In her incisive assessment of environmental theater, Una Chaudhuri calls attention to its "dream of fullness," its "fantasy of limtless theatrical signification, an infinity of meaning resulting from the infinite possible reconfigurations of theatrical space" (1995:23). And, to the point, she concludes that "environmental theater is burdened with an ideology whose primary characteristic is that it obscures itself, denies its presence" (26). Following Althusser, we can say that this is one of main characteristics of ideology as such. Environmental theater's cornucopia of sense-perceptions was but one specific instance of ideology adopting a specific material manifestation in advanced capitalism. Another specificity of this ideological operation is its ability to present itself as new with astonishing regularity: in the 1980s, environmental theater reappeared as participatory, and two decades later as immersive theater. In each of its incarnations, environmental staging is fueled by large technological and cultural changes.[14] The latest one bears directly on behavior, the foundational conceptual premise of theories of performance and of ideological apparatuses.

BEHAVIORAL EXTRACTION

From March to November 1972, Willats and his collaborators visited dozens of households in West London, conducted several rounds of interviews, distributed and processed at least two sets of questionnaires, amalgamated and presented their findings, collected feedback, presented it yet again, and shared final conclusions with communities involved in this project. The following year, he organized in Edinburgh his most complete social resource project, for which he could enlist the help of a mainframe computer in a nearby laboratory. That indicated what was coming. Had they ever showed up in Nottingham, visitors from the twenty-first century would not have jumped out of strange vehicles, wearing silver space outfits. They would not have gone door-to-door, handed out questionnaires, talked to residents, collected answers, build bulletin boards, and so on. If these visitors had come even from a near future, only some forty years removed from Willats's early social resource projects, they would have come from a behavioral heaven, where canvassing is done continuously and the "residents" are the "operators" at the same time. Toward the end of the second decade of the twenty-first century, Harvard psychologist Shoshana Zuboff named this materialized cybernetic utopia "surveillance capitalism." This is a far cry from mid-century "big brother" dystopias about a metastasized totalitarian state, and even from contemporary forms of military and industrial surveillance. "Surveillance" here describes a new logic of capitalist production, which has behavior as its main commodity.

From labor routines to military exercises, to athletic feats, to stage enactments, industrial capitalism strove to situate, organize, and harness elements of the performance apparatus for its own purposes. If in the 1970s certain artistic and theoretical practices engaged the performance apparatus, four decades later this apparatus became indispensable for mining raw material in new extraction economy of surveillance capitalism. From the time of the publication of Althusser's ideology essay and the beginnings of performance art, which coincided with the neoliberal turn in economy, the locus of surveillance moved from repressive to ideological state apparatuses, which is to say, from state agencies to private corporations. According to Zuboff, only with the advance of digital technologies was capitalism able to fully monetize this operation by commodifying the totality of human behavior, in and outside of the workplace, or on- and offstage, as it were. As she puts it succinctly, "Surveillance capitalism unilaterally claims human experience as free raw material for translation into behavioral data"; it uses this data to produce a "behavioral surplus" that takes the form of "behavioral products"; finally, these products are traded in a marketplace that Zuboff calls the "behavioral futures market" (8). She insists on the distinction between "digital" and "surveillance" capitalism.

While it is spearheaded by digital giants such as Apple, Amazon, Google, Facebook, and Microsoft, what defines surveillance capitalism is not that it relies on digital technologies, but the purposes for which digital technologies are used. Zuboff is adamant that "surveillance capitalism is not technology," but "a logic that imbues technology and commands it into action." In other words, it is "a market form that is unimaginable outside of the digital milieu, but is not the same as the 'digital'" (15). Put somewhat crudely, the "digital" is to surveillance what the internal combustion machine was to industrial capitalism: a means that provides access to its raw material and secures circulation of its products. Instead of natural resources (ore, crude oil, land), the raw material now comes from what Althusser called the superstructure, that "instance" in the structure of capitalist society which is charged with the "reproduction of the relations of production" (1971:128). Fredric Jameson suggests in *The Political Unconscious* that, while classical Marxism understood the idea of the relations of production in narrowly economic sense, Althusser's theory of the levels opens for analysis the complex relationship between the infra- and superstructure. Ideology becomes the key element in the "synchronic system of social relations as a whole" (1981:36). Within this social order, the literary "work in the narrow sense" has been "reconstituted in the form of the great collective and class discourses" of which the text is but one individual instance (76). Departing from Althusser, Jameson is asking for a more granular approach to the critique of ideology in literary studies, and in doing so isolates the *ideologeme* as "the smallest intelligible unit of the essentially antagonistic collective discourses of social classes" (76). If we follow Jameson, we can ask if there is a place for a "smallest unit" in the study of performance. Would not something like "performeme" be the next logical step in the analysis of those "strips of behavior" that constitute performance? Setting aside the klutzy sound of this neologism, the absence of this kind of category from performance theory is not surprising if we consider that it inherited from traditional theater and dance scholarship the notion of gesture as the way of conceptualizing those smallest meaningful units of behavior. Positioned between the everyday, or non-aesthetic, and aesthetic behavior, gesture provides the opening between these two levels: through gesture, the everyday enters aesthetic performance, and the other way around. And also, if it can be readily aestheticized, gesture can just as easily become the material for commodification. The logic of reproduction de-aesthetisizes gesture and turns it into the *performeme* as the smallest commodifiable unit of behavior. The discovery of behavioral surplus hinges on the ability of new technologies to capture and process these behavioral particles and package them as commodities.

Zuboff takes 9 August 2011, the date Apple topped Exxon as the world's most highly capitalized corporation, as the symbolic moment when this new logic of capitalism eclipsed the old industrial one (2019:27). In the latest form of capitalism, the most precious raw material is not a natural, but an ideological, product. According to Zuboff, the key moment in the emergence of surveillance capitalism was the discovery of behavioral surplus. The everyday use of online functions, from shopping to paying bills to searching for information, produces traces of behavior, which is in the lingo of digital technology commonly referred to as "digital waste," or more intuitively, as "digital breadcrumbs." This behavioral data was never just trash, as it was used to modify and improve still-developing digital technology. Zuboff suggests that the turning point in the industry, and in the logic of capitalism, came once companies such as Google produced sufficient computing power and established proprietary methods that enabled them to collect "more behavioral data than it needed to serve its users." "That surplus, a behavioral surplus, was the game-changing, zero-cost asset that was diverted from service improvement toward a genuine and highly lucrative market exchange" (81). The pivotal instance in this change of the game was the status of the "user." In the age of mass media, it became well established that the viewer, or user, was considered the product rather than a consumer in this kind of economy. One needs not go further than Richard Serra's 1973 video piece *Television Delivers People*.[15] With the rise of surveillance capitalism, the users are no longer products, but rather "the sources of raw-material supply" (70). This transformation of the status of users depends on predictability of their behavior: "Surveillance capitalism's unusual products manage to be derived from our behavior while remaining indifferent to our behavior. Its products are about predicting us, without actually caring what we do and what is done to us" (70). One of the basic tenets of behaviorism, as monstrous as it might have appeared in the early 1970s, that behavior is predictable and prescriptive, became one of the founding blocks of surveillance capitalism.

The arena of surveillance capitalism is not constituted visually, but behaviorally. Zuboff points out that Google established "proprietary methods" that "enable it to surveil, capture, expand, construct, and claim behavioral surplus, including the data that users intentionally choose not to share" (80). Behavioral data mining extracts seemingly insignificant details about users, their "thoughts, feelings, interests" that are "constructed from the wake of unstructured signals that trailed every online action" (68). Importantly, what Zuboff leaves out from her consideration are some of the key insights of performance theory, such as the one about the restoration of behavior: before they are harvested, behaviors are produced. If the ideologeme, which Jameson describes as "an amphibious formation, whose structural characteristics may be described as its possibility to manifest itself either as a pseudoidea . . . or a protonarrative," makes possible the ideological analysis of literary texts, then the performeme, relieved from the aesthetic glow of the gesture and its psychological underpinnings, allows us to engage in ideological analysis of performances (86). A consideration of the performance apparatus demonstrates that this production is cultural and historical. One doesn't "climb" into the performance apparatus the way one enters an aircraft, a tower block, or, for that matter, a theater space, but rather internalizes it. In other words, in order to enter the performance apparatus, one has to be already inured to it. Behaviors of "users" are not spontaneous, and if they are invested with interests, that is because of their ideological constitution. Far from being "raw," users' data come not only from their thoughts and feelings but also from their actions and behaviors, that is to say performances, which are commodifiable precisely because they have been constituted as such. Behavioral extraction is inseparable from behavioral production. Production of behaviors is not an invention of surveillance capitalism. In fact, it has been one of the central mechanisms of capitalism from its very inception. Commodity production generates new behaviors, which coalesce into massive "lifestyles." Commodities are not outside of the bodies, and the world of commodities is not just the milieu in which the bodies enter. Instead, they enter the bodies through gestures and habits to produce new behaviors. These behaviors are what drives commodity production. One of common misconceptions about capitalist modernity is that it was engaged exclusively in the production of mass and uniform behaviors.

Zuboff takes neoliberal ideology and the policies it produced in the 1970s and 1980s as prerequisites for the emergence of surveillance capitalism. She is well justified in her assertion that the neoliberal belief in the unmistakability of market forces displaced "democratic contest and deliberation with an ideology of atomized individuals sentenced to perpetual competition for scarce resources" (39). However, Zuboff is primarily interested in these individuals as objects, or raw material for the extraction of behavioral data, and not as subjects. The mechanisms of subjectivation constitute the process of the "enrichment" of individuals—in the same way uranium is enriched—that makes them into raw material worthy of behavioral extraction. In his writings produced in the formative years of surveillance capitalism, Maurizio Lazzarato paid attention precisely to that which Zuboff neglected when he declared that for "modern-day capitalism subjectivity is the product of a world-wide mass industry" and that "subjectivity is a 'key commodity' whose 'nature' is conceived, developed, and manufactured in the same way as an automobile, electricity, or a washing machine" (2014:55). No amount of expansion of the repressive state apparatus and proliferation of ideological state apparatuses would be sufficient to explain this explosion in the mass production of subjectivities. In fact, the mass industry of subjectivities does not resemble in any way the modes of production characteristic of industrial societies.

If the subject is produced discursively, in the first decades after the Second World War cybernetics and neo-behaviorism were the discourses that fostered the dream of an industrial-grade subjectivation. In "Psychology and Ideology," a shattering critique of B. F. Skinner, the leading figure in

American neo-behaviorism, Noam Chomsky demonstrated that the basic premises of this social science, the determination of behaviors by the environment and reinforcements, are consistent with the capitalist ideology. According to Chomsky, behaviorist ideas of a "technology of behavior" and a "design of a culture" are consistent with "a police state in which rigid laws are enforced by people who are themselves subject to them and the threat of dire punishment hangs over all" (1973:343). By the time critiques of this kind were published, it was already clear that the "police state" technology of behavior is unproductive, and that in order to survive, capitalism has to shed any overt appearance of totalitarian enforcement of behaviors. That, however, did not mean that some of the postulates of behaviorism did not carry over to its next, "more flexible," phase. In fact, some of them were foundational for its constitution. In one of his analyses of *Edinburgh Social Model Construction Project*, Willats wrote that the aim of his undertaking was to move participants from a descriptive, to a predictive, and finally to a prescriptive mode (1974b:10). Here, importantly, he was drawing on John Dutton and William H. Starbuck's early work on artificial intelligence, *Computer Simulation of Human Behavior*. This kind of cybernetic research went into the foundations of surveillance capitalism.

The crucial change was in the scale and method of the production and harvesting of behaviors: while industrial capitalism attempted a replication of behaviors on a mass scale, its surveillance successor went in the opposite direction, toward their miniaturization and individualization. As Walter Benjamin demonstrated in "On Some Motifs in Baudelaire," one of the most striking effects of capitalist mass production of commodities was the invention of new behaviors and their personalization in the form of skills. In order to become reproducible and transferable, behaviors have to be broken down to their smallest units. The credit for the discovery of the smallest commodifiable unit of behavior goes to Benjamin:

> In the mid-nineteenth century, the invention of the match brought forth a number of innovations which have one thing in common: a single abrupt movement of the hand triggers a process of many steps. This development is taking place in many areas. A case in point is the telephone, where the lifting of a receiver has taken the place of the steady movement that used to be required to crank the older models. With regards to countless movements of switching, inserting, pressing, and the like, the "snapping" by the photographer had the greatest consequences. Henceforth a touch of the finger sufficed to fix an event for an unlimited period of time. The camera gave the moment a posthumous shock, as it were. ([1940] 2003:328)

In the early twenty-first century, the invention of the touch screen propelled simple gestures of tapping and swiping to hitherto undreamed of ubiquity and power. Who tapped and swiped before 2010? Now billions of people do, across the globe. And furthermore, these humble gestures are hardwired into an economy that spans worldwide and drives the production of new wealth on the order unseen since the apex of imperialism. This gestural revolution is not only technological: it is first and foremost ideological. These trillions of light brushes of fingertips on glassy screens are all but random. They just might turn out to be the most massive performance training in the history of humankind.

These performemes are ideological in nature, insofar as they come in response to a summons that endows them with purpose and meaning. These are never one-off gestures. Instead, they are performances that are constituted iteratively. Like performative utterances, they are, as Butler argues in her reformulation of Althusser's thesis, "part of the continuous and uninterrupted process to which we are subjected, an on-going subjection (*assujettisement*) that is the very operation of interpellation, that continually repeated action of discourse by which subjects are formed in subjugation" (1997a:27). It is this repetition that endows the behavior of the subject with an appearance of thinglike solidity. As we have seen with twice-behaved behavior, repetition is the hallmark of ritualized behavior. In her important consideration of ritual aspects of Austin's speech acts and Althusser's interpellation, Butler concludes that "ritual is material to the extent that it is productive." It, indeed, produces "the belief that appears to be 'behind' it," as in Althusser's example of Pascal's dictum that religious behavior (prayer) will produce religious belief (25). It is, as she asserts in another place, central to the "ideological work of acquiring skills, a process central to the formation of the subject" (1997b:115). Which is to say: "To master a set of skills is not simply to accept a set of skills, but to reproduce them in and as one's own activity. This is not simply to act according to a set of rules, but to embody rules in the course of action and to reproduce those rules in embodied rituals of action" (119). Butler's focus on the discursive production of gendered and racialized behavior is well justified, but it takes attention from the ideological operations embedded in technology. We are well advised to recall Habermas's warning from what now appears as prehistory of technological revolution.

"Technology and Science as 'Ideology'" goes further in its investigation of routinized behavior than Althusser does in his invocation of Pascal in "Ideology and Ideological State Apparatuses." Habermas argues that if we understand a "behavioral system of action" as a feedback loop of "rational decision and instrumental action," then it is possible to "reconstruct the history of technology from the point of view of the step-by-step objectivation of the elements of that very system" (1970:87). He proceeds to detail that process: "At first the functions of the motor apparatus (hands and legs) were augmented and replaced, followed by energy production (of the human body), the functions of the sensory apparatus (eyes, ears, and skin), and finally of the governing center (the brain)" (87). This is how far Habermas could go in 1968. Following this step-by-step procedure, we can now witness the pervasive objectivation of the faculties of the "governing center" itself. For, it is important to keep in mind the final point of Pascal's reflection on the mechanics of prayer and belief: "For we must make no mistake about ourselves: we are as much automaton as mind" (in Bourdieu 1990:48). Production and dissemination, prediction and prescription of behaviors has been one of the vital operations of advanced capitalism. While this *communication* of skills, their transmission and internalization, comes in waves with the introduction of new technologies, it is not reducible to technological innovation. Safety matches, the rotary telephone, the analog camera, the film projector were mechanical aspects of apparatuses positioned in relation to a behaving body. Unlike them, screen-based digital devices minimize the tools (smartphones being the Swiss knife of digital capitalism), which become dematerialized and absorbed into conduct of their users. If the old devices were attached to and promoted the "automaton" part of the self, the new ones are integrated in what Pascal calls the "mind." They are not only a metaphor of the psychic apparatus, as cinema used to be, but its integral part.

Published in 2019, Zuboff's *The Age of Surveillance Capitalism: The Fight for a Human Future at the New Frontier of Power* book is already falling behind the latest technologies of behavioral extraction and objectification of the mind. Little did I know when I started this book that by the time I finished it, "psychedelic capitalism" would become a budding industry, and even more significantly, that digital technologies based on large language models would begin a gradual replacement of "symbolic action" that Habermas and his Frankfurt school friends took as the bedrock of humanity itself. Late in 2022, as I was working on the revisions of this book, a whole new industry based on the idea of the generation of linguistic, visual, audio, and code content was in the offing. The early signs were already there. That August, the news broke out that a game designer won at the Colorado State Fair Fine Arts Competition for the work *Théâtre D'opéra Spatial* produced with the help of artificial intelligence (AI) image generator DALL-E. That November, OpenAI, the same startup that produced DALL-E, launched ChatGPT, a language generator of unprecedented power and efficiency. Far exceeding similar chatbots such as Siri and Alexa, ChatGPT demonstrated capacity to produce undergraduate-level scholarly papers, poems, basic coding, and even musical compositions. In the months after, the media was abuzz with reports from the AI frontiers. Like many other institutions of higher education, my university scrambled to come up with new policies that would prevent or at least curtail cheating on final papers and exams (here the irony being that the university where I work was instrumental in initiating and sustaining the digital industry known as Silicon Valley). The academic paper, as we know it, seems to be on its way out.

As I write this, we are only in the first months of ChatGPT era, and it is far too early to offer any definitive answers to many questions concerning the broad accessibility of AI. Still, some things are already clearly discernible. Importantly, AI generators are mimetic machines: they excel in Alan Turing's "imitation game," but they don't understand what animates anti-mimetic practices. They can generate a Dadaist poem, but they don't know what it is and the significance of that gesture. Next, and no less important, is the fact that AI latches onto our need for meaning-production: even that content which is in itself nonsensical begins to emanate meaning in its encounter with the reader. Being mimetic, AI generators are, as their early users observed, "people pleasers." They excel in answering questions by summarizing concepts stored in gigabytes of online data they are canvassing (consider the efficacy of this algorithm in comparison to Willats' canvassers "from the 21st century"!). When it comes to critical inquiry, they are just clunky machines. In other words, they execute, but they don't perform. They are, essentially, ideological machines. They are, without doubt, at the very frontier of that objectification of the mind that Althusser and Habermas dreaded, and which is the true purpose of ideology. In other words, they are more efficient than any other apparatus in accomplishing the goal that ideology always strove for. In that sense, there is not much that is new about them, which does not make them less onerous.

Thus far, there has been more fearmongering about AI than true attempts to engage this new technology in a truly critical way. Consider the twenty-two-word statement from AI techno-capitalists issued only months after they made this technology widely available, in which they likened its potential for destruction to nuclear warfare and pandemics.[16] The problem is not in the steady rise of new technologies, but in the perpetual decline of the critique of ideology. In another text from 1968, Habermas has positioned them side by side:

> Raising the productivity of technically exploitable knowledge, which in the sphere of socially necessary labor leads to the complete substitution of machinery for men, has its counterpart here in the

> self-reflection of consciousness in its manifestations to the point where the self-consciousness of the species has attained the level of critique and freed itself from all ideological delusion. The two developments do not converge. Yet they are interdependent. ([1968] 1971:55)

A little more than half a century later, the former has outpaced the later by far. That makes the urgency of self-reflection on our involvement with ideological apparatuses, which are *only peripherally tied with technology*, all the more compelling. The name of the new capitalist game is not the production of new technologies, but turning physical and mental behaviors into commodities that can be harvested and monetized. Performance art and performance theory came to understand, early on, that if behaviors can be the object of industrial production, they can also engage in the production of counter-behaviors. If a performance apparatus can be harnessed for the production and extraction of behaviors, then the understanding of its operations can make it useful in the creation on behaviors that are not extractable. One of the key ideological lessons of the performance apparatus is that this is no longer enough. Our ability to create strategies of resisting and overcoming surveillance capitalism and its imperial logic that goes from everyday search engines to apocalypse-inducing AI hinges on the production not only of new behaviors but of new subjectivities: subjectivities capable of reflecting on the ideological implications of these apparatuses and acting on that reflection, which is to say, inhabiting, exploring, and cultivating the terrains of behavior, twice behaved and otherwise, that remain inaccessible to them.

THREE | Agit-Funk

A Love Lesson for the Apparatus

ELEGY AND IDEOLOGY

The symbiosis of ideology and its apparatuses is so fundamental that it seems that neither one of them could survive on its own. There is no ideology without its material apparatuses, and, vice versa, it is ideology that secures the efficient operations of apparatuses. It seems that the uncoupling of ideology from apparatuses would almost certainly result in the disintegration of capitalist state. But how do they find one another? Does ideology devise its apparatuses, or, conversely, do certain material conditions, say, of production, yield an ideological order? What happens if an apparatus remains outside of the state ideology? When does its outsider status become its essential property? Can a political apparatus simply pick an ideological order for itself, disregarding Althusser's dictum about ideology as the imaginary relationship of subjects to the material conditions of their existence?

In the course of the twentieth century, a number of political parties and movements have done precisely that. On 1 February 1976 the Congress of Afrikan People (CAP), a movement established in 1970, which the poet and activist Amiri Baraka had chaired since 1972, changed its name to the Revolutionary Communist League (Marxist-Leninist–Mao Tse-tung Thought). The leadership of RCL (M-L-M) explained its decision in its unofficial organ, *Unity and Struggle*, in June 1976. Then, in its next issue, printed in October of the same year, it issued the first part of a long document entitled "RCL's Position on Party Building." It concludes with a glossary of sorts: an enumerated series of conclusions and definitions used in the position paper. RCL's working definitions of theory and ideology are in bullet point 4: theory is "the summed-up experience of the working-class movement taken in its general aspect and as put forward chiefly by 5 great teachers—Marx, Engels, Lenin, Stalin, and Mao." Noting that theory and ideology are "at times . . . used interchangeably," the authors declare that the latter represents "the stand, worldview and methodology of the proletariat, i.e., dialectical and historical materialism" (1976b:16). The momentous transition from the Pan-Africanist Congress of Afrikan People to the Maoist Revolutionary Communist League was engineered and driven by Baraka. The publication of these proclamations and position papers came exactly a decade after the completion of the four-year span from 1962 to 1966, which Fred Moten described as Baraka's "tragic period" (2003:94). Moten recognized the sources of this "tragic" or "elegiac" state to be Baraka's "political homelessness" and "political despair," or "despair about the organization of things" (93, 94). The period from 1972 to 1976, which can be said to constitute Baraka's "ideological period," appears to be an attempt to reverse the "tragedy," find a political home, and reignite confidence in the "organization of things." The pivotal moment in this period was the year 1974, during which he made his transition from Black nationalism to anti-revisionist communism, a term that the radical Left in the West used for an anti-Trotskyist and anti-Khrushchevite doctrine: effectively, Maoism. Indeed, he concludes one of the key statements from that pivotal year, the talk entitled "Toward Ideological Clarity," which he gave at the African Liberation Support Committee (ALSC) conference at Howard University, with this call for action: "It is a time of ideology and it is a time of organization" (1974c:31). At first glance, it might appear that this proclamation marks the beginning of the poet's decisive transformation into a politician.

But what if "ideology" and "organization" don't presuppose, but instead oppose, one another? What if they don't represent a reversal of Baraka's "tragic period," but rather its outcome? In that light they can be seen as belonging to that group of oppositions—"emotion and structure, preparation and spontaneity, individuality and collectivity"—which Moten recognized as the "conceptual apparatus" that "Baraka uses to represent music" in his texts on jazz from the mid-1960s (129). Ten years later, this expansion of the conceptual apparatus no longer entails only a discursive representation, but also sonic production. Namely, a vinyl record Baraka produced in 1976 showcases a juxtaposition of ideology, as understood in RCL's position paper on party building, with a kind of organization explicitly proscribed in that same position paper. This 45-rpm record, almost forgotten and often excluded from Baraka's discographies, represents precisely that "artifact of the recording, the necessary reduction of process to product, the containment and replication of the sense of excess" which Moten talks about (118). At the center of this black disc is a bright red label inscribed with a set of distinguishing marks. The name of the band is the Advanced Workers with the Anti-Imperialist Singers. On the A-side of the single is the song "You Was Dancin Need to Be Marchin So You Can Dance Some More Later On,'" with "Better Red Let Others Be Dead" on the B-side. Baraka, Jio Williams, and Winston Sims are credited with writing both songs. Sims is listed as the arranger and Baraka as the producer. The name of the record label, People's War, is printed above its emblem: a black silhouette of protesters, one raising a clenched fist, and the other waving a flag.

From his first recording with the New York Art Quartet in 1965 to his CD with William Parker, *I Plan to Stay a Believer: The Inside Songs of Curtis Mayfield,* released in 2010, only four years before his death, Baraka collaborated with a series of renowned jazz musicians. In his discussion of Baraka's "collaborative sound recordings," Anthony Reed calls attention to "a different theoretical function of *voice* in his thinking, not just as a sign or reflection of racialized presence but the continual *production* of racial difference as inchoate political consciousness, mobilized against the standardizing impulses of mode of life built around the alienation of labor power from the laborer" (2021:107). While Baraka collaborated with jazz musicians, off and on, over a long period of time (his recording sessions with the New York Art Quartet coming almost forty years apart), his excursion into funk in 1976–77 involved a whole new sense of *production*. In his sessions with the Advanced Workers Baraka took on the responsibilities of the lyricist, producer, and stage leader. With these *working musicians*, he performed in venues that ranged from Newark, New Jersey, bars to the prestigious Jazztage music festival in Berlin, Germany. Reed observed that "Baraka's Marxist poetry pursued an immediacy that made it more score-like, 'less and less about the text' or written word" (105). In his work with the Advanced Workers, this poetry becomes fully immersed in the production of live music, giving it, in turn, a clear political tenor: it is not only, as Baraka put it, "speech *musicked*" but (popular) music *politicked*.[1] Here he is in "You Was Dancin Need to be Marchin," reciting:

> But this was an army of workers
> Led by the science of revolution,
> An army of workers who grasped the science of revolution.
> And when they said "party," they meant an anti-revisionist
> revolutionary communist party.
> And when they said "party," they meant an anti-revisionist
> communist party.
> And if you asked them what truths their party taught,
> They'd say Marxism-Leninism–Mao Tse-tung thought,

And if you asked them what truths their party taught,
They'd say Marxism-Leninism–Mao Tse-tung thought.

So much for ideology. When it comes to sonic organization, the Advanced Workers had nothing in common with the organizational principles that the RCL propagated in its position papers published at the very same time this record was released. Writing about George Clinton's genre-defining early 1970s bands Parliament and Funkadelic, funk scholar Tony Bolden pointed out that kinesis, particularly dance, is at the core of the music they created (2013:29). Like Clinton's bands, which eventually merged into P-Funk, the sound of the Advanced Workers is marked by shifts between irregular and steady rhythms, and by the efforts of the musicians to upend and reinvent the conventional role of their instruments. Like limbs in a dizzying dance, each band member seems to be on a different tangent, while actually moving together with the others in the same direction. On their single, especially its A-side, the Advanced Workers organize the syncopated drums, burping bass lines, sharp guitar riffs, and rising vocals, which in funk often remain buried, under the cumulative force of its internal rhythmic oppositions: the drive of a steady forward motion. The inimitable Kodwo Eshun asserts in *More Brilliant Than the Sun: Adventures in Sonic Fiction*: "As a homeopathic agent, 'Funk not only moves, it can remove' the sensations of feeling walled-in, closed-up, cased in armour. It squirms like tapeworm, heaving and contracting along your intestines. It's a basssnake that undulates the inert abdomen and pelvis in S waves, snakemotions that sidewind along the things" (1998:150). The setting that the Advanced Workers wanted for their movement is not the dance floor, but the street. The organization of the music enacts the idea expressed in the lyrics: "You was dancin' need to be marchin' so you can dance some more later on."

Later on, in his *Funk Lore* collection of poems, Baraka attempted to capture in verse this complex temporal structure of irregularity and progression:

Plays on & on place after place into future past
It's passing It the is the is was been & going
Going is blowing gone is blown
Why the Funk remember
Why the Funk keep all we hearts

Like marching could be wind & noises

So:

> All them to come was here when they left
> all us who left here is now
> about to come
> cause we in love
> what keep us breathing
> is keep us a spirit
> a point to pointing
> a go to going
> & we keep coming
> Oh baby, is nighttime
> Joe Williams say nighttime
> is the right time (1996:93)

Joe "Jio" Williams, who composed all the songs for the Advanced Workers, was part of the New Jersey funk scene from its very beginnings. He and Clinton had known each other since their youth but were not in the same bands. Like Clinton, who started his music career with a community doo-wop group based in the Silk Palace barbershop in Plainfield, New Jersey, Williams also had his own vocal band, the Supremes (it had to give up that name soon). He signed a contract with a small recording label, Hull Records from New York, and introduced Clinton to the label. In the late 1960s, both Clinton and Williams discovered Sly and the Family Stone and started to "funkify" their sound. Around the time Clinton put together Funkadelic and reformed his first band under the name Parliament, Williams established his band Nbuda Funkshun (which later dropped the "Funkshun" from its name). Like Clinton's, Williams's funk was rooted in a "decidedly working-class black aesthetic" (Wright 2008:33). Unlike Clinton, Williams never broke through beyond the local New Jersey club scene, and he remained closely tied with the working class from which he hailed: his day job was as a barber, which is how he met and befriended Baraka. In 1976, Baraka approached Williams with the idea of making a funk record, and they invited the guitar player Winston Sims to join them. The first lineup of the Advanced Workers was a full-blooded funk formation consisting of members of prominent bands such as the Commodores, Parliament, Funkadelic, and Kool and the Gang, all of whom Williams and Baraka recruited through Sims. Williams remembers that they rehearsed at the Spirit House, Baraka's Newark headquarters, and recorded the single in one studio ses-

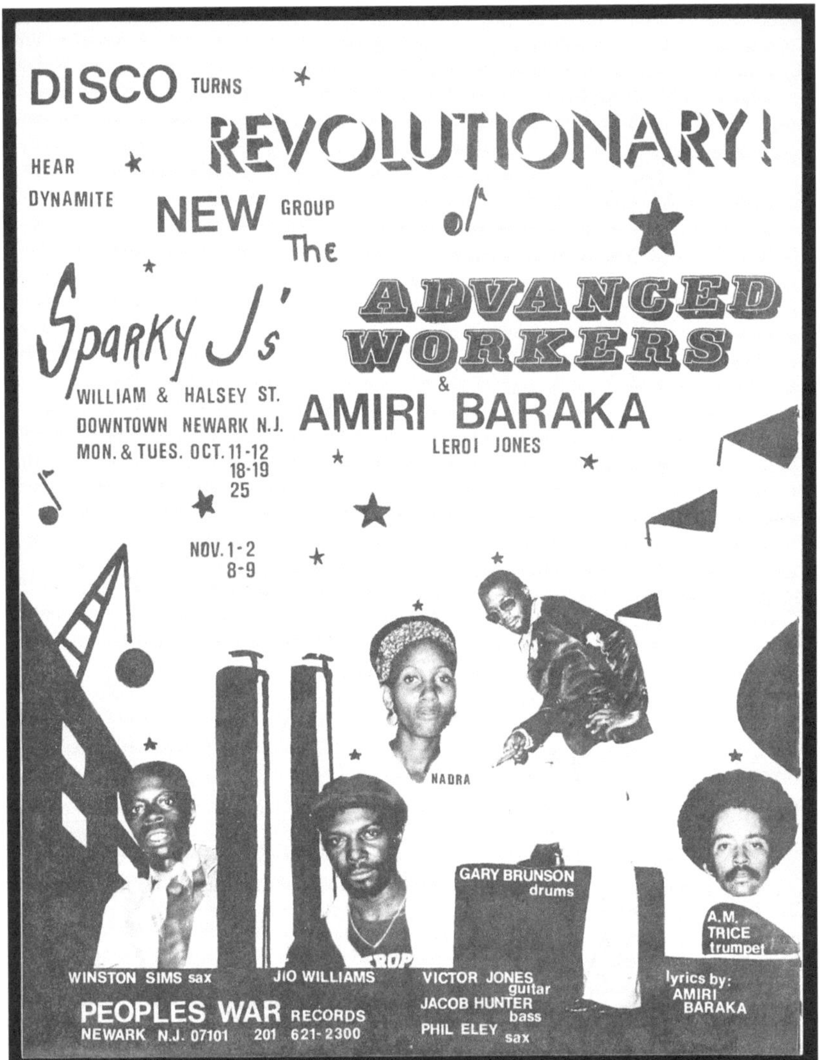

Figure 2. Amiri Baraka and the Advanced Workers Poster: Disco Turns Revolutionary

sion. The second incarnation of the Advanced Workers was in fact Williams's Nbuda Funkshun, which for the occasion of Jazztage music festival in Berlin performed under the name Advanced Workers.[2] The concert they performed on 3 November 1977 was recorded and released on the LP *Amiri Baraka and the Advance* [*sic*] *Workers*. This turned out to be their only live recording and the evidence of the force, precision, and joy of their funk.

On pages of *Unity and Struggle* and on fliers for their performances, the Advanced Workers' single record was advertised with the slogan "Disco turns revolutionary." In the Berlin concert, Baraka introduced "You Was Dancin Need to Be Marchin" as a critique of the kind of art that capitalist society uses to pacify the working classes: "This tune is dedicated to ya'll who every time when we tell you to come to a rally, or every time we tell you to support a demonstration, you tell us you are going to the discotheque."[3] In contrasting discotheque and street, dancing and marching, Baraka presented not only two forms of kinesis but also the movement of the history of Black music, which was subjected to a series of cultural appropriations. In the deluge of the worldwide phenomenon of disco, heralded by the rise of Van McCoy's "The Hustle" to the top of pop charts only a year before the release of "You Was Dancin Need to Be Marchin"—with its drum machines, dance suits, high heels, box-office hit records and films, light shows, and even its drugs of choice—the rhythmical structures of funk were degraded from musical kinesis to movement in place. Funk's response to this cultural theft was perhaps best epitomized by Clinton's P-Funk, where "P" no longer stood just for "Parliament" but also for purity. The Advanced Workers suggest that an integral part of this purity is due to the social position of funk as a continuation of Black working-class music. Baraka said as much in the title of his collection *Funk Lore* and in the verses of his eponymous poem:

> We are the blues
> ourselves
> our favorite
> color
> Where we been, half here
> half gone (1996:95)

Long before he teamed up with Williams to start a proletarian funk band, in the final pages of *Blues People* Baraka wrote that in the 1950s jazz critics and "hobbyists" attached to the form of jazz known as hard bop the idea of "social alienation" and plain "weirdness," which were encapsulated in the word "funk": "*Funky* (a word with as dubious a place in polite society as *jazz*) became the treasured adjective, where once *cool* had been, with *soul*" (1963:219). "Even the adjective *funky*, which once meant to many Negros merely a stink (usually associated with sex), was used to qualify the music as meaningful"—and then he adds, parenthetically: "the word became fashionable and is now almost useless" (219). In the process of appropriation of Black music into white mainstream, funk came to signify the remnant that is inassimilable by and even unrecognizable to musical entrepreneurs: "This smell now, real or not, was made a valuable characteristic of 'Negro-ness.' And 'Negro-ness,' by the fifties, for many Negroes (and whites) was the only strength left to American culture" (220). However short-lived, Baraka's stint with the Advanced Workers was his hands-on investigation of the political potential of this placelessness of radical Black musical forms and of the social formations to which they belonged.

APPARATUS IN SEARCH OF IDEOLOGY

In her "Notes on Funk," Adrian Piper places this musical form on the historical continuum of Black music in America:

> Funk constitutes a language of interpersonal communication and collective self-expression that has its origins in African tribal music and dance and is the result of the increasing interest of contemporary black musicians and the populace in these sources elicited by the civil rights movement of the 1960s and early 1970s. (1996:195)

If both Piper and Baraka embraced funk at certain points of their careers, that is because they recognized it not as a form of entertainment, but as a particularly effective and meaningful mode of Black political performance. For Baraka, as for Piper, funk's force comes from its embeddedness in Black musical tradition, which he sees as inseparable from what Cedric J. Robinson called Black radical tradition. In *Black Marxism,* Robinson makes an important distinction between Black and Western radicalism.[4] The former is not a variant of the later; instead, "it is a specifically African response to an oppression emergent from the immediate determinants of European development in the modern era and framed by orders of human exploitation woven into the interstices of European social life from the inception of Western civilization" ([1983] 2000:73). Baraka's blues, as well as Piper's funk, belong to this tradition.

As unexpected as it seemed when it happened in 1974, Baraka's turn from Black nationalism to orthodox communism is consistent with his unrelenting commitment to that tradition. Robinson traces its sources to precolonial Africa. He suggests that Black "revolutionary consciousness" came "from the whole historical experience of Black people and not merely from the social formations of capitalist slavery or the relations of production of colonialism" ([1983] 2000:169). This positioning of African culture as the foundation of Black radical tradition echoes the argument that Baraka made in *Blues People* against the idea of the cultural uprooting of enslaved Africans. According to Baraka, slavery and its abolition informed the social position of African culture in America, not its sources and its internal dynamics. While the musical properties of the blues reach back to slavery and beyond to African cultural heritage of enslaved workers in the American South, the blues acquires its specific social position with the changes that the Black community experienced with the abolition of slavery: "What is so often forgotten in any discussion of the Negro's 'place' in American society is the fact that it was only as a slave that he really had one. The post-slave society had no place for the black American" (1963:55). The end of slavery brought about a structural transformation of the community of formerly enslaved workers, marked both by its separation from white society and its internal stratification.

This dual social division left the blues, quite literally, down and out: out of white society and with other Black Americans; and down in relation to the newly emerging Black middle class. Tracing the beginnings of social stratification within the community of enslaved laborers back to divisions based on the nature of labor tasks such as house and field slaves, and onward from there to ministry and other professional trades (teachers, lawyers, medical doctors), Baraka holds that the members of the Black bourgeoisie "swallowed the socio-economic concepts of their white upper-class whole" (54). He concludes that in doing so, they created "a separate meta-society, one whose members strove to emulate exactly the white society" (54). He takes the Black church as the model of this "meta-society," in which the "lowest rungs of the social ladder" are occupied by "backsliders" (sinning churchgoers) and the "heathen" (48). Baraka argues that, as a social category, "bluesman" is not limited to musicians or even the consumers of that music. Instead, it designates an entire underclass that refuses to "swallow" the assimilationist attitudes of the Black middle class, and in doing so exposes the paradoxical nature of its ideology. This underclass, together with its lifestyle, music, and poetry, escaped appropriation by withdrawing from white mainstream and rejecting the Black bourgeoisie. It is on this tradition that Baraka draws in his "phonographic poetry." As Reed suggests regarding "Black Dada Nihilismus," which Baraka recorded with New York Art Quartet in 1964, "Sound's circulation within and beyond existing economies of circulation and value . . . is crucial for this poem's staging of the new black music as a blacker, unappropriable art" (125). This aspiration was further radicalized in his work with funk in the following decade.

In his writing about "blues people" no less than in his work with "funk people," Baraka shows that while from its very inception blues had been associated with a certain musical form, it is not reducible to it. Blues is not only a musical style, and a bluesman or blueswoman is not only a musician. If in relation to the middle classes of both races, the bluesman or blueswoman is the "lowest" and the "Blackest," then categorizing blues as "folk" culture would be yet another form of cultural appropriation: it is, more than anything else, a proletarian culture (1968:179). Due to the particular historical conditions of their enslavement and their subsequent limited liberation, Black workers developed a culture with traits distinct from the cultures of the working classes in other capitalist societies. This "class conscience" was evident, as Robinson put it, in "the structures of the mind" that had distinct cultural origins, and one of its manifestations was its refusal to embrace white bourgeois culture indiscriminately (2000:169). Baraka suggests that instead of imitating white culture, bluesmen and blueswomen accepted their own apartness and their difference, which allowed them to adopt or refuse elements of predominant culture as they saw fit. He sees the blues as an expression of the social and cultural unavailability of Black people to the forces of assimilation that were, and are, coming both from within and from without their community.

Improvisation is at the core of the blues in more than one way. It is not only a defining principle of a musical style but also a mode of survival. "Blues people," not "blues music": for Baraka, blues is not just music but also an *asocial social entity* that exists in perpetual condition of exile from the nation-state and its institutions. The difference between bluesmen and blueswomen and the social configuration from which they are forever banished is not just economic and racial but first and foremost epistemic. Baraka holds that it is not only memory, or history, but a deep physical knowledge of slavery that is "at the root of the legitimate black culture" in the United States (1963:136). Music gives this knowledge a form that can be perceived, experienced, and participated in: "Music, as it might seem, is the result of thought. It is the result of thought perfected at its most empirical, *i.e.*, as *attitude*, or *stance*" (152). Already on the first page of *Blues People*, Baraka states unequivocally that blues is not about chords, scales, rhythmical structures, and orchestral arrangements, but about the "customs, attitudes, desires" of Black people in America (1). For him, blues is more than a musical form or a lyrical pattern, but less than an institution insofar as it is not and has never been recognized by the state as one of its organs and equal to them. Blues is a complex arrangement of behaviors, expressions, affects, experiences, and relationships that were shaped into a distinct social entity by virtue of its exclusion from and persecution by the state. Seen not only as a musical form but also as a social formation, blues offers important insights into the nature and functioning of the apparatus as such.

Of course, there is no argument with Althusser that the materiality of ideology in an apparatus "does not have the same modality as the material existence of a paving-stone or a rifle" (1971:156). Nor is there any question that behaviors, attitudes, and rituals are created through interaction with things that range from massive architectural structures to tools (or weapons) of everyday use, or with objects with no obvious practical use, such as artworks. Equally important is the social fact that all of these objects have the legal form of property. Under the capitalist mode of production, there is a direct correlation between ideology and ownership, to the point that capitalism itself can be said to be an ideology of ownership. Modern slavery is a unique combination of ideological and repressive state apparatuses that reduces individuals to the status of commodities, such that they can participate in market circulation only as objects. As Althusserian legal scholar Bernard Edelman observed, in capitalist society the subject in law is defined by the right of ownership. If "the freedom of ownership is the juridical consequence of the free ownership of oneself," then "the slave, the object of ownership, can hardly be conceived as a subject in law" ([1973] 1979:29). It is precisely human behavior violently removed from property ownership that Baraka recognizes as the foundational element of "blues" as social practice forged within communities subjugated to the state ideology of slavery. The enslavers could rip anything from the hands of enslaved workers, including their own children, but they could not take away their voices, gestures, and movements: "These nonmaterial aspects of the African's culture were almost impossible to eradicate" (16). Here, be-havior—harkening back to *aveir* and *avoir*, "having" and "possession"—reaches its full meaning as a property inalienable from the body. As "music, dance, religion do not have *artifacts* as their end products," they became the foundational elements of an apparatus specific to enslaved African workers and their descendants, which after the abolition of slavery achieved expressive, affective, and social behavioral complex that came to be known as *blues* (16).

If apparatuses are seamlessly fused with ideologies, then the nexus that holds them together is the subject. Slavery reveals the economic side of subjecthood, which dictates that individuals can own objects and generate wealth only insofar as they are "possessed" by ideology. This aspect of subjectivation is based on a reciprocal relationship between the subject and property, and it is this relationship that underlines Althusser's scene of interpellation. It is not surprising that his "theoretical theater" consists of shards of behavior (greeting, hailing) caught in fleeting moments, just before they become irretrievably enmeshed with tangible objects, that is, before relationships between people become transmuted to commodity relations. The spotlight in this "little theoretical theater" is ever-present and unavoidable: the voice of power, as exemplified by the police officer, summons the individual into subjectivity. There is a sense of inevitability in this recognition of the subject by ideology, even if—and precisely because—this scene is based on the subject's misrecognition. Following on Althusser's acknowledgment of the possibility of "bad subjects" who don't comply with "juridical and social formation of the subject," Judith Butler observes the "range of *disobedience* that such an interpellating law might produce" (1993:122). She points out that "where the uniformity of the subject is expected, where the behavioral conformity of the subject is commanded, there might be produced the refusal of the law in the form of the parodic inhabiting of conformity" (122). While expanding and correcting Althusser, this by now classical argument about queer performativity retains his positing of an internal coherence of the law and its uniformity of meaning. Here the scene of interpellation is determined by the centrality of an indisputable power. The call comes from one place, it goes in one direction, and it summons the individual in one way. This operation of power places equivocation, distortion, and infelicity on the side of the subject. However, what both Althusser and Butler disregard is that ideology speaks through a multitude of apparatuses, that it uses an array of voices, and that it produces a number meanings, some of which appear to contradict one another. If an apparatus is a social edifice that acquires its material existence through the process of subjectivation, that does not mean this process is uniform and unidirectional. Interpellation of an individual into subjecthood involves a process of negotiation and harmonization among a number of apparatuses. The paradox of Black subjecthood is that some of these apparatuses violently deny that very subjecthood. This little theoretical theater is double. The Black subject is summoned simultaneously into subjecthood and objecthood.

To clarify, the operations of ideology not only summon individuals as subjects but also have the power to shut out these individuals from its apparatuses, thus preventing them from attaining subjecthood. From Althusser's perspective, it is hard to imagine a call from power that doesn't summon but rather repels. Frantz Fanon shows that the same "theoretical scene" can produce a process of inverse subjectivation:

> "Look! A Negro!" It was a passing sting. I attempted a smile.
> "Look! A Negro!" It was true. It amused me.
> "Look a Negro!" Absolutely. I was beginning to enjoy myself.
> "*Maman*, look, a Negro; I'm scared!" Scared! Scared! Now they were beginning to be scared of me. ([1958] 2008:91)[5]

This is a call, all right, but this time it doesn't invite but instead rejects. Ideology can drive (*pellere, in Latin*) the subject in or out: what Althusser sees only as a centripetal force of *interpellation*, Fanon sees as a centrifugal operation of *repellation*, or rejection. This operation that selectively prevents an individual from attaining the status of the subject is fundamental for the production of the form of collectivity that Baraka identifies as "blues people." People, not citizens. According to Baraka, the foundational illusion of what he calls the "Black bourgeoisie" is its belief that the only way to become recognized as "citizens . . . would be to *disappear* completely, leaving no trace at all that there had ever been an Africa, or a slavery, or even, finally, a black man" (1963:124). This act of renunciation still doesn't secure for a member of this class the place of the protagonist in the "theoretical theater" of interpellation. Baraka recognizes blues as a statement of the recognition that regardless of his or her social attainment, a Black person always remains exposed to the force of *ideological repellation*, and that this force is deadly. If there is an ideological aspect of blues, it is precisely in its refusal of this ideology of the emerging Black middle classes.

For Baraka, blues is an expression of cultural, social, and, more than anything else, ideological unrecognizability of a "certain kind" of Black people by the forces of assimilation. While in the first decades of the twentieth century professional musicians could join the ranks of the Black middle class, "Such a thing as a *middle-class blues singer* is almost unheard of" (140). Blues is the worldview of the *people* without the state, from which it follows that it is also an apparatus without ideology. It offers historically grounded evidence that there are apparatuses outside of state ideology, and that an *anideological* apparatus, the very contradiction in terms as far as Althusserian analysis is concerned, is possible. Baraka's work during the period that intervened between his tragic and ideological periods, marked by his attempts to develop and organize Black artistic and political institutions, is informed by his understanding of blues as a paradoxical (an)apparatus. These attempts are guided by Baraka's recognition of the limitations and shortcomings of blues as an apparatus: its lack of formal organization, the absence of planning and intentionality, its reactivity, its inefficiency when it comes to social change, its resignation to devising strategies for subsistence in an oppressive system that comes together with its inability to assert its political agency, and its availability for appropriation and exploitation, which results in its repeated retreats into "subculture" (1963:132, 141, 166). So, when a decade later Baraka wrote a series of political statements asking for "ideological clarity," these calls came from his deep familiarity with the limited effectiveness of an apparatus that is missing a clearly defined ideological framework.

UNITY-CRITICISM-UNITY

"Where is the revolution brothers & sisters?" wrote Baraka in his poem "Today" from the collection *Hard Facts*, which marked his ideological repositioning of the mid-1970s:

> Where is the mobilization of the masses led
> by the advanced section of the working class?
> Where is the unity criticism unity? The self criticism
> & criticism? Where is the work & study? The
> ideological clarity? ([1975] 1979:253)

At the time he wrote the poems that were included in this collection, Baraka also put together a number of political dispatches, such as the internal memo "Creating Unified Consciousness" that was distributed to the members of the Congress of Afrikan People. Speaking in 1973 from his position of CAP chairman, he explained that the direction "unity-criticism-unity," which he charted for the upcoming period, amounted to a process of "seeking unity, criticizing our deviation from the values and the ideology, and at the end of our discussion seeking unity again" (in Simanga 2019:102). He concluded by proclaiming: "We must have ideological clarity before we move on the next higher level of development, which is true NATIONAL MOVEMENT. *If we are serious and involved actually with revolution we will do what we must to see that these things come into being*" (102). Poet and CAP community organizer Michael Simanga reports that Baraka and the leadership of the movement proclaimed 1974 the "Year of Ideological Clarity" (2019:105). Indeed, that year was pivotal in Baraka's maneuvering of CAP to the new ideological position of radical Marxism.

This shift did not come out of nowhere. In "Black like Mao," Robin Kelley and Betsy Esch show that a number of Black intellectuals, activists, and movements, from W. E. B. Du Bois to the Black Panther Party, found in

Mao's China a new, non-Western paradigm of successful revolutionary action. "It is our contention," they write, "that China offered black radicals a 'colored,' or Third World Marxist model that enabled them to challenge a white and Western vision of class struggle" (1999:8). Focusing more specifically on Baraka's turn to Maoism, Robeson Frazier emphasizes the impact that some leaders of African decolonialization movement had on him. He singles out the president of Tanzania, Mwalimu Julius Nyerere, and his brand of socialism, which was ideologically, politically, and economically closely aligned with China, and takes Baraka's participation in the Sixth Pan-African Congress, which was held in the capital of Tanzania in June 1974, as decisive for his ideological change (Frazier 2006:152). However, it seems that by the time he traveled to Dar es Salaam, Baraka had already completed his journey from Black nationalism to internationalism of the radical Left. Simanga points out that he signposted this ideological transformation in three speeches that he delivered in the first half of 1974: "Revolutionary Party: Revolutionary Ideology," which he gave at the Midwest Regional Congress of CAP held in Chicago March 31–April 1 (105); the second a few days later, at the Second National Black Political Convention in Little Rock, Arkansas (11); finally, "Which Road toward Black Liberation" at the ALSC conference at Howard University in May (113). All of this suggests that Baraka's ideological transition was deliberate, planned, and very public.

In the first of these speeches, Baraka forcefully argued for a shift of the organization's platform from nationalism to socialism. Departing sharply from ideological positions he had built over the previous four years, which he still espoused in public statements he made in January 1974, he claimed that while both of these ideological positions are based on an adherence to African culture, nationalism is bourgeois and "metaphysical" in nature, while socialism is progressive and scientific. Moving from one position to another calls for changes that range from CAP's organizational structure to the values reflected in its members' lifestyle: "We must finally convince ourselves that merely by dressing in Afrikan clothes and speaking Swahili and cultivating a superior diet, no revolution will transform the total lives of the majority of people in our national community, nor substantially support the world Afrikan liberation movement" (1974a:4).[6] Ideological change called for altering of the fabric of behavior.

Baraka's radical political and ideological shift from Black nationalism to Marxism-Leninism was the subject of extensive self-criticism, which informed scholarly interpretations of his work. In *Freedom Dreams: The*

Black Radical Imagination Robin Kelley cites the influence of Black Marxists such as William Watkins, with whom Baraka engaged in "work & study" of Marxim-Leninism. This was coupled with the "painful lesson he learned about the limitations of black 'petty bourgeois' politicians," particularly the first Black mayor of Newark, Kenneth Gibson, whom he helped get elected (2002:103). And as Komozi Woodard shows in *A Nation within a Nation: Amiri Baraka (LeRoi Jones) and Black Power Politics*, this disillusionment with Black elected politicians was, for Baraka, also a lesson about the material nature of ideological apparatuses, which he learned when his urban redevelopment project in inner-city Newark was thwarted. It was supposed to include Kawaida Towers, a housing complex named after the Black nationalist doctrine of Maulana Karenga, who had a formative influence on Baraka during his Black nationalist period (1999:224). Ideology is as real as real estate. In a capitalist society, mechanisms of interpellation are just as vulgar and violent as those of repellation, and they operate by means much more complex than those of the hailing voice of a street cop. Baraka witnessed the basic operations of ideological co-optation in urban Newark, New Jersey, and in neocolonial Dar es Salaam, Tanzania.[7] In another verse from "Today" in *Hard Facts* he relates these experiences in a direct and unapologetic way:

> Skinny niggers taking 4 hours to prepare a special
> Afrikan stu meanwhile regular
> Black folks eat watermelons, okra, fried chicken, turnips, all from
> Afrika.
> Abstract metaphysical shit talking bores
> counter revolutionary, selfish, unserious pseudo
> imitators, red baiters, poets forever in residence
> Black studies pimps in interesting tweed jackets
> Frauds in leopard skin, turbaned hustlers w/skin
> type rackets, colored capitalists, negro
> exploiters . . . ([1975] 1979:253)

Here, "abstract metaphysical shit" refers to the Black bourgeoisie; in the introduction to *Hard Facts*, he explains:

> Earlier our own poems came from an enraptured patriotism that screamed against whites as the eternal enemies of Black people, as the sole cause of our disorder & oppression. The same subjective mystification led to mysticism, metaphysics, spookism, etc., rather

> than dealing with reality, as well as an ultimately reactionary nationalism that served no interests but our newly emerging Black bureaucratic elite and petty bourgeois, so that they would have control over their Black market. ([1975] 1979:238)

It turns out that the ideological repositioning of CAP in the watershed year 1974 was, for Baraka, a way to stay consistent in what Reed calls "the work of negativity" in his thought: "His opposition to 'bourgeois art' implied a social alternative whose power derived from its opposition . . . to abstractions disconnected from the rhythms and concerns of everyday living" (131). For Baraka, "ideological clarity" demanded fidelity to the apparatus he discovered in the blues. His own, and CAP's, shift from nationalism to radical communism came from a deep consistency with that "work of negativity" which is recognizable already in *Blues People* and which affected all of his previous political, poetic, and existential breakups. CAP's repositioning to the radical Left can be seen as an expression of Baraka's recognition that the choice is not between bourgeois ideology that necessarily involves co-optation and a position outside of it, based, in the case of Black nationalism, on the rejection of Western values and forms of life, but in relationship to interests as the driving force of ideology. Here Éric Alliez and Maurizio Lazzarato's distinction between "egoist" and "disinterested" interests is relevant: the former "produce no localization, no territoriality, no particular groupings (the market is deterritorializing, universalizing and its relationships are 'abstract')," while the latter "produce community ties and thus territorialized, localized, singular groups" (2016:142). When it comes to Baraka, the first is aligned with politics, and the second with poetics. Contrary to dismissive readings of his Marxist poetry of the middle and late 1970s, it was not that his political realignment transformed his art, but the other way around.[8]

In the introduction to *Hard Facts*, Baraka gives a clear indication that his turn away from the "metaphysical shit" of the Black bourgeoisie is part of the trajectory he started on a decade earlier, with his disavowal of Greenwich Village avant-garde poetic circles for their inability to distance themselves from the middle class: they became "old American academics reflecting on our gardens & the newest frog to croak there—even if the garden is the Lower East Side" (238). Baraka's crossing over to the radical Left can be seen as a part of a much longer series of personal transformations than his involvement in electoral politics, Pan-Africanism, and urban renewal in Newark. More than all of these apparatuses, at stake for him was the apparatus of poetry, its architectonics and sonics, which he started exploring in the late 1950s. What was at stake here was not finding, but losing, his voice; or to use his favorite formula from the late 1970s, the sequence of unity-criticism-unity, where the second unity can never be the same as the first one. It demands a profound transformation both of the subject and of the society and its apparatuses.

According to this dialectical schema, if Baraka's first "unity" was with the Beat poets of the Lower East Side and "criticism" his rejection of the Beats from the position of Black nationalism, than the second "unity" is with "the omnieyed, multinational mass" (Baraka [1975] 1979:236). In other words, Baraka's transition to the radical Left is the final in a series of gestures rejecting the American modernist poetics of Charles Olson and Robert Creeley, which had a formative influence on his poetry. Even in the mid-1970s, it could easily be construed that Baraka was still following the precepts of Olson's poetics of "projective verse." Motion as the main organizing principle of funk has a strange resonance with Olson's first tenet about poetry, that it is "a *kinetic* thing": the syllable and the line animate the breath into poetic figures akin to dance (1959:3).[9] But who dances here, and what dance? What has been celebrated as Olson's insistence on the "particularity" and individuality of the poet (as opposed to the impersonal laws that have traditionally guided poetry) can also be seen as bourgeois individualism to boot. There is much that goes unobserved in Olson's understanding of "the kinetic of the poem" as a tangible presence of the poet comparable to "what we call the objects of reality" (20). In the second part of the essay, Olson develops this idea further:

> Objectism is the getting rid of the lyrical interference of the individual as ego, of the "subject" and his soul, that peculiar presumption by which western man has interposed himself between what he is as a creature of nature (with certain instructions to carry out) and those other creations of nature which we may, with no derogation, call objects. (10)

How could a Black poet not recognize that these lines could only be written from the position of a white subject who can afford to forget the history of "natural" objects in America? Olson's call for the renunciation of subjectivity comes precisely from this willed political and historical ignorance: "For a man himself is an object, whatever he may take to be his advantages, the more likely to recognize himself as such the greater his advantages, particularly at that moment that he achieves an humilitas sufficient to make him of use" (25). That only a bourgeois poet can idealize (and even ideologize) this kind of "objectism" is not obscured by Olson's seemingly self-mocking address to his poet friends as "citizens" in the third tenet of his projective verse manifesto (17). Baraka understood what was going on there, and he indicated that recognition by including the epigraph from Olson at the head of chapter 9 of *Blues People,* in which he indicts Black bourgeoisie for the price it was willing to pay for its admission to the status of citizenship in American society.

PARTY FUNK

In his calls for the ideological transformation of CAP, Baraka is explicit about his sources. In "Revolutionary Party: Revolutionary Ideology," the list of priorities for the projected party is also a list of ideological principles: first comes "Black Liberation Party," then Marx, Lenin, and Mao, who are followed by the trailblazers of African socialism: the leader of the liberation movement in Ghana, Kwame Nkrumah; the first president of independent Tanzania, Julius Nyerere; the first president of Guinea, Sékou Touré; and the foremost Marxist theoretician of Lusophone Africa, Amílcar Cabral. The final spot is left for the leading figure of Black cultural nationalism, Maulana Karenga, whose name completely disappears from "Towards Ideological Clarity" and other documents Baraka produced after 1974. His adherence to the Chinese model of a communist revolution was not atypical for radical Black politics of that period. In his work on the Black radical imagination Robin Kelley maintains that, of all international communist doctrines, the Chinese Cultural Revolution "seemed to have the most direct impact on black radical movements in the United States" (2002:91). He cites responses to the Cultural Revolution from Black activists, ranging from the exiled communist activist Robert Williams, who, only months into the revolution echoed its basic tenets in his article "Reconstitute Afro-American Art to Remold Black Souls" (1967), to its impact on some of the most prominent Black political movements of the 1960s, such as the Black Panther Party. Kelley holds that, even though it arrived on the scene very late, Baraka's RCL was the "movement with perhaps the deepest roots in the black cultural politics of the 1960s that developed a Marxist-Leninist-Maoist position" (102). Of all Marxist movements in the second half of the twentieth century, Mao's Great Proletarian Cultural Revolution can be seen as an event that bridges the temporal, geographical, and cultural gap that separates Althusser and Baraka.

In its issue for November–December 1966, published only months after the launch of the movement to transform Communist China, the journal *Cahiers marxistes-léninistes* featured the unsigned article "On the Cultural Revolution." The journal was the organ of the Communist (Marxist-Leninist) Youth Union, which emerged after a split within another communist group made up in large part of Althusser's students from the École Normale Supérieure. Although the article first appeared anonymously, it was later confirmed that the author was Althusser himself. This article is not significant only because it displays Althusser's attitude toward the Cultural Revolution, but because it offers one of his early engagements with ideology and its apparatuses. Right at the outset, he points out that the true nature of the Cultural Revolution is not political or economic, but ideological. This revolution in the ideology of the masses is the logical and necessary continuation of the previous two revolutionary phases, and it comes from the Chinese Communist Party's recognition that "stopping halfway" in the revolutionary process was no better than a regression back to capitalist economic, political, and ideological patterns ([1966] 2010:6). This section of the article offers a fairly straightforward interpretation of Chinese official sources. Althusser's intervention comes with his analysis of the purpose of ideological revolution in a socialist state: if political revolution transforms the organization of a society, and economic revolution radically reorders relations of production, in which social sphere does an ideological revolution intervene? Althusser takes a decidedly Marxist approach to this question: "Like all 'levels' of society, the ideological is made up of *objective social relations*. Just as there are social (economic) relations of production, there are also political social relations and 'ideological social relations'" (15). If political relations are transformed with the help of party leadership, and economic relations through the redistribution of wealth, ideological relations are transformed through cultural work. It is at this point that Althusser offers an early insight about ideology inhering within the material strata of society:

> What, in fact, are these relations made of? There [*sic*] are not only made up of systems of ideas-representations, but systems of conducts-behaviors as well; therefore, both "theoretical" and "practical" systems. The ideological includes not only the systems of ideas (*ideologies* in the strict sense), but also systems of practices of conduct-behavior (*mores* or customs [*moeurs*]). (15)

From this it follows that "an ideological revolution should necessarily be a revolution not only in ideas—or ideologies—but also in practical conducts and behaviors—or customs" (15). Sensing that this kind of revolution within a socialist state can easily turn into a system of purges, as already seen in Stalin's USSR, Althusser warns that "in no case, even against the bourgeois class enemy (crimes being punished by law), should one come to 'blows' and have recourse to violence, but always to reasoning and persuasion" (8). As it turned out, precisely because it aimed to intervene in and transform behaviors and customs, the Chinese Cultural Revolution turned into a mass reeducation effort that used violent means to achieve its goals.

Published ten years later, on the other side of the historical divide marked by the Third World revolutionaries' disillusionment with Chinese internal and international politics, the documents of the Revolutionary Communist League (M-L-M) seem to take the vanguard role of the Party as the main takeaway of the Cultural Revolution. The Maoist "ideological revolution" resonates through Baraka's political writings of 1974. The position paper published in *Unity and Struggle* in June 1976, in which the RCL explains the decision to change its name, identifies party building as its "central task" (1976a:6). Elaborating, word by word, the organization's new name, the document states that "Revolutionary" represents the "fighting spirit and fighting organization"; "Communist" is a declaration of political lineage: "We must call ourselves Communist Party—just as Marx and Engels called themselves"; "League," importantly, because "as a *pre-party* formation we must continue to struggle to build a revolutionary organization based on democratic centralism" (7, emphasis added). Finally, the bracketed abbreviation "M-L-M" echoes the same position as "Bolshevik" in the name of the Russian Communist Party under Lenin, who used this designation to distinguish his faction "from the opportunism of the Mensheviks" (8).[10] The position paper on party building, published in November 1976, abounds with long quotations from Stalin. The document repeatedly cites the Soviet leader's emphasis on propaganda during the "pre-party" period. To point:

> At this stage of party building, in the pre-party period, we hold that Political Line is key line, which means that the theoretical form of class struggle, the ideological struggle over correct political line, that is the application of the theories of M-L-M to the concrete conditions of the U.S.A. in the concrete practice of making proletarian revolution in the U.S.A. must take precedence, and that our chief form of practical activity is propaganda. (1976b:11)

Already in "Towards Ideological Clarity" Baraka espoused a view of the party as the driving force for accomplishing ideological and political goals of the class. As such, its success depended on its ideological resolve and organizational efficacy. If for Althusser *representation* was the central operation of ideology, for Baraka it was *organization*. For him, the party is an apparatus. In the same way in which apparatus is directionless without ideology, ideology is powerless without its apparatuses.

Before he engaged in the study of Mao and Stalin, Baraka had plenty of practical knowledge about the apparatic nature of political parties. Drawing on his extensive experience with establishing and running nongovernmental institutions such as Black Arts Repertory Theatre/School (BART/S) during the Black Arts movement in the mid-1960s, Baraka was very much aware of the basic elements that go into building an organization from the ground up.[11] The ready-made audience, willing artists, and federal funds that BART/S received from Office for Economic Opportunity through the Harlem Youth Opportunities Unlimited Experience were not enough. In retrospect, Baraka acknowledged that the key missing component was ideology: "We had no stated ideology except 'black,' and that meant many things to many people, much of it useful, much of it not" (1984:318).[12] This experience certainly informed his turn to the left and his attempt at party building. In "The Pan-African Party and the Black Nation" (1971a), a position paper addressing the issue of organizing a political party, Baraka laid out areas of activity, organizational schema, and funding sources for a Black party that would start in the United States and then develop internationally. Five years before the publication of "RLC's Position on Party Building," Baraka was very much aware that an effective party depends on the successful integration of an ideological platform and an organizational structure. This document conveys his understanding that a working party has to exceed its purely organizational parameters and become an apparatus in a sense almost identical to Althusser's. "A political party is an organ of consciousness," wrote Baraka (1971a:26); and "It must also provide a value system, a way of living, that will ensure *predictability of behavior, ultimate authority, and a means of security*" (25). His statements on party building from the mid-1970s were a radical reversal of the convictions he presented in his position paper on the Pan-African Party that "theoretical ideology must be subservient to the commonality of our experience, and by working together the gap between so-called ideologies will disappear and strong working relationships develop among black people of seemingly widely-divergent, theoretical, political ideologies" (26). This is where leopard hats, African stew, and poets in residence come in. The ideological clarity comes from honoring "the need for a vanguard party whose members recognize the necessary difference between themselves and the revolutionary masses

LOCAL PYRAMID AND CIRCLE STRUCTURE FOR ORGANIZING LOCAL, STATE, OR REGIONAL OFFICES.

The local CAP office should be structured, keeping in mind the need for the formation of a cadre of dedicated workers and a circle of operational unity in the community.

The pyramid or the cadre should consist of the dedicated working leadership and membership of the local CAP office. It is from this cadre that the local thrust — initiators of ideas and actions — should come.

The circle of operational unity should encompass as many local leaders, politicians and organizations as possible. This will prevent the concept of isolation, alienation and eventual elimination, through pooling of ideas, resources (economics, political and survival).

This circle of operational unity serves the dual purpose of being a vehicle for mobilizing, organizing and politicizing the total community and in turn serves as a buffer between you and the negative forces. Through this type of community contact the base of our cadre should increase and hopefully encompass the entire community organized behind a Pan-African nationalist ideology.

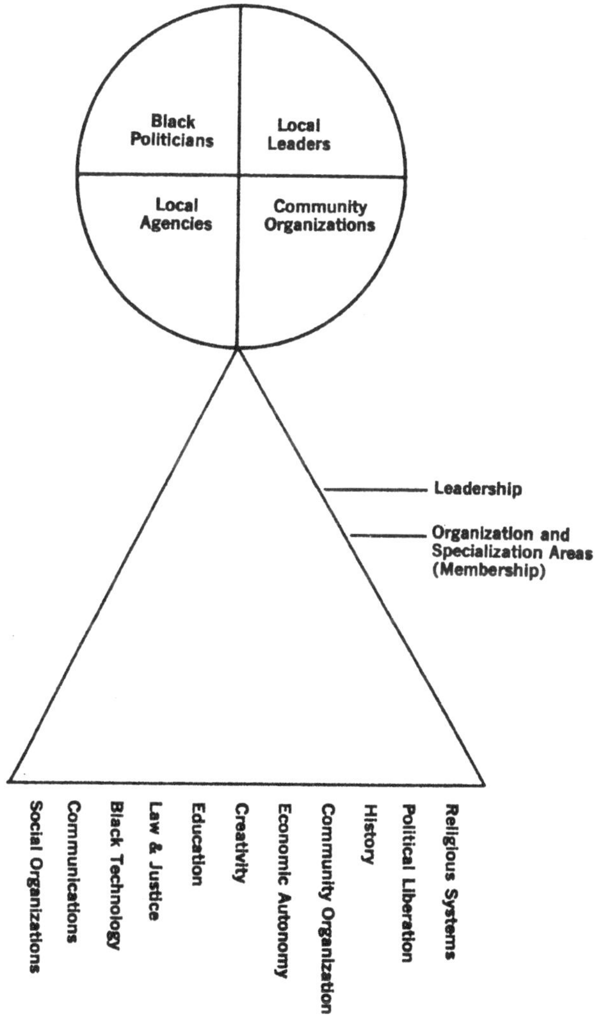

Figure 3. Amiri Baraka: Local Pyramid and Circle Structure for Organizing Local, State, or Regional Offices

in terms of a firm ideology, programmatic commitment, and discipline, before they go to the masses to interact with them and give them leadership" (1974c:93).

What remained constant in Baraka's plans for building a Black nationalist or a Maoist party was the lesson he drew from his study of the incomplete apparatus of "blues": that a movement vitally depends on its compositional structure. The year 1971 was as much "a time for organization" as was 1974 or 1976: "The process of organizing in all the areas of political power is the one constant of our survival. All areas!" (1971a:30). Unlike in position papers on party building from his Maoist period, Baraka included in "The Pan-African Party and the Black Nation" elaborate graphs outlining this organizational structure. The second graph presents the organizational schema of local, regional, and state offices (Figure 3).

The caption added to this diagram reads like a working definition of an ideological apparatus: "This circle of operational unity serves the dual purpose of being a vehicle for mobilizing, organizing and politicizing the total community and in turn serves as a buffer between you and the negative forces" (1971a:31). It is important to remember that these lines come from a political organizer who was first and foremost a poet. Baraka's statements on party building were, quite literally, exercises in projective writing: they were spatial and temporal templates for establishing meaningful relationships between great numbers of individuals. Olson "swears" that the line comes "from the breath, from the breathing of the man who writes, at the moment that he writes, and thus is, it is here that, the daily work, the WORK, gets in, for only he, the man who writes, can declare, at every moment, the line its metric and its ending—where its breathing, shall come to, termination" (1959:6). And he chastises: "Contemporary workers go lazy RIGHT HERE WHERE THE LINE IS BORN" (6). Not "advanced workers"! Baraka's graph speaks to the insufficiency of the syllable, the breath, and the line as the building blocks of a poem. The advanced work of projective verse does not stop at the line or at the page. It is multidirectional, and it extends both in space and time. The advantages that Olson sees in work facilitated by the typewriter can't accommodate this kind of bodily writing. The assemblage that Baraka envisions includes bodies, groups, actions, and words, but also sounds, images, hollers, and odors (funk!). The apparatus is an action poem irreducible to a typewriter metaphor. Consider the vision of the discursive machine Baraka produced during the same period when he drew the party organizational graphs:

> A typewriter?—why shd it only make use of the tips of the fingers as contact points of flowing multi directional creativity. If I invented a

> word placing machine, an "expression-scriber," *if you will*, the I would have a kind of instrument into which I could step & sit or sprawl or hang & use not only my fingers to make words express feelings but elbows, feet, head, behind, and all sounds I wanted, screams, grunts, taps, itches. I'd have magnetically recorded, at the same time & translated into word—or perhaps even the final xpressed thought/feeling wd not be merely word or sheet, but *itself*, the xpression, three-dimensional—able to be touched, or tasted, or felt, or entered, or heard or carried like a speaking singing constantly communicating charm. *A typewriter is corny!!* (1971b:156)

This is the theoretical prelude to the work in which Baraka was to engage only a few years later. Already in 1976 he was building the party and leading a funk band. At the same time, he chaired the Afro-American Commission that produced a position paper on the Black national question, one of the most important documents that the RCL issued. While doing that, he contributed a regular column to *Unity and Struggle* and produced a steady stream of pamphlets addressing questions such as the busing crisis in Boston and ideological conflicts with other factions on the radical left. During that time, Baraka also organized the Yenan Theater Workshop, with which he staged his play *What Was the Relationship of the Lone Ranger to the Means of Production?*, and which also devised the collective theater piece *Images of Struggle and Revolution*. These theater productions were linked with the Anti-Imperialist Cultural Union (AICU), a wide-ranging association of artists on the left, which included former members of Art & Language (New York), individual conceptual artists, and artists engaged in institutional critique. The Visuals Workshop of AICU worked on Yenan's productions and other AICU projects, such as the journal *Main Trend*.[13] All of that on top of writing poetry, doing readings, and giving lectures. If, as he put it in an interview from that time, "the real revolution" is "the upsurge of work," then this was it ([1979] 1994:160). What animated this personal revolution, and what at the same time this revolution animated, was the realization that no ideology is limited to a single apparatus. The state is in the business of endlessly multiplying its apparatuses. In the late 1970s, Baraka fostered an alternative system of ideological apparatuses that germinated through the cracks of capitalist hegemony. Each of them required a different form of social organization and a different mode of engagement. For a brief period in 1976–77, Baraka's funk band Advanced Workers was a pulsating center at the intersection of all of these micro-apparatuses.

"Advanced Workers" is a direct reference to the "Summary" section of

RLC's position paper on party building. In this section, which draws on Lenin's statement in his pamphlet "A Retrograde Trend in Russian Social-Democracy," Baraka speaks of an "advanced worker" as "one who is class conscious, politically active, can win the confidence and trust of the masses, educate and organize the proletariat, studying and actively seeking answers to questions thrown up by the movement and society, consciously accept socialism and will become a communist based on their contact with M-L-M," etc. (Revolutionary Communist League (M-L-M) 1976b:16). While the phrase "the advanced workers" reflects Baraka's ideological position, organizationally and functionally the RCL and the Advanced Workers appear as polar opposites. Taking a cue from Stalin's *Foundations of Leninism,* that "the logical basis of all opportunity is the theory of spontaneity," the leaders of RCL (M-L-M) saw "combating spontaneity" as one of the primary tasks in the process of party building (1976b:3). In the second part of the position paper, printed in the May–June 1977 edition of *Unity and Struggle,* they explain that "the workers movement is spontaneous and not based on the science of proletarian revolution" so that it is "the job of the communists (the Revolutionary theoreticians) to introduce the science of M-L-M, the science that will lead the proletariat under the leadership of the communist vanguard party to victory in armed struggle to overthrow the bourgeois state" (1977:6). The "theory of spontaneity" stands in sharp opposition to the doctrine of party discipline, which came from Lenin to Mao, via Stalin's steely mediation. This doctrine does not belong to the science of M-L-M, but to the militarist doctrine of L-S-M—Lenin-Stalin-Mao—invoked several times in RCL's papers on party building: "The Party constitutes the officer corps and general staff of the proletariat, who direct the struggle of the latter in all its forms and all spheres without exception, and combine diverse forms of the struggle into one whole" (1976a:6). The vanguard position that the Party takes in relation to the working class requires a militantly hierarchical organization of its apparatus.[14]

Both the Party and a musical form such as the blues are related to, as Baraka put it, "the needs of the group," but in completely opposite ways. The latter is characterized by an absence of uniformity: "It was assumed that each man had his *own* blues and that he would sing them" (1963:82). And onward from blues, "primitive jazz," Baraka maintains, "was a communal, collective music" in which individual "solo-like statements" were "dominated by the form and intent of the ensemble" (156). These forms of "collective improvisation" Baraka characterized specifically in terms of "spontaneity" (156, 181). Once uniformity is introduced to a jazz ensemble, "catatonia and noncommunication" set in (181). As with music, so with political organization: Baraka recognizes that the forms of orchestration invented by ensembles are expressions of the needs of larger communities. The individuality prioritized by early blues players carries over to the "sloppy ensemble style" of uptown New Orleans orchestras and is recognizable in "the autonomy, even anarchy" of the small-band form preferred by bebop musicians (111, 184). What jazz critics saw as "sloppy" and "anarchic" was in fact a unique form of organization not *for*, but *in* performance. In other words, that is the principle of funkiness that Baraka recognized so astutely and so early, and which returned to Black music with the rise of the funk band in the 1970s.

There is certain similarity between the development from small blues bands to great jazz orchestras from the mid-nineteenth to the mid-twentieth century, and the growth of funk bands in the early seventies, which would start from a core group of musicians and then keep adding, reaching the extremes of P-Funk mobs of over twenty musicians performing onstage. The historian of funk Rickey Vincent points out that this unique form of musical collectivity was driven by the principle of maintaining equality among band members, "both in music and in attitude" (1996:16). In funk, collective improvisation was not modal or melodic, but motional. Each player moves freely between enforcing and subverting the traditional role of her or his instrument, riffing off each other and changing roles. Vincent: "The drums and bass had their traditional roles as organizers of the rhythmic pattern, but the advent of new keyboards gave the pianist a dual role as rhythm and lead instrument, depending on the situation. The goal was for every player to improvise at his or her best, while staying 'locked' with the others" (17). Here the "others" are not just the band members onstage but also the dancers in front of them: Marshall Jones, bassist for the Ohio Players, spoke of focusing on dancers on the floor and taking cues from them for his rhythmical patterns (in Bolden 2013:12). In this instance, who is organizing whom?

In the lyrics he wrote for the Advanced Workers and in the poems he read during its concerts, Baraka liberally cites from Mao Zedong, whom he also honored in the name of the Yenan Theater Workshop. In interviews from this period, he praised not only Mao's political views but also his aesthetic judgments. He often referenced his "Talks at the Yenan Forum on Literature and Art," not hesitating to characterize it as "the best book on literary criticism" he had "ever read" ([1978] 1994:137). In itself, that raises the question of reconciling the Advanced Workers' irreverent funk with Mao's praise for "Soviet experience" and his advocating for socialist realism ([1942] 1965:87). How did Baraka reconcile the complex rhythmical structures of "Better Red" or "You Was Dancin'" with Mao's demand that art become a "reflection of life" on a "higher plane, more intense, more concentrated, more typical, nearer the ideal, and therefore more universal than actual everyday life," which smacks of hard-core Zhdanovism (82)? Far from "typifying the contradictions," Baraka's band funkifies them, taking them far from the "ideal" and "universal" to address the specificity and uniqueness of Black experience in the United States.

The Advanced Workers' funk is uncompromising and hard-driving. The work of this group of professional musicians, best captured in the live recording of their performance at the 1977 Berlin Jazztage festival, is characterized by the impeccable rhythm structures of Theodor Mathews on drums and Thomas Lewis on bass, and by Barry Eversly's piercing guitar licks and high-flying solos, which the guitar prodigy Eddie Hazel of Funkadelic introduced into funk. And if Clinton experimented with integrating elements of white hard rock into Black music, the Advanced Workers brought striking blues elements into their funk. This deep bluesification of dance music comes out in the singer Joe Williams's harmonica that's buzzing and sawing through a sturdy funk groove, and in the hoarseness of Larry Lewis's voice, which shows up midway through the concert, and last but not the least, in Baraka's delivery of his poems. Some of them were included in his appropriately titled collection *Poetry for the Advanced*. Live performances of "An American Oppress Story!" and "Like, This Is What I Meant!" were captured in the recording of the Advanced Workers' Berlin set. The contradictions of Baraka's agit-funk are especially revealing in "Like, This Is What I Meant!" Similarly to some of his other poems from the period, this number starts with a poetic credo:

> Poetry makes a statement
> like everything
> like everything poetry
> makes a statement
>
> It is a "being of words"
>
> produced by the life
> of (DAH da da Dah!)
> "The pOeT" (1979:294)

In concert, the driving rhythm of bass, drum, and keyboard rolls in the background as Baraka reads his first stanza. He then invokes Chairman Mao:

"Take Class Struggle
as the key link," sd Mao, "Act according
  to the past principles"

So that even in our verse
The roar of raging mass
is heard (1979:294)

This is where the bass guitar jumps in with a full-bodied, heavy riff, adding emphasis. And from there on, the antiphonal interaction between Baraka's words and the band's voice-like instruments sets in. To Baraka's

"Countries want Independence
Nations want Liberation
People want revolution," Chairman Mao
  has sd (295)

Eversly responds with a shrill solo vignette. And a couple of verses later, the chorus of background vocals (Mary Davis, Jio Williams, and Larry Lewis) join the rhythm section with their melodic "Yeahs." But the call-and-response doesn't allow the voice, the poem, to monopolize the foreground. Sounds and hollers jump out in front of verses and pull them back into the background. The poet-performer now must leave the page behind to wrestle with music for attention:

Poetry must sing, laugh & fight
Poetry must reveal, probe and light
Poetry must take class struggle
  as the key link (294)

Backing vocals assert themselves and prod the poet forward. They are, as Baraka said of another ensemble of poet-musicians, like "blue wings flapping up a hurricane of funk" (1984:337):

must remold its world view
to take up the struggle
for the mighty

That's how this last line reads on the page. But in performance, it enters a different logic, which dictates that it's no longer sufficient for the poet to just utter the word, so instead he accelerates into "mighty, mighty, mighty, mighty, mighty working class." He is on board now, and interjects "yeahs" between his verses. In the last stanza, it all comes together. It's no longer a poem, it's a song:

So that even
in our
verse
even in
our dancing
even in
our song
yeh
in our pure lover song. (297)

And again, one iteration of "pure" is not enough. Instead, in performance, it is "pure, pure, pure, pure lover song." Repeated, "lover" sounds like "love," which finally funkifies the poetic statement. But what is "love" doing here, the funk love, P-love, sensual love of pleasure in syncopated rhythms? How does that measure against Mao's aphorisms about class struggle and revolution? Did Baraka miss Mao's repudiation of love in "Yenan Talks"? There he lectured that "it is a basic Marxist concept that being determines consciousness, that the objective realities of class struggle and national struggle determine our thoughts and feelings. But some of our comrades turn this upside down and maintain that everything ought to start from 'love'" (74). This is socialist realism, for sure, and not funky at all.

So what is this "pure lover" doing in Baraka's political funk? Is he paying lip service to Mao while proposing and propagating something completely foreign to the Chinese revolutionary leader's steely realism? Or is he reversing the relationship between Black experience in the United States and international Maoism, so that he doesn't try to adapt his art to its ideological apparatus but instead impart this experience to it, that is to say, to teach, and in doing so add to radical Marxism a whole new repository of lived knowledge? Unity, but then also criticism? Indeed, the performance of the verse about "pure lover song" carries with it a fundamental insight from blues. It is knowledge about the apparatus as an assemblage not only of relationships, bodies, and behaviors but also of emotions. And the fundamental emotion of blues, despite its name, is not melancholy and sadness, but love: love not as elation and cheerfulness, but as an emotion that is as autonomous, inviolable, and class-conscious as this music. It is not

Mao's love misunderstood as class solidarity, or even the psychoanalytic insight that Althusser took for granted from Jacques Lacan about loving as giving what one does not have to someone who does not want it. That love is conditioned by a subject-object relationship. Blues is the kind of love in which the subject and the object are forcefully collapsed onto one another. And so is funk, but it doesn't stop there. As we have seen, in this collapsing of subject and object Piper finds the distinctive feature of performance art.

The lesson that Baraka offers to Mao is the one he learned from blues: it carries the insight about love that is not an experience of a desiring subject, but love constituted through violent removal of a desired object. It is non-objective, pure love. The knowledge of slavery that was, as Baraka recognized, the fundamental knowledge of blues speaks of this love as the only possession, the only thing that can't be taken away, given or taken, bought and sold. In "The Changing Same (R&B and New Black Music)," the closing chapter of *Black Music*, Baraka writes that blues is about love and that, if one wants to know about this love that blues knows, one should not read the Moynihan Report, which details the generational devastation of Black families under the ideology of racism, but instead should listen to Junior Walker's "(I'm a) Roadrunner": "And this missed love that runs through these songs is exactly reflect [*sic*] of what is the term of love and loving in the Black world of America Twentieth Century" (1968:183). It is in these lines that Amiri Baraka / LeRoi Jones, the prolific author of liner notes, captures what Daphne Brooks in her magisterial *Liner Notes for the Revolution* identifies as "the Black radical marvelous" (2021:10). Missed love, love gone, love snatched away, is, paradoxically, the only property that the owned person can own, the core of her subjectivity. Ideology and its apparatuses need to account for this love, for this absolute ownership of love as lack. The repressive state apparatus can easily become violence concentrated, just as ideological state apparatuses can became blatant systems of co-optation. However, there are other social arrangements that don't lend themselves as easily to mechanisms of repression and appropriation.

The party is an apparatus of accord. It is organized hierarchically. The body at the top takes over and possesses all of the subordinated bodies, without question or dissent. The band is an apparatus of discord. Its main organizing principle is the questioning of organization. Each body responds to another, pushes back and receives, denies and is denied, objects and subjects. Any body that comes to occupy the center does that only tentatively and temporarily. Baraka captures this performance in an offhand remark from his autobiography: "Jackie had the most strange presence and he would conduct the band (really like Diz) with head, arms, legs, butt, even his eyes shooting in all directions" (1997:81). The conductor is being conducted. In the band, the bodies enter other bodies, so that each body becomes an ensemble: the head argues with the arm, and eyes with tongue. It is a disorganized organization, a torrent in an organism, which brings into question both the torrent and the organism. That is the existential condition of Black radical tradition, what makes it unlike all other Western (and Eastern!) radicalisms. A direct descendant of blues and jazz orchestras, the funk mob is a multicentric and multidirectional assembly of production, an open exchange of impulses and responses. To paraphrase Kodwo Eshun, in the mad science of the funk band, M-L-M is science gone glad.[15] The band is undiagrammable: as such, it is the action-critique of the hierarchical, scriptural, and logocentric logic of the communist party that Mao (following Stalin, following Lenin) advocated for. As for the bodies, so for the apparatuses. In his work with the Advanced Workers, Baraka offered a self-critique of his idea of the apparatus as a device that secures predictability of behavior. In the process, he offers a critical insight about the performance apparatus, which is always located between other apparatuses. It springs up at points of their intersections and areas of overlap. Performance labors to push against these apparatuses to de-routinize their operations. The experience of the Advanced Workers and Anti-Imperialist Singers as a dynamic node in a network of apparatuses is fundamental for understanding the emergence and elaboration of the performance apparatus.

FOUR | Situation

On Performance Dramaturgy

PROJECTION

If ideology, as Althusser claims, has no history, apparatuses certainly do. In her article "Theater, an 'Original Apparatus'?," published in the journal *Appareil*, French theater scholar Sophie-Aurore Roussel recognizes in the Greek tragic theater the earliest and paradigmatic formation of the "aesthetic apparatus" in the West. In several ways, the theory of the aesthetic apparatus, which emerged in France in the first decade of the current millennium, attempts to depart from the apparatus theory from the 1970s that was rooted in Althusserian critique of ideology. In the introduction to her edited volume *Miroir, appareils et autres dispositifs* (Mirror, Apparatuses, and Other *Dispositifs*; 2008), Soko Phay-Vakalis offers a working definition of the aesthetic apparatus as "a technique that makes the event 'appear,'" noting it can't be "reduced to a technique (machine, tool, instrument), to the *dispositif* in Foucauldian sense (prison, hospital, army)," or "to a medium of communication (radio, press)" (2008:8).[1] She dates the beginning of this resurgence of interest in the apparatus to the conference at Beaulieu College of Art in 2001 and the program "Arts, Apparatuses, Diffusion" held the following year at the research center Maison des Sciences de l'Homme Paris Nord. The proceedings of the Beulieu conference were published in 2006 under the title *L'art au temps des appareils* (Art in the Age of Apparatuses; 2006) edited by Pierre-Damien Huyghe. The emergence and development of the aesthetic apparatus theory was initiated and paced by the philosopher of aesthetics Jean-Louis Déotte, who during this period published a series of monographs and articles that include *L'époque de l'appareil perspectif* (The Epoch of Perspectival Apparatus; 2001), *L'époque des appareils* (The Epoch of Apparatuses; 2004), and *Qu'est-ce qu'un appareil?* (What Is an Apparatus?; 2007). While they come from various disciplines (aesthetics, theater, cinema studies, media studies, art history), the proponents of aesthetic apparatus theory share the method of taking a specific "technique" as the defining moment in their historizations of apparatuses. For Roussel, it's Greek tragic theater; for Phay-Vakalis, the mirror; and for Déotte, the perspective in visual arts.

In his article "Alberti, Vasari, Leonardo: From *Disegno* as Drawing to *Disegno* as Projective Milieu," Déotte takes Jean-François Lyotard's idea of the "norms of legitimacy" as "major relationships between law, power, and knowledge" to be his guideposts in charting three broad "epochs" of the apparatus. The first one is that of narration, that is, of the myth, which has the ritual body as its "preferred surface of inscription" (Déotte 2007:52); the second one is the revelation of the law, which, as evidenced in major monotheistic religions, takes the book as its preferred surface of inscription (53); finally, the third is an "indefinite deliberation," for which representation, both political and aesthetic, is "essential" (53). If the first norm of legitimacy finds its ideal surface of inscription in the ritual and the second one in the book, then in the third one finds it in representation, and more specifically, in the Renaissance discovery of perspective in painting, architecture, and theater. Déotte takes this latter norm of legitimacy, characteristic of "modern, non-ancient conditions of deliberation," as the foundation for his theorization of the apparatus. According to him, the representation is made possible by separation and projection, and both of these properties are found in a certain architectonic organization of theater: in modernity, "everything happens as if the separation carried out by the proscenium frame of Italian theater became the condition of politics and knowledge: a transfer of power is taking place from representatives to representatives, those in the auditorium and those on the stage" (53). For Déotte, the perspective as materialized in the proscenium theater is more than a technique of representation: it is the "projective and representative arch-apparatus" (54). As such, its principles govern the operations of a number of its historical incarnations, from camera obscura to easel painting, museum, photography, cinema, and video. Further, once established as the paradigm, this "arch-apparatus" it not limited to different technologies of visual representation, but includes instances of "projective" philosophical procedures, such that of René Descartes, whose treatises Déotte takes as the prime example of "projective writing" (2019).

Arguing that "it is representation that makes presence possible and not the other way around," Déotte changes the status of "representation" from a mechanism of replication to the very condition of the possibility of presence (54). The main consequence of this inherently paradoxical nature of representation is political in nature: according to Déotte, representation generates a mode of "being together," which is no longer an effect of some ideal "naked presence" but of "projection," that is to say, of mediation. Representation brings together the artistic with the inherently social nature of performance: "It can be the fact of a simple spokesperson, of an abstract work. The central thesis is that the *One*, in order to be, must split, become *Two*, in different ways" (54). And it is here that this theorization of the apparatus leaves behind the aesthetic and the technological to engage the political. Phay-Vakalis completes her definition of the apparatus by suggesting that, being a "technique that makes the event 'appear,'" the apparatus generates a "community": "In significant ways, it influences and modifies our values, conceptions, and ways of doing things" (2008:8). In her discussion of the Greek tragic theater, Roussel observes that the word "democracy" appears for the first time in Aeschylus's *Eumenides*, which she takes as an indication that "theater can be seen as an apparatus by means of which the community is established and contemplates itself in the very moment of its formation" (2016). And Déotte suggests that "the apparatus of an art that becomes the core backbone of any given society" makes possible the historization of the "notions of habitus, of *ethos* (death), of *hexis* (manner of being), of the techniques of the body: this is inevitable because the apparatuses configure the appearance of that which appears and impose the models of behavior on singularities" (62). If it is apparatuses that seem to frame and regulate the forms of "deliberation" and not the other way around, that is because this group of theoreticians scrupulously excludes ideological considerations from their theorization of the apparatus. They seek their sources in thinkers such as Lyotard, Jacques Rancière, and Walter Benjamin, while carefully shunning Althusser, Baudry (disregarding the centrality of perspectival painting in his theory of cinematic apparatus), and others who in the 1970s made ideology the central concern in their theorizing of the apparatus.

This exclusion of Althusser is all the more perplexing if we take into consideration the degree to which his "little theoretical theater" conforms to the apparatus as theorized by Déotte. Namely, the process of interpellation, which is the very engine of Althusser's idea of ideological apparatuses, is strictly projective: here, the one (the individual) comes into subjectivity only in the presence of the other (the power figure), whose voice is projected as a summons. Furthermore, it underscores the linear nature of this projection. Taken as the "projective arch-apparatus," perspective gives a stamp of linearity to systems that it generates. On the one hand, this leads Roussel to emphasize analogical relations between sections of individual Greek tragedies, which leads her to assert that analogy is the "motor" of this "original" apparatus of Greek tragic theater (2016). On the other hand, while the linearity and projectivity of a certain kind of representation supports a diachronic approach to apparatuses (from the camera obscura to the proscenium stage, cinema, video, etc.), it completely leaves out their synchronic relationships. If the passage from *One* to *Two* is central for modernity, it is because this splitting is, first and foremost, an internal division: its signal property is not projectivity, but self-refection, that is to say, critique. Taken to its final conclusion, the idea of the "passage from One to Two" as an internal critique suggests that *modern theater* as a social and aesthetic apparatus was not completed with the invention of the perspectival stage or with new systems of acting, but with the inauguration of a profession that enacts and formalizes that self-critique of the theatrical medium. The case in point is the figure of the dramaturg, which seems to confirm, on the level of the apparatus, Althusser's dictum that the critique of ideology needs to come from within ideology. Taking all of this into consideration, we can say with some certainty that modern theater reached its completion as an ideological apparatus with the decision of a group of businessmen in the German city of Hamburg to set up a permanent theater dedicated to the performance of national and European dramatic canon, and to invite the scholar and dramatist Gotthold Ephraim Lessing to serve as its in-house critic.

DRAMATURGICAL APPARATUS

The date of the inauguration of a fully operational theater apparatus coincides, then, with the opening of Hamburg National Theater on 27 April 1767. The theater folded only eight months later, on 4 December 1767, but that did not matter for the apparatus. Once the structure of an ideological apparatus is fully realized, its individual instantiations become almost incidental. A close investigation of the corpus of writings that Lessing produced in Hamburg, collected and published under the title *Hamburgische Dramaturgie* (Hamburg Dramaturgy), opens possibilities for identifying a specific moment in which the apparatus of modern theater was completed. While in his texts from this period he mostly concerned himself with the mechanics of dramatic plot and with the bashing of French neoclassical drama, in his letter dated 5 February 1768 Lessing seems to discuss the theater in a completely different register. He starts his letter no. 80 with a straight-on questioning of the very purpose of theater as an institution: "Why bother with the laborious work of dramatic form? Why build a theater, costume men and women, rack one's memories, invite the whole city into one place, if I do not want to produce anything more with my work and its performance than some of the feelings that could be produced by a good story, read by anyone curled up at home?" (2019:251). He goes on to assert that neither Germany nor France, nor, for that matter, any other nation in Europe, has achieved a *truly* tragic theater. Part of the reason for this failure is the physical state of their theaters. He takes the Hamburg playhouse with which he was affiliated as an example:

> There was another factor that kept back the high pathos from our scenes and prevented the action from becoming truly tragic, and this was the small, badly constructed theater with its paltry decorations.—What could be done on a couple of dozen boards, packed with spectators to boot? What pomp and apparatus could be used there to captivate, enthrall, and deceive the spectator's eye? What great tragic action could be performed there? What freedom could the poet's imagination have there? (253)[2]

Even if Lessing backpedals in order to reconcile his argument with Aristotle's famous disregard for "spectacle" in the *Poetics*, it is obvious that the critic, who in his letters discussed at length not only dramatic poetry but also issues of acting, stage effects, and the civic role of theater, cannot reduce the "dramatic form" solely to dramatic text. Lessing's comments on the Hamburg theater offer evidence of an emergent distinction between the future fields of narratology and dramaturgy that will come to full fruition some two hundred years later, in the mid-twentieth century. While the literary discipline of narratology analyzes structural and compositional components of narratives, including but not limited to drama, dramaturgy as critical discourse and theatrical practice takes into account institutional, representational, personal, and social forces that shape theatrical performance. In the same way in which narratology exceeds traditional literary genres (poetry, novel, drama) to address the nonliterary (life story, biography, news reports) as well as narratives presented in other media (film, television, radio, digital technologies), dramaturgy is not concerned only with dramatic theater, and easily crosses over to other representational regimes (film, television, digital media) and modes of performance (dance, political events, and other sociological phenomena).[3] Dramaturgy of some sort is present in any structured event that takes place within, or in relation to, an ideological apparatus.

Since the last decade of the twentieth century, this recognition has led to a vast expansion of dramaturgical discourse. Peter Eckersall astutely observed that, now, "we can talk about the dramaturgy of political campaigns, of sporting events, religious gatherings, concerts, lectures, media campaigns, exhibitions, urban spaces and so on" (2018:241). In its widespread lexical use, "dramaturgy" came to rival "curating" and terms derived from it (curatorship, curatorial, etc.). However, if "we can talk" about dramaturgical structure in all of these areas, that doesn't mean that dramaturgical practice is at home in most of them. Indeed, as Eckersall is careful to caution, "Not everything is dramaturgy" (242). In the same period during which critical use of the term "dramaturgy" expanded far beyond dramatic theater, the expansion of dramaturgy as practice was limited mostly to dance, another traditional performance form that has a longstanding relationship with dramatic theater.

Dance scholar and dramaturg Bojana Cvejić points out that a number of prominent choreographers of "new" or "conceptual" dance of the 1990s and 2000s in Europe, such as Xavier Le Roy, Boris Charmatz, Eszter Salamon, and others, have been working within the "institutional framework of theater." She notes that "whereas in the 1960s and 1970s Neo-Avantgarde tendencies attempted to detheatricalize dance, theater, and music," retheticalization of dance in the past three decades rejected "the performative promise of the real in liveness and presence as an illusion always already produced by theater." Instead of renouncing theater, new choreography "reorients its focus on theater as an apparatus whose givenness should be explored, altered, and even undone" (2015:97). Conceptual choreography doesn't accept the "institutional framework of theater" as, to use Brecht's locution, "incognito." Fully aware of the ideological nature of the theatrical apparatus, performances of conceptual choreography often counter the institutions within which they reside. As Cvejić points out, "Being a construct, the apparatus can be transformed, reinvented according to its power to produce performance and its subjects" (97). Regardless of significant differences between theatrical apparatuses in the United States and continental Europe, dance dramaturgs such as Marianne Van Kerkhoven, Katherine Profeta, and Cvejić herself have recognized that new choreography and new dramaturgy are able to use the institutional narrative of the theater apparatus in part because of dance's inherently theatrical structure—from the presence of the choreographer as the institutionally recognized "author" to ensembles of dancers in most of these works, to their use of the physical properties of theater, such as stage, lights, costumes, and the auditorium. Even if it is explicitly nonnarrative, dance has theater's institutional narrative to work with or against.

This uneasy, yet mutually enabling, cohabitation of different kinds of performance practice and their institutional frameworks seems to leave out performance art. Even as it accomplished unprecedented levels of institutionalization, performance art seems to be resistant not only to dramaturgical studio practice but also to dramaturgy as a critical discourse. Performance artists work with curators, not with dramaturgs; and similarly, dramaturgy seems ill equipped for critical analysis of performance art. To put it rather bluntly, we can practice dramaturgy in a performance art studio only insofar as we find meaningful ways to talk about it. The challenge that performance art poses to dramaturgy as a critical discourse and as an institutional practice comes from its refusal to sublimate its action into theatrical narrative. If it narrates, it does so differently. In order to engage performance art, dramaturgy has to go to its own roots: not to drama as a staged narrative, but to the etymological meaning of drama as action.

SITUATION

In 1977, San Francisco-based artist Terry Fox exhibited for the first time his piece *A Metaphor*, which consisted of two tall wooden stools with round seats, one upside down and attached to the other at the bottoms of their legs, thus forming a symmetrical structure. Along the axis of this construction ran a string attached to the center of the bottom part of each stool. Midway through the string, right at the imaginary plane where the legs of two stools meet, there was a small cardboard disk with a labyrinth printed on it.

A black-and-white photograph of this object was pinned on the wall next to it alongside an extensive label. The stools Fox chose for this installation resemble the one that Marcel Duchamp used as the base in his readymade *Bicycle Wheel* (1913, 1951); yet, this was not a readymade. Fox's installation, which included a chair, its photograph, and a text, was also reminiscent of Joseph Kosuth's conceptual art piece *One and Three Chairs* (1965). However, whereas Kosuth used a dictionary definition of "chair" for the textual segment of his installation, Fox's text was far from a dry lexicon entry. It addressed the observer directly:

> In order to grasp the object, you need to make a few visual adjustments. Imagine the lower stool to be half imbedded in the earth and pretend an underground river flows along the floor through the center of the stool. A well rises from the river along the string to ground

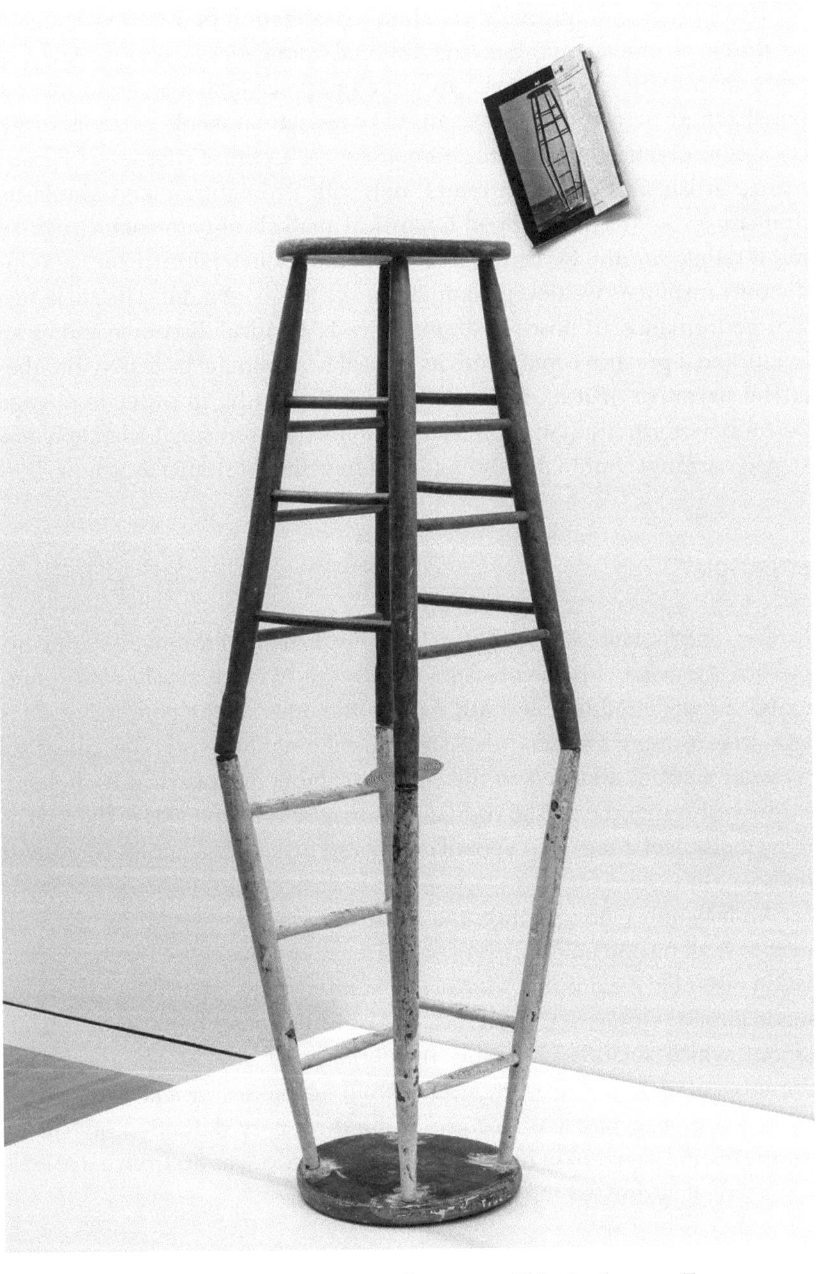

Figure 4. Terry Fox: *A Metaphor*, 1977. Courtesy of Marita Loosen-Fox.

> level, halfway up the stool. This well is covered by dolmen made of large stones. Its vertical stone walls support a single massive stone as roof, under such enormous pressure that it is taut and resonant. This dolmen is in turn covered by an enormous mound of earth whose apex lies under the object at the center of the string. On the top of this mound is a huge stone bell, the cathedral of Chartres, whose vault reaches to the seat of the stool. The string connects the vault with the water table of the underground river. In the center of the string, exactly 37 meters from the top of the vault and 37 meters from the water table of the well, is the labyrinth. This labyrinth is connected by the string to the powerful currents both in the underground river and in the atmosphere surrounding the roof of the cathedral. These currents pass as vibrations along the string from both ends to the center of the labyrinth. The labyrinth is 40 feet in diameter with a path of blue and white stones leading 300 yards into the center and back. This course flows in 34 turns through 11 concentric rings for 552 steps and leads to a large white stone at the center. There is a piton connected to a metal ring imbedded in the first step of the labyrinth, and a red Maltese cross is painted on the vault above. Movement through the labyrinth forms a pattern in the air tracing a triptych of interconnected crosses. ([1977] 1982:63)

The symmetrical arrangement of *A Metaphor* transforms this assemblage consisting of two humble wooden stools into an object resembling a minimalist sculpture. Yet the string that runs along its axis with the print of the labyrinth attached to it disturbs this simplicity and turns this object into something that art historians might describe as a post-minimalist installation. Further, the detailed caption adds to it an emphatically conceptual dimension. It turns the spectator's attention away from the sculptural properties of the work and invites her to consider the object not only in relation to its immediate surroundings but also in relation to that which is purely imaginary: the underground river, the dome, the water and air currents, and the vibrations of the string. What we end up with is a sort of spatial rebus consisting of an object, an image, and a text. *A Metaphor* transports not the meaning, but the spectator; and it does that not by means of symbols but by means of the simplification and miniaturization of the basic geometrical proportions of an architectonic structure halfway around the world from where it was exhibited. If we were to try to solve this puzzle, the answer could be a cathedral in the French city of Chartres. Fox discovered the cathedral and its labyrinth in 1972, and had subsequently produced a number of works related to it. *A Metaphor* is a simplified model of the cathedral that invites the spectator to circumnavigate it, to explore and "enter" it through the text. It seems that at some point, this journey around and into the structure could coalesce into a story.

In his discussion of narratives in visual art, Nelson Goodman focuses on the relationship between the "the order of occurrence" (the sequence in which certain events happen) and "order of telling" (the way in which they are presented in a work of art) in a number of paintings and other visual works, from Pieter Bruegel's *The Conversion of Saint Paul*, to Jacopo del Sellaio's *The Story of Psyche*, Lorenzo Ghiberti's relief *The Garden of Eden* from the Florence Baptistry, and a screen from a painted biography of Prince Shōtoku Taishi from the Hōryū-ji Temple in Nara. What all of these works have in common is that they depict episodes from well-known mythical or historical narratives. In each of them, cultural mores, conventions of the period, and the artists' personal interventions determine the presentation of the story ("the order of telling"). While Goodman is correct to point out that visual arts have their own nonlinguistic ways of presenting mythical and other stories, what he completely disregards are narrative forces at work in the immediate proximity of the works, that is to say in their institutional and cultural settings. This prompts the question of how, and to what degree, the meaning of, say, Ghiberti's *The Garden of Eden* changes with its transfer from the baptistry door in Florence to the exhibition gallery in the Louvre to the page of the book *On Narrative* in which Goodman's article is published. It is not only the content of the work but also the mode of the audience's engagement that determines the difference between the narrative and the dramaturgy of the visual work of art. In *A Metaphor*, both the order of telling and order of occurrence are literalized: the narrative, if there is any, is spelled out in a text that is an integral part of the work, while the "occurrence" is no longer an action that is depicted in the work but is instead something that happens to the beholder.

A Metaphor was part of the exhibition *Metaphors for Falling* at Site artist space in the South of Market area of San Francisco. This was Fox's first public showing of his works inspired by the labyrinth in the Chartres cathedral. Apart from the stool piece, the display included pendulums, drawings, paintings on black glass, and other pieces that were "piled up in the corner of the gallery, 'flea market' style" (so much for the order of telling) ([1977] 1982:64). But that was not all. At the entrance to this fourth-floor walk-up space Fox installed a suspended object (another pendulum) hanging at eye level, and had a piton bolted into the floor directly underneath the pendulum. Focused on the hanging object, visitors would not watch their step and more often than not, they would trip over the piton. According to Fox, "This was a way of disorienting the visitors both mentally and physically and thus preparing them for the exhibition" (64). So, apart from being a sculpture, an installation, a model, a rebus, and of course, a metaphor, *A Metaphor* was also a participatory work that reached its completion only in the act of engaged witnessing by a spectator shocked into a heightened state of attention. The spectator's experience was no less an element of this art project than the stools, the string, the photograph, and the text on the label. In short, what Fox created in Site gallery was not just an installation, but a *situation*, a term he used to describe his performances.

This term first appears in the title of a joint performance Fox did with Vito Acconci and Dennis Oppenheim, *Environmental Surfaces: Three Simultaneous Situational Enclosures*, in Reese Palley Gallery in San Francisco in 1971. In his segment of the performance, Fox used a number of diverse objects such as a bar of soap, water, flour, and Fab laundry detergent, as well as a prerecorded track of his breathing juxtaposed with amplified sounds of him inhaling and exhaling during the performance. Fox discussed the compositional principles he used in this work in an interview he did with Willoughby Sharp, the owner and editor of the art magazine *Avalanche*:

> What I am involved in is creating certain kinds of *spatial situations*. I am dealing with objects in a space and their relationships with each other, and how my mood alters them. The way I move a flashlight is going to affect not only the quality of the light but also my relationship to it. Two flashlights aimed at a bar of soap mean much more to me than anything the spectator could imagine. They create a certain translucence, a modification of materials that I find very interesting, like the idea of two flashlights eventually melting the soap. (1971:87)

As in *A Metaphor*, the situation in this performance consists of a complex interaction between objects, sounds, bodies, images, experiences, and ideas involved in performance. And it is the ideas that lend to the situation its expansive and unforeseen dimension: in the same way in which the spectator is invited to imagine an underground river flowing deep under the two stools nailed together, in *Environmental Surfaces* Fox's idea that light could dissolve matter (a bar of soap) is an integral part of performance, even if the spectators have no way of knowing that. Clearly, this notion of the situation is a far cry from the conception of the situation understood as a wrestling arena of free wills that Jean-Paul Sartre advanced in his short essay "For a Theater of Situations": "If it's true that man is free in a given situation and that in and through that situation he chooses what he will be, then what we have to show in the theater are simple and human situations and free individuals in these situations choosing what they will be" ([1947] 1976:4). In his theater, Sartre places "situations" in service of a linear dramaturgy in which he manipulates characters' choices and decisions into a philosophical lecture demonstration, leaving almost nothing to the imagination of the spectators.

Of course, Sartre's was not the only nor the most prominent idea of the situation in relation to the arts of the post–Second World War Europe. In fact, Fox's found performances from the late 1960s, which he later named "Public Theater," are much closer to the Situationist International idea of "fortuitous situations" than to Sartre's philosophical stage machinations. For example, in 1969 Fox sent invitations to a select group of friends to see a salesman's pitch at Woolworth variety store in San Francisco, a piece he later named *Buying and Selling*; and the same year, he did another "public theater" piece named *What Do Blind Men Dream?*, for which he hired a blind female singer-accordionist and her boyfriend to play in front of an empty construction site on Union Street instead of in their usual spot on Market Street in the busy downtown San Francisco area (Lewallen 2015:25). These public interventions are reminiscent of Guy Debord's program of "the construction of situations, that is to say, the concrete construction of momentary ambiances of life and their transformation into a superior passional quality" ([1957] 1980:22); also, they seem very well aligned with the concise definition of the situation as a "unitary ensemble of behavior in time" offered in the first issue of *Internationale Situationiste* ([1958] 1980:43). Fox traveled extensively in Europe during the 1960s, and on several occasions he pointed out that witnessing the May 1968 uprising in Paris, in which the demonstrators used a number of strategies devised by the Situationists, strongly influenced his early performance work. However, by 1970 he had turned away from staging "Public Theater" interventions toward performances that foregrounded his idea of the situation as a relationship between objects, bodies, and ideas that often didn't include invited or random spectators and participants. For example, *Push Wall* (1970), in which he pressed his body against a brick wall in an alley, and *Corner Push* from that same year, in which he tried to squeeze himself as much as possible into a corner of Reese Palley Gallery in San Francisco.

Toward the end of the decade, in an interview with Robin White published in the Oakland art magazine *View*, Fox returned to the notion of the situation. As if summing up his performance work of the 1970s, he claimed that this form had been "bastardized" and turned into entertainment, so much so that he was not even sure if he would categorize his live art practice as performance:

> Performance has changed so much. It's almost impossible to talk about performance anymore. That word means something different from what it used to. There must be a better word, we could say "situation." I make a situation. The actual situation is what's going on in the space we're in. And situation involves everybody there, and there is a blend when everybody starts participating. (1979:5)

He then offered an example of a "situation" he did in Montana, where he played an instrument in a boat in a tunnel, and for the duration of the performance people came and sang, played, and listened. But audience participation is not what constitutes "blend" in Fox's performance. "Everybody" is not just every human body, but also every object, sound, image, idea, and sensation involved in the performance. This situation is not a springboard for a dramatic action, as in Sartre, nor an instance of Situationist *dérive*. A theory of situation that could engage performance art more productively than these two schemes also comes from France, and from the time period close to the years when Sartre and Debord came up with their concepts of situation. Unlike them, the author of this theoretical intervention has been by now largely forgotten, and his book doubly so: the case in point is French philosopher of aesthetics Étienne Souriau and his book *Les deux cent mille situations dramatiques* (Two Hundred Thousand Dramatic Situations), which Flammarion published in 1950.

STELLAR SIGNATURE

Souriau was a philosopher, not a theater scholar. *Two Hundred Thousand Dramatic Situations* was his only book on dramatic theory, and it belonged to a wider corpus of his aesthetic research: it was preceded by his major work of comparative aesthetics *La correspondance des arts* (Correspondences between Arts; 1947), and followed by his book on film, *L'univers filmique* (Film Universe; 1953). It can be said that in these and his other works on aesthetics from that period, especially his essays "Du mode d'existence de l'oeuvre a faire" (Of the Mode of Existence of the Work to-Be-Made; 1956) and "Essai sur les limites de l'art" (Essay on the Limits of Art; 1959), Souriau was developing and expanding the ideas he presented in his philosophical works *L'instauration philosophique* (Philosophical Instauration; 1939) and *Les différents modes d'existence* (*The Different Modes of Existence*; 1943).[4] In their introduction to the new edition (and English translation) of Souriau's *The Different Modes of Existence*, Isabelle Stengers and Bruno Latour characterized *Two Hundred Thousand Dramatic Situations* as "one of his curious books" (2015:59).[5] That is an understatement.

In *Two Hundred Thousand Dramatic Situations*, Souriau takes as his starting point the premise that there were a limited number of dramatic plots, an idea that was prominent among theater professionals and scholars in the nineteenth and early twentieth centuries, including dramatists such as Goethe and theater-makers such as Russian and Soviet theater director Vsevolod Meyerhold. This hypothesis came from the Italian dramatist Carlo Gozzi, who in the late 1700s suggested that all dramatic plots could be boiled down to thirty-six elementary situations. In France, Georges Polti updated and elaborated this theory in his influential *Les trente-six situations dramatiques* (*The Thirty-Six Dramatic Situations*, 1895). Souriau proposes that this number is much larger: 210,141, to be precise, but he rounded it down to "just" 200,000 (1950:11). His goal was not to outdo Polti, but to redefine the idea of the situation in the arts by focusing on case studies he took from theater. However, the way he did that was highly unusual. It is no wonder the book never made it outside of France and that even there it became quickly outdated, as Souriau draws on examples from French nineteenth- and early twentieth-century plays that were already half-forgotten at the time of his writing. As if that was not enough, he adopts astrological symbols for his dramaturgical notation of situations. While stating explicitly that he has no interest in astrology, he explains that he could have used conventional symbols (letters, numbers) but that the zodiac signs worked well for his conception of the situation (1950:80). This allows him to compose situational formulas of great elegance and simplicity, which at the same time seem obscure and quirky to most of the readers interested in the subject.[6]

As he took his existential philosophy into the field of comparative aesthetics in the late 1940s, Souriau made sure to establish a clear distinction between "existential" and "existentialist" in Sartre's sense of the word. In *Two Hundred Thousand Dramatic Situations* he points out that the true drama of the situation is not to be found in existentialist theater. Whereas "all theater—the true eternal theater of masterpieces—is existential," existentialist drama is "getting away from existence" to become "the genre of the theater of ideas, of plays with a thesis" (69). Within his scholarly work—which includes a number of essays on poetry, cinema, and painting—*Two Hundred Thousand Dramatic Situations* stands out as his most comprehensive book on a single art form. Why drama and not the novel or opera, or some other representational art form? Souriau is very explicit about his sources and aims. To begin with, he is clear that his notion of the situation has nothing to do with Polti's, who identifies it with a basic plot structure. Instead, Souriau holds that the situation is not a "fact of drama" but the "fact of life," and states that for him, the situation has "exactly the same meaning found in . . . the existential philosophy of [Karl] Jaspers" (68). If "situation" is one of the peripheral ideas in Sartre's existentialist philosophy, it is central to Jaspers's existential outlook in his works on psychology and philosophy, such as *Psychologie der Weltanschauungen* (*Psychology of the World Views*, 1919) and the three-volume *Philosophie* (*Philosophy*, 1932). In the latter, he writes that "what we call a situation is not just a reality governed by natural laws. It is a *sense-related reality*—neither psychological nor physical, but both in one. It is the concrete reality which means advantage or detriment, opportunity or obstacle, to my existence" ([1932] in Peach 2008:61). While Souriau acknowledges the importance of Jaspers's idea of the situation for his work, he does not follow the German philosopher's emphasis on "boundary situations" and their division into four specific kinds (struggle, suffering, guilt, and death). Instead, he seems to be driven by the idea that the theater, unlike other arts, has its own specific situations, which corresponds to the "extra-dramaturgical" or existential situation (69). Unlike Jaspers's existential situations, theater has to contend with a "beyond" that he sees as both symbolic and concrete. Its symbolic nature is an extension of the dramatic diegesis, and its concrete nature is the apparatus in the narrow sense of the term: the mechanism of theater as the medium.

Souriau takes as his starting point the idea of an artwork (any artwork, as he points out, and not only drama) as a certain self-contained world or "universe" (1950:14). In theater, this world has its limited space (stage), time (duration of the piece), characters, et cetera. Within the black box of the stage, "Everything is positive, valid, and fully materialized," and "Beyond this space, everything is a matter of imagination alone," while "What really surrounds the box—the backstage and the dressing rooms where actors rest, talk, and put on makeup, where machinists prepare scene changes—none of it counts, none of it exists" (18).[7] What Souriau calls the "scenic microcosm" nests within the theatrical macrocosm. The scenic microcosm is supported by, and at the same time itself supports, the macrocosm of theater's representational apparatus, which is steeped in the world consisting of a multitude of social macrocosms. By now it is clear that Souriau sees the world of drama in a way radically different than do Polti, Sartre, and, for that matter, Debord: this "universe" is not linear and successional, but spatial and concentric; at the same time, it is not simply submerged in the social world, but has a clearly defined relation to it. A dramatic situation is irreducible to a plot, and it is even "antagonistic" to it (48). The situation emanates from the "scenic core" of the work, which Souriau depicts as "a solar system"; with its "evolutions, revolutions, various combinations of aspect and movement, instances of attraction and repulsion, and arrangements of moral forces in varied figures," this system shapes and coordinates its universe (29). In short, the situation is the "structural figure drawn . . . by a *system of forces*"; "It is a system of oppositions and attractions, of convergences in moral shock or destructive explosion, of alliances or hostile divisions, which we must identify in order to understand them" (55). The site of the situation, its "situ," is not reducible to the locale, the theater as mechanical apparatus: it is an intersection of forces that expands and evolves in multiple directions. In theater, Souriau recovered a regime of radial and energetic communication that survived the onslaught of the culture of the line, which began with the proliferation of phonetic writing and, especially, print.[8]

Scholars gathered around the journal *Appareil* argue that, in theater, this linearity has a decisively projective quality. If performance art offers an alternative configuration to proscenium theater, then Souriou's situation does the same in relation to the "aesthetic apparatus." To be clear, while the idea of "theatrical macrocosm" is important to Souriau, he was not interested in theorizing it as an "apparatus." Surely enough, his work does not figure in the *Appareil* school of writers' texts on the subject. Far from confirming their theories of the apparatus, his conceptualization of the situation offers an important alternative to their thesis about the projective and linear nature of representation and constitutes a working model of a polycentric field of apparatuses. Souriau captures the idea of the situation in a range of figures such as tapestries, roses (as in the "rose of winds"), knots, constellations, and, most often, musical chords (49). At the very basis of his idea of the situation is a set of relationships and their combinations and permutations: the title of the middle chapter of Souriau's book is, tellingly, "Ars Combinatoria." But this is not a blind game of combinatorics. Multiple elements establish relations that move, evolve, intersect, depart, clash, and transform. The "action" is not a unidirectional unfolding based on a series of analogies, but an energetic field that makes these variations possible and is at the same time their effect. It places characters "into arrangements, both architectural and dynamic, that qualify as situations," so that the play amounts to a "kaleidoscopic succession of situations" (38). Kaleidoscopic: they don't proceed successively one after another, but expand and collapse, intersect and interweave, overlap and multiply, and move in all directions at once.

For Souriau, the situation is "a dynamic form: the essential and intrinsic shape of the system of forces that characters incarnate at a given moment" (38). Souriau is an existential philosopher, and he sees characters as beings, existences. They can be constituents of a constellation such as Oedipus, Jocasta, and Laius, but also members of a society, or objects in a room, philosophical systems, and even artistic disciplines. On the one hand, in *Correspondence between Arts*, his book of comparative aesthetics published only three years before *Two Hundred Thousand Dramatic Situations*, Souriau talks about individual arts as "characters." On the other, in the essay "Of the Mode of Existence of the Work to-Be-Made," which followed his two hundred thousand situations by a few years, he talks about "the work" as a character caught up in a "drama" of making, or form-giving. There are two more "characters" in this scenario: "the work in the mode of concrete presence," that is, its materialization; and "the man who is responsible for all of that" (2015:229). The "dramatic microcosm" is just one possible instantiation of the situation. In its true scope, it ranges from art as a human activity to an individual artwork. Souriau's comparativism is situational: *correspondence* between the arts is not just any relation, but precisely that complex web of evolutions, revolutions, attractions, and repulsions that constitutes the aesthetic milieu. And a situation is always at the intersection between micro- and macro-worlds, between internal properties within individual works and external relations between them:

> The essence of the dramatic thing is precisely in the presence, influence, and operation, through living beings, of a certain stellar signature that comes from without; or a functional force that in its fury, grace, or infatuation makes from [characters] marionettes that are wistful, stunning, painful, terrified, melancholy, gently persistent, or enthralled like a moth by a lamp; reduced, against their will and in contrast with their vivacity and complexity, to be only a force in the narrative, a vector, a directional dynamic impulse. (1950:68)[9]

In the white box of the gallery, everything is positive, valid, and fully materialized to an even greater degree than in the theater's black box, as performers, actions, images, and objects are not veiled in the diegetic narrative of the drama. Here the "world of the work" not only washes over the macrocosm of its physical site but clashes with the site's basic properties. In theater, the narrative structure of the beginning, middle, and the end, and the line-by-line dialogue, conceal and suppress the stellar assemblage of the situation buried deeply underneath. By removing narrative layers, performance art brings out into the open those long-dormant dimensions of live art. If *Push Wall* and *Corner Push* were situations that clearly and almost schematically presented the dynamics of opposing forces (body and wall), Fox's other performances fully actualize the situation in its multidirectionality and interaction of elements to produce the effect of a (dis)chord. In his performance *Timbre*, which took place on 13 March 1976 in Cushing Memorial Amphitheater on Mount Tamalpais in Marin County, just north of San Francisco, the architectural properties of the site served just as an initial setup for the exploration of radial properties of the situation. The cardinal elements of this 4.5 hour performance were two "instruments," as Fox called them: a musical contraption he made out of a wooden box and strung piano wires, and a Cessna 172 single engine airplane that flew overhead (1982:67). The artist placed the instrument in the prompter's box partially filled with water to alter its resonance, and strummed the wires each time the airplane would fly overhead. The airplane left after two hours, and the artist continued beating the wires even as the audience members, who hiked up the mountain to the amphitheater, started leaving at dusk. He finished the performance alone in pitch darkness (Fox 1979:14). In *Timbre*, the radial range of the situation spans from the stone prompter's box to the outer reaches of the amphitheater's circle; from the foot of the hill to its top, and from the drone of the piano wires to the roar of the airplane engine.

Souriau emphasizes the importance of the "*stellar center*" of the situation: the "stellar organization of the work's universe is the fundamental condition of the theater: a certain point of interhuman tension constitutes its core; enclosed in the scenic box, it radiates the cosmos of the work" (1950:24). We can easily transpose this idea to performance art, where the tension is not only between dramatic characters but between performers' bodies, objects, sounds, and so on. In relation to this tensional center of the work, everything else is incidental: "This flexibility, this implicit palpitation of the real, by turns deployed in all its vastness and reduced to bare necessity, is inherent in the very nature of the theater. What remains indispensable in all cases is that this 'core' exists—a central constellation sufficiently exact, hard, and luminous to impose a nuclear structure on the universe represented" (29). Again, we can say that in a performance art piece such as *Timbre*, the "palpitation of the real" is not symbolized through an act of representation, an operation that exposes the "central constellation" that furnishes the "nuclear structure" of the piece. In *Timbre*, the central constellation is the relationship between the two instruments. However, that is where the problem begins: while it provides the work with its "nuclear core," this relationship at the same time exposes the limits of that core. The player of the instrument and the airplane pilot are the principal performers in this piece, but the pilot certainly cannot hear the drone from below, nor can the player strumming the piano wires hear the Cessna once it gets out of his earshot, lands at the airport, rolls on the tarmac . . . The core of the situation is purely relational and conceptual, like vibrations in that string at the axis of *A Metaphor*, triggered by the currents of the imaginary underground river below and the fantasmatic air currents above.

The situation's stellar center becomes even more precarious in Fox's other works, such as *Levitation*, a piece he performed in 1970 in Richmond Art Center, across the bay from San Francisco. Fox described the performance in great detail in his *Avalanche* interview:

> I wanted to create a space that was conductive to levitation. The first thing I did was to cover the sixty by thirty foot floor with white paper and to tape white paper on the walls. The floor had been dark, but it became such a brilliant white that if you were at one end of it, it glared, it hurt your eyes to look at someone standing at the other end. It was such a buoyant space that anyone in it was already walking on air. Then I laid down a ton and a half of dirt, taken from under a freeway on Army Street, in an eleven and a half foot square. The mold was made with four redwood planks each twice my body height—I used my body as a unit of measure for most of the elements in the piece. . . . I fasted to empty myself. . . . I drew a circle in the middle of the dirt with my own blood. Its diameter was my height. According to the medieval notion, that creates a magic space. Then I lay on my back in the middle of the circle, holding four clear polyethylene tubes filled with blood, urine, milk, and water. They represented the elemental fluids that I was expelling from my body. I lay there for six hours with the tubes in my hand trying to levitate. The doors were locked. Nobody saw me. I didn't move a muscle. . . . I was trying to think about leaving the ground, until I realized I should be thinking about entering the air. For me that changed everything, made it work. I mean, I levitated. After the fourth hour I

> couldn't feel any part of my body, not even my chest expanding and contracting. My legs and arms were probably asleep. I felt I was somewhere else. I'd gone. I'd left my body. (1971:70–71)

This work stages, quite literally, the stellar multidirectionality of the situation: a body in a circle, inscribed in a square, which is inserted in a (gallery) cube. Here, "everybody" clearly doesn't apply to audience members, who entered the space only toward the end of performance, but to the carefully selected and arranged elements, up to and including the event of levitation. Like the soap bar melted by light, the underground river in *A Metaphor*, and the relationship between the two instrumentalists in *Timbre*, the "stellar core" of *Levitation* is dematerialized to the highest degree possible. And this is precisely where Fox's situation departs from Souriau's: whereas in the latter, the "central constellation" provides the work with its "nuclear structure," in the former it is made conditional to the point of incredulity. This is the main difference between the situations that animate theater and performance art as two distinct forms of live performance.

What Fox recognized more clearly than many other performance artists of his generation is that performance has to include its own conceptual horizon. For Fox, performance art is fundamentally an existential situation. It became "bastardized" once it became "like" theater and other live representational arts. In the *View* conversation, published in 1979, he already recognized that performance was at the precipice of being fully integrated into art industry: "In New York, if we go to the Kitchen, it costs five dollars each, ten dollars to see somebody play a pre-recorded tape, I mean, it's really ridiculous. And it's gotten to the point where the audience sits on chairs, you know, and if there are no seats available, they close the door" (1979:6). The problem here is just as much in "pre-recorded tape" as in the adoption of theatrical conventions (tickets, chairs, and even reservations). According to Fox, performance art betrays its "original impetus" not only by adopting conventions of the theatrical apparatus but also by importing wholesale its representational apparatus. If performance art is in itself a boundary situation, then it has to be able internalize its own limit. That is the central condition of Fox's situation.

THE ANGEL OF WORK

Does that mean that no performance form other than the situation of a solitary artist performing in a gallery or in a site-specific location—anywhere but in a theater—is capable of finding and internalizing its own limits?

What happens if the situational assemblage of objects, images, experiences, ideas, et cetera includes more than one body? If it turns out, as it often does, that in that case the limits have to be agreed upon, and are because of that palpably apparent, do they have to remain external to performance, that is to say, outside of the situation? Finally, does the performance dramaturgy of the situation survive in a more theatrical setup of a performance group?

Matthew Goulish, the founding member and dramaturg of Chicago-based performance collective Every house has a door, opened the lecture "Performance and the Limits of Fiction," given at the San Francisco Art Institute, by interrogating what he calls "the fundamentals of performance." Starting from the premise that the "fundamental is an element that is present in every instance," Goulish proposes that one such element in performance is the floor. He continued by asking: "What might a performance look like that does not involve a floor? Let's propose: every instance of performance involves a floor. Therefore, we may consider the floor a fundamental of performance practice. After this proposition, we will talk about the possibility of the floor. In order to do that, I will begin by talking about the ceiling" (Goulish 2014). The ceiling doesn't offer support to the weight of objects and bodies involved in performance. Not being involved in every instance of performance, it is not fundamental in the same way the floor is. It can be said that the ceiling acts as the floor's other: it is not foundational, but aspirational element of performance. As such, it provides a perspective on the floor, a point from which to reflect on it, the route that Goulish recognizes and takes. Performance practice takes place between the floor and the ceiling, whatever they might be: asphalt floor and concrete ceiling of a parking garage, sprung floor and fly space of a dance theater, raised floor and lowered ceiling of a modern office building, grass and blue skies, anywhere.

Consider the following exercise:

1. Write an impossible task on a piece of paper.
2. Pass the paper to the person next to you.
3. Make a movement that illustrates the impossible task you have just been given. Take a few minutes to make this movement. Construct the movement so it can be repeated the same way time after time, and simplify it so that it can be taught to someone else.
4. Repeat this impossible task movement for exactly 1 minute.
5. Move to a different place in the room. Stand beside a different person. Repeat the impossible task movement for exactly 1 minute. (Goat Island 1997:8)

These instructions are followed by a list of ten impossible tasks. They include operations such as "Tie a knot in a rope of water," "Watch the back of your head," and "Jump in the air with both feet off the ground and stay suspended for 5 minutes" (10), that is, levitate between the floor and the ceiling. "Impossible Task Exercise" comes from *Schoolbook*, a small, spiral-bound volume published by performance group Goat Island for their first summer school program, held in 1996. In 1987, a group of Chicago-based artists that included Goulish, Lin Hixson, Adrian Blundell, Karen Christopher, Mark Jeffrey, and Bryan Saner decided to make performances together and adopted the name Goat Island for their collective. The members of the group realized that there was no funding for the kind of work they wanted to do, so they each committed to making a monthly contribution to a common account that would help them fund their work and rent a rehearsal space (2007:117). They ended up renting a gym space in Wellington Avenue Church in Chicago, where they rehearsed and performed all of their works over a period of two decades.

While in Goat Island, Hixson performed the task of director; the group did not have a dramaturg. Still, it did have a good amount of dramaturgy involved in their performance-making process. Today, a collective performance of dramaturgical function, or dramaturgy without a dramaturg per se, is usually described as "diffused dramaturgy." In Goat Island, performance dramaturgy was integrated into the entire process of performance-making and accomplished by the whole group. After Goat Island folded in 2007, Goulish and Hixson formed a new performance collective, Every house has a door. Instead of working with a more or less permanent group of performers in one space, they formed partnerships with a number of different individual artists and institutions. Hixson continued working as a director, and Goulish assumed the role of dramaturg. One of continuities between Goat Island and Every house has a door is recognition of the necessity of performance dramaturgy; one of the differences between the two collectives is that in the latter the position of the dramaturg has been formalized.

Performance dramaturgs are free from considerations about plausibility of the narrative, believability of dramatic characters, verisimilitude of language, historical accuracy of set, costumes, and props, and so forth; in short, they are not concerned with the details that cohere into an illusionistic representation. One of the things that performance dramaturgs do is to provide a critical reflection, in the fashion that Lessing did in theater, on the very medium that they engage. In other words, performance dramaturgs complete the apparatus of performance. That does not mean that performance art can escape its own apparatic nature by simply depriving itself of an internal critic; doing that would just mean that in absence of that person, someone else would take over the critical, that is to say the dramaturgical function. Goulish was fulfilling this dramaturgical role when he stated, in "A Poetics of the Thing Outlived," a collaborative lecture he did with Hixson: "We consider performance that mode of presentation that makes relations apparent before us" (2015b:10). Which relations? Not relations among dramatis personae, between protagonists, antagonists, and episodists, but between bodies onstage, and onward from there: between bodies and performance space (floor, ceiling, if there is one, and walls, if there are some), objects, texts, noises, lights. And this relationality is not limited to any individual performance piece. Like Terry Fox, Goat Island knew that a performance has to include its own impossibility; unlike him, they never referred to their performances as "situations." They needn't do that. To be in a performance group is already to enter a constellation of forces that constitute a performance situation. If to make performance art is to actively seek a limit situation, then to organize a performance collective is to push against the limits of the apparatus of art.

Starting, as he often does, with a correspondence between philosophy and performance, in one of his dramaturgical notes Goulish outlined two approaches to performance-making that could be seen as an exposé on his approach to performance dramaturgy. The first concerns "the selection of material that will guide the performance." This, as Goulish offered, can be seen as a "form of curation" (Daddario et al. 2020:429). These "materials" are not exclusively textual, but they often have a textual function, which this dramaturgical approach subverts: Goulish doesn't see them as providing the foundation, but instead a guidance to performance. The second approach is a take on composition, which is one of the main practical tasks of conventional dramaturgy. Only this time, composition is an art of finding a way for the various materials to coexist, rather than of fitting together disparate parts. As Goulish put it, this approach boils down to "conceptualizing how the performance as a whole will occupy the same universe as the material selected, how it will reflect or amplify that material's set of concerns as we understand them, and how we will structure and sequence the parts clearly in the time we have in the room in which we meet" (430). But there is also a third approach, which transforms these standard dramaturgical procedures of selection and configuration and turns them into performance dramaturgy. Goulish doesn't comment on it in any of his dramaturgical notes, but Hixson does in her short text on the performance *Scarecrow*. Here is her description of Goulish's dramaturgical work in this piece:

> A paper leaf falls differently each time it falls. Sometimes, it spins. Sometimes, it takes off. Sometimes, it launches into the air. Then drops. Matthew, performing in *Scarecrow*, sets the paper leaves in motion, pitching and sending them afloat. In turn, the leaves animate Matthew. He swivels, flicks his wrist, bends his knees, and lets go. It is here in the air that the mystery occurs. For one cannot control where the leaf falls. One time it is here. Another there. Between hand, paper, air, and floor, a micro-event occurs like a falling star. (Daddario et al. 2020:427)

Performance dramaturgy is not about striving to establish a narrative order of consecution and consequence and then showing how they align. Unlike traditional theater dramaturgy, it does not try to eliminate chance from performance, but rather invites and welcomes it. It is open-ended and responsive. It not only renounces the (art) object but also repudiates any predetermined object-ive. This kind of dramaturgy makes sure that the performance doesn't drift into the straits of a linear narrative, and if it does get there, performance dramaturgy needs to inquire how that informs nonnarrative and nonlinear aspects of *actions* that come together in the performance. In short, this is a dramaturgy not in search of completeness and totality, but in service of openness and inquisitiveness. Unlike in traditional dramatic theater, the collective performance dramaturg is not positioned outside the performance, a script-master and proprietor of papers, but a script-partner, twirling around with paper leaves and leaves of paper. This dramaturgy isn't a process of imposing order on the materials, but instead of responding to them. It doesn't answer to the materials gathered (curating), or to a system it implements (composition), and not even to performance as a medium. Performance dramaturgy responds to the process of making, the *work*, in the sense of both the piece (artwork) and the work that goes into it.

This ethics of the work informed both the diffused dramaturgy of Goat Island and Goulish's dramaturgical practice during and after this period. Several of his *39 Microlectures* are dedicated to the idea of the work: "A work is an object overflowing its frame" and "Work is an event in which the human participates; the human is an organism that works" (2000:102). It seems that "the work" came to Goat Island members as the most natural way to address what they do. Referring to Pina Bausch and Tadeusz Kantor, Hixson suggested that "they made you come to the work, instead of thrusting the work at you" (in Bottoms and Goulish 2007:91). Bryan Saner, who supported himself by working as a carpenter, spoke about performance work but also work as wage-earning labor (Bottoms and Goulish

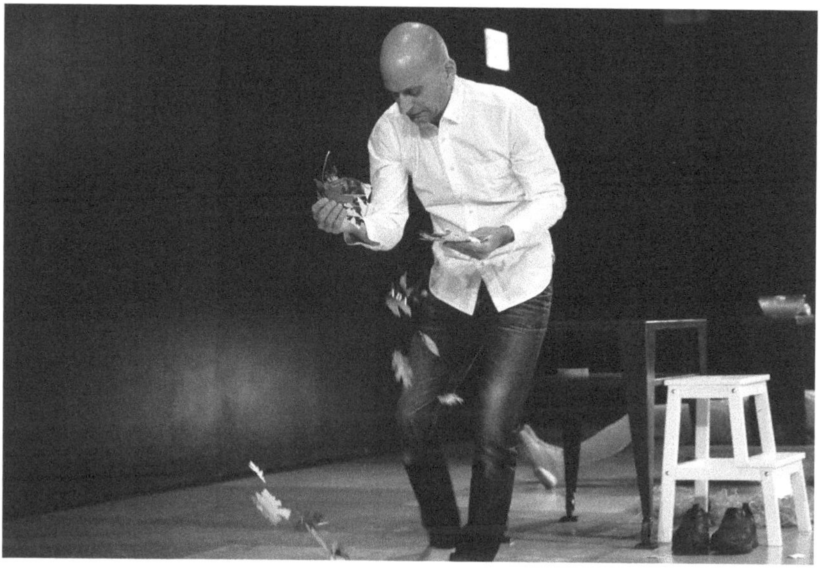

Figure 5. Matthew Goulish in *Scarecrow*, a performance by Every house has a door and Essi Kausalainen, Steppenwolf Theatre Lookout Series, Chicago, 30 November 2018. Photo credit: Hadley Austin and Yoni Goldstein.

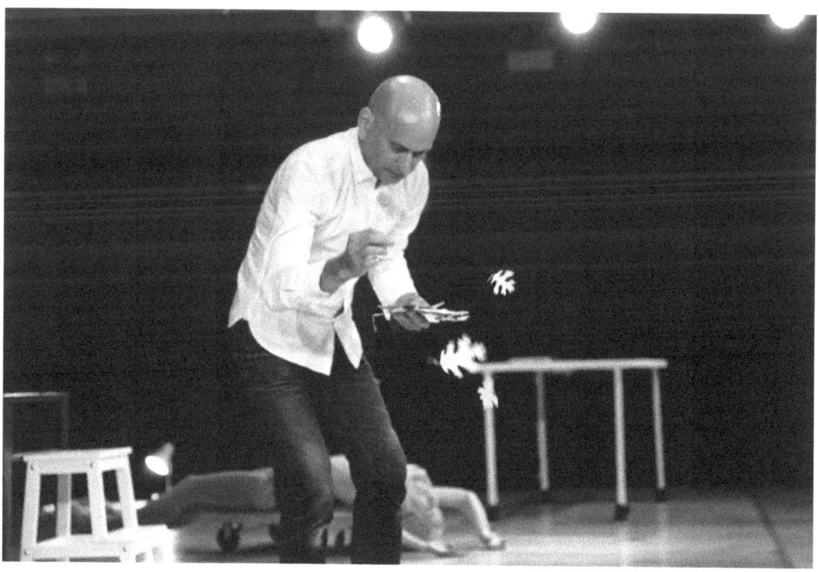

Figure 6. Matthew Goulish in *Scarecrow*, a performance by Every house has a door and Essi Kausalainen, Steppenwolf Theatre Lookout Series, Chicago, 30 November 2018. Photo credit: Hadley Austin and Yoni Goldstein.

2007:117). Karen Christopher commented on the process: "Through our working process, we generate much more material than we will actually make use of in the end," so that "eventually the work begins to make itself" (in Bottoms and Goulish 2007:120). The work is taxing (physically and financially), excessive, and uncontainable. It pushes back and makes its own demands. It is untamable: the way to approach it is through collaboration, inter-action, not command. It asks for complementarity, not one-sidedness.

It is this kind of complementarity that Souriau offers as an answer to the problem of "the existential incompleteness of every thing" ([1943] 2015:220). He starts one of his key philosophical works, *The Different Modes of Existence,* in the same way he could open an exploration of drama: "Did Hamlet, the *Primavera,* Peer Gynt exist, do they exist, and in what sense?" ([1943] 2015:97). Do they exist in the same way that thought, matter, and God exist? Or are they different modalities of existence? Souriau identifies "thingly" (*réique*) as the most fundamental mode of existence that characterizes the object.[10] In his discussion of this mode, Souriau offers a thought experiment: a sculptor working on a piece of clay, transforming it from raw matter into a sculpture, thus bringing the virtual to intersect with *réique* existence. With each gesture of the sculptor, "the physical reality of the material" approaches the point of convergence with the "spiritual reality of the work to-be-made" (128). He developed this same idea, using the same example, in a lecture presented in 1956 to the Société française de philosophie, "Of the Mode of Existence of the Work to-Be-Made," which can be read as his statement of method and a point of integration of his philosophical and aesthetic work (or of philosophy and art).

The work to-be-made is not a hypothesis, a plan, and certainly not a projection. Its mode of existence is that of a "real being" that is "still virtual and in limbo," but which also has its concreteness ([1956] 2015:229). Souriau sees the work to-be-made as a character in the process of making, partnering with the work in its concrete presence and the person who mediates between the two, the maker. If they are engaged in a drama as real personages, or characters, that means the maker is just one of the beings who are mutually engaged in a series of interactions. To be in possession or in command of this process is an illusion: the virtual work to-be-made makes its demands, just as the physical thing offers its resistances. Forcing the latter brings the danger of eradicating the former. The only path toward the completion of that which is "existentially incomplete" is by way of complementarity, which comes through recognition and acceptance of restraints that each character in this drama imposes on the others. What is the being at the center of this system of correspondences? Souriau offers the expression "the Angel of work" to indicate "something that appears to come from another world and to play a heraldic role" (230)—"heraldic" in the sense he gives to constellations of forces in a situation. The "agent" or the maker, the third character in this drama, "must yield before the work's own will, must work out what it is it wills, and must renounce himself for the sake of this autonomous being, which he seeks to promote in accordance with its own right to existence" (232). The work comes only through agents' willing limitation of their own agency. The sculptor doesn't reveal the figure in the piece of marble, but negotiates the way to bring the figure out of its virtual existence. The work to-be-made "establishes and maintains a *questioning situation*" (232). Agents respond to the question of the work: in responding, all they do is assist the work in its passage from one mode of existence to another.

What brings Goulish close to Souriau is not his explicit engagement with or even stated interest in situations, but their shared belief in a continuity between philosophy and art. While Goulish explores performance as an established artistic practice, Souriau intuited it as an art form that was just beginning to emerge as he was writing his major works on philosophical aesthetics. In *Different Modes of Existence,* he presents phenomenal existence in terms that strikingly resemble the way in which he would talk about the situation a few years later. Surely enough, the phenomenon "is and claims to be just what it is," but it is also "presence" and "radiance" ([1943] 2015:133). And not only that: the phenomenon has "the particular quality of a strange musical chord"; and it is "discrete," "self-enclosed," "stellar and microcosmically limited" (133). Not surprisingly, Souriau suggests that "the phenomenon owes all of its radiance to the art" immanent to it, "which is rekindled by the ideas of harmony and architectonics. Yet, it owes its radiance not to abstract art that we can separate from the phenomenon through comparison and generalizing induction, but to concrete art that is effectively and singularly at work in its present existence" (138). It is quite possible that Souriau turned his attention to the situational dimension of theater because of its ability to receive "the body proper" as a "foothold for the phenomenon in the cosmos of *réique* [thingly] entities," at the same time as it accommodates what he calls "fictional beings," "the beings of representation," "false beings," and even "certain beings of pure logic" (151, 97–99). If the situation resembles phenomenal existences, and if it can accommodate things and bodies, all of that is held together through a virtual existence at its core, "that kaleidoscopic"—here is again that catchword for the situation—"interplay of beings or monumentalities that will never exist; that has no other reality than that of being conditioned hypothetically or in advance" (156). In short, like the situational, "The virtual is a conditioned conditioning, dependent on the fragment of reality, which is foreign to its own being, and which is like its evocatory formula" (158). And in the opposite direction, the situation encompasses, if not a transcendental existence, then its own "transcendentalization," or an "inter-ontic relation": "in the relation of architectonic subordination—we could say of 'composition' (in the aesthetic sense of the term)—that forms the correlative *situation* of the two [or more] elements whose relation changes" (168; emphasis added). It is here that the situation departs from traditional art forms and approaches a mode of existence strikingly evocative of performance art. It is that mode expressed in the "verbality of the verb": the event, whose "grandeur" is "accounted for neither by its transitive or dynamic, nor even by its being singular and *hic et nunc*, but by its being the 'what is done,' by its being that which takes place" (172). Souriau sees the event as time-bound, relational, transitional, and above all, actional. In engaging with every modality of existence, be it phenomenal, objectal (*réique*), corporeal, or fictional, an individual can attain and hold an agential position (demiurge, creator). However,

> In opting for action, he will plunge into a completely different kind of reality, he will opt for a completely different manner of being. All that is verbal will now be vain, and all that is stable in the ontic will become spectral. Properly speaking, there will no longer be a universe of discourse. There will only be this action, which belongs to the kind of the event. And in order to establish himself in it, in order to situate himself in it, existing in the sense that the action exists, he will have to sacrifice (an enormous, frightening sacrifice) all the ontic solidity and stability belonging to him and even to the world which, from the other point of view, appeared to be the very model of substantiality. His reward? Simply this plunge into a kind of existence that then offers to him alone, and not without some vertigo, participation in the real, through the very operation of the facts of the action. (178)

Was there ever a more detailed, almost tangible, intuition of an art form that will prioritize action over everything else, and that will some three decades after this writing come to be known as performance art? Looking forward, this intuition prompted Souriau to explore the kaleidoscopic combinatorics of the situation; looking back, he was led to this through his early interest in certain forms of nonfigural art.

The beginnings of Souriau's formulation of the kind of aesthetic arrangement that he would eventually identify as "situation" are discernable in his early essay "L'arabesque" (1928). Poised at the very limit of Western art, the arabesque offers a completely different arrangement of form and material than representational arts. Unlike many of his contemporaries, Souriau was not fascinated by its similarity with abstract art, which was just reemerging in the West.[11] Nor was he engaging in an orientalist exercise of mastering the aesthetics of French colonial acquisitions. Instead, he found in it a concrete art that provides the kernel for his thinking about the phenomenon and the situation. The way to the arabesque is not through embellishment of simple forms, but precisely the opposite, through reduction. He invites the reader to picture an image of a lion carved onto a dagger, and then a flesh-and-blood animal rumbling through the wild. He then poses the question: "What will be left of the carved beast if the roaring beast disappeared? Only an arabesque, an intrinsic form, graceful or savage, consisting of curves engraved in steel. And such form is self-sufficient: it carries its justification in its own qualities" (1928:113). Reduction, again. "*Imago leonis*": "nothing aspires to the expression of vivacious essence, to the manifestation of nature. But forget and ignore the beast, and only consider the skillful manner of the brush, the contour that separates pattern from background; try to become attentive to the song expressed by lines, take them for the ones in arbitrary ornament or an intriguing floral design." In this kind of "stylistic pattern" Souriau recognizes a "contour of being" (115). This "contour" is much more than a simple outline, a cameo: "We only enter fully into arabesque art once we have passed the frontier, when the form of second degree breaks and takes on the sophisticated form to submit to the first degree form, and is only a memory and a hint" (115). Arabesque is not only a visual curio. Like music, it has a temporal dimension. However, the time of the arabesque, like the time of the situation and of the chord, is not linear, but radial. As a form of temporality, the situation enters history and at the same time contests its foundational assumption about unidirectional progression of chronological time.

One never knows when one will run into a situation, when one will come across an arabesque, a contour of a performance radiating in time. In the spring of 2019, the Chicago Cultural Center hosted the exhibit *Goat Island Archive—We Have Discovered the Performance by Making It*, curated by Nicholas Lowe. The first room in the Sidney R. Yates Gallery and Exhibition Hall contained several vitrines with artifacts from Goat Island performances, from *Soldier, Child, Tortured Man* (1987) to the collective's final

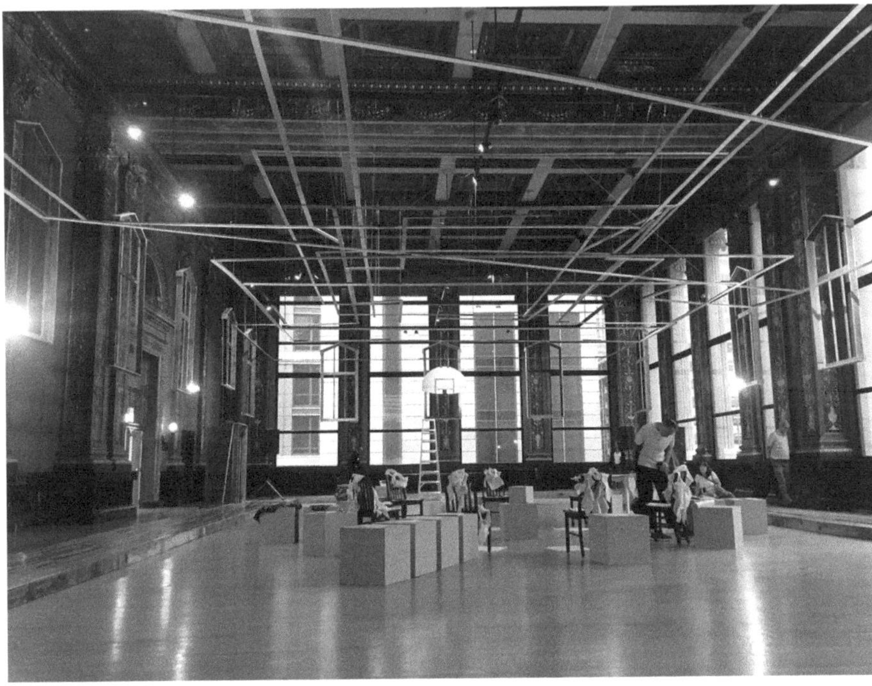

Figure 7. Bryan Saner: Recreation of Wellington Avenue Church, Chicago Cultural Center, 2019

work, *The Lastmaker* (2009). In the far left corner of the room were chairs arranged in front of a screen showing video recordings of performances. Next to this viewing setup, there was a small corridor that led to the next room. This large hall featured a recreation of the rehearsal space from Wellington Avenue Church where Goat Island devised and rehearsed performances over the two decades of its existence. Only, there were no walls: they were indicated by window- and doorframes positioned exactly as they were in the church hall. And there was no ceiling: in its place were the floor patterns from all performances, positioned one on top of another, and hoisted up in the air. And there it was, the arabesque: the contours of actual bodily movements, positions, and arrangements. The songs expressed by these lines were performances, and their superimposition over one another, the historical accumulation of movements and actions. Looking up, one entered the situation that reversed the floor and the ceiling, the foundational and aspirational, the objectal (*réique*) and the virtual. This reversed perspective offered the outline, from within, of the performance apparatus.

Here we have two complementary forms of performance: the first one is solo, and it engages the idea of the situation while showing no interest whatsoever in dramaturgy; the second one is collective, and it includes dramaturgical procedures but leaves the concept of the situation aside. What they have in common, however, is their explicit rejection of projectivity and of the perspective as the visual technique or as a writerly, performance, or philosophical procedure. Their questioning of the projective and perspectival approaches to representation is best exemplified in their engagement with the phenomena of verticality: we find it in Fox's stools and droning dialogue with the aircraft, and in Goulish's reflection of the fundamental-aspirational axis of floor and ceiling, and in the arabesque formed by the vertical displacement of the floor. This adoption of verticality frustrates and complicates linear progression and promotes radiality: an axial point is open to all directions at once. These artistic practices not only expose the limitations of the aesthetic apparatus theory but also provide an important correction to Althusser's "little theoretical theater": to view it in isolation from other theaters and as a bipolar power relation risks a vast simplification. What can the situation tell us about the apparatus? An apparatus is not determined by unidirectional flows of power and by strict divisions. Instead, it is an arrangement organized through circulations and transformations, expansions and contractions, overlaps and flows. Ideological interpellation never comes from a single source, but from a constellation of calls—and an individual's response to these calls goes out simultaneously in many directions. In this theoretical theater, the subject is situational, or it is not at all.

In the modern capitalist state, there is no zone free from apparatuses. Ideology doesn't tolerate a vacuum: any gap that opens up within or between apparatuses is quickly filled by other, often unrelated apparatus. Apparatuses allow and encourage the interlacing of logics: here the aesthetic seamlessly turns into the political, the political transforms into the economic, the economic into the mathematical, which feeds the literary, and so on. The apparatus has its symmetries, its complementarities, its choreographic turns: its organizing principle is beauty as much as power. The situation suggests that there is no such thing in an ideological apparatus as the aesthetics of politics, or the politics of aesthetics: the aesthetics *is* the politics. The secret of the apparatus is that it conceals these multiple transformations and restorations through an illusion of creation. There is nothing new in the apparatus, except the apparatus itself. Its main aim is its own perpetuation. Apparatuses have their own logics and dramaturgies.

Understanding them can offer ways of resisting, altering, or sending the apparatus in any direction. Dramaturgical analysis of the apparatus can offer a direction for political action. Like ideology—from which it is inseparable—it has no outside: all it can offer is its own ideality as false transcendence. The apparatus, like the situation, internalizes its own limit: it contains, deeply within, its own conceptual and functional fault lines.

FIVE | Disassembling the Self

Toward a Revolutionary Subject

THE XYC OF INSTITUTIONS

The title of Althusser's essay "Ideology and Ideological State Apparatuses" could have easily been "Ideology and Ideological State Institutions," so lax is his use of these two key terms. One need not go further than his initial definition of ideological state apparatuses (ISAs) as "distinct and specialized institutions"; this explanation is followed by a list of apparatuses, which he also introduces as "institutions" (1971:136). From the beginning to the end of the essay, Althusser seems to make no effort to establish meaningful distinction between ideological apparatuses and institutions: already in the preliminary section ("Reproduction of Labour-Power"), he brings up "State institutions like the Church" and "other apparatuses like the Army" in a single sentence (128);[1] he adds no clarity when, in one of key segments of the essay, he refers to "public" and "private institutions" as ideological apparatuses (137); and finally, Althusser summarizes his essay by stating that ideologies are "*realized* in institutions, in their rituals and practices," adding "in the ISAs" to the end of the sentence, as if to confirm the indistinction between the two (171). In general, he seems to be uninterested or unable to clarify the difference between the general idea of institution and his new, ideologically charged notion of the apparatus.[2]

Althusser's students offered several explanations for this lack of inquiry into the nature of apparatuses that is so evident in his work. In his essay "Althusser and the Rue D'Ulm" Etienne Balibar takes a biographical approach, pointing out his teacher's immersion in and dependence on institutions, from his internment as a prisoner of war in Germany during the Second World War to his dependence on the support he received in asylums following the accident in which he killed his wife Hélène (he received a lenient sentence due to his diagnosis of manic-depression). In between these two cardinal events he spent decades at the École Normale

Supérieure on Rue d'Ulm in Paris as a resident faculty member. Commenting on the intense overlap of the private and the public that defined Althusser's position at the École, Balibar suggests that it was for him, "more than any other institution, the very model of the 'ideological state apparatus' that 'interpellates individuals as subjects'" (2009:107). Jacques Rancière, another prominent member of the circle of Althusser's students at ÉNS, singles out another institution his teacher was committed to throughout his adult life: the French Communist Party (Parti communiste français, PCF). In *Althusser's Lesson*, published in the thick of intense realignments on the Left during the post-1968 decade, Rancière focuses much of his critique of his former teacher's political philosophy on his unwavering fidelity to the PCF. He sees the "theoretical apparatus" that Althusser developed during the 1960s—"the distinction between instances, the construction of the time specific to each instance, the severing of science from ideology, the epistemological break"—as fundamental to the role of "Althusserianism" in service of the PCF ([1974] 2011:28). He writes that "the nascent French Maoism inherited from Althusserianism the view that political apparatuses are instruments for the application of party lines" (54). Therefore, Althusser's failure to distinguish between apparatus and institution, key terms in his critique of ideology, finds an explanation in the history of the proletarian Left in France, which was, as Rancière explains, "weighted down by a *neutral* understanding of organization as the instrument for the application of a line founded on the positivity of a class ideology" (54). According to this view, the Party organization, with its hierarchy, policies, procedures, and rituals, is no more than a transmitter of the values and goals of the class it claims to represent.

In "On the Theory of Ideology: Althusser's Politics," appended to *Althusser's Lesson*, Rancière dispenses with the presumption of the Party's neutrality and the neutrality of institutions in general. "Ideology," he asserts, "is not simply a collection of discourses or a system of representations." Instead, "The dominant ideology is a *power* organized in a collection of institutions" (2011:142).[3] Rancière's main objection was that during the 1960s, Althusser disregarded class struggles and power relations *within* political institutions on the Left in favor of elaborating the "scientific" nature of dialectical materialism. Institutions are not mere channels that secure the unobstructed flow of power. Their participation in the distribution of power is much more complex: they cohere into larger ideological formations, but they also capture, contain, and redistribute power. Importantly, that which contains ideology also takes charge of it, which is to say, it is the site of ideological production. These relations of power, made visible by the near breakdown of state institutions in the spring of 1968, which Althusser refused to engage even as he wrote about the centrality of apparatuses and institutions for the production of ideology, became the subject of inquiry taken up not only by a whole generation of political philosophers but also by the generation of artists who came of age during this period.

Despite, or perhaps precisely because of Althusser's reluctance to submit institutions and apparatuses to close scrutiny, his critique of ideology became associated with the institutional critique of art. In one of the most telling instances of this correlation between Althusser's theory and artistic practice, Benjamin Buchloh concludes his much-discussed article "Conceptual Art 1962–1969: From the Aesthetic of Administration to the Critique of Institutions" by suggesting that while other conceptual artists "mimed the operating logic of late capitalism and its positivist instrumentality in an effort to place its auto-critical investigations at the service of liquidating even the last remnants of traditional aesthetic experience," Daniel Buren, Hans Haacke, and other representatives of the first wave of institutional critique from the late 1960s "turned the violence of that mimetic relationship back onto *the ideological apparatus* itself, using it to analyze and expose the social institutions from which the laws of positivist instrumentality and the logic of administration emanate in the first place" (1990:143; emphasis added). On the one hand, Buchloh builds this argument on his discussions of mimetism from the early 1980s, specifically on his assessments of appropriation art published in *Artforum* and his catalog essay for the exhibition *Art & Ideology*, which took place at the New Museum in 1984 and for which he served as one of five invited curators.[4] On the other hand, this conclusion hinges on the importance of conceptual art's engagement with institutions of art. According to Buchloh, unlike minimalist or pop art, which questioned traditional aesthetic criteria such as taste and uniqueness, conceptual art engaged in "a critique that operates at the level of the aesthetic 'institution'" (136). Therefore, the main intervention of conceptual art in its formative phase "circa 1969" was not in the "dematerialization" of art, that is, in the reduction and elimination of formal, visual, or structural properties of the art object, but in the recognition that these properties "are always already inscribed within the conventions of language and thereby within institutional power and ideological and economic investment" (136). The object survives, but its meaning is contingent upon its institutional placement. Having recognized conceptual art as "the most rigorous elimination of visuality and traditional definitions of representation," Buchloh proceeds to analyze precisely those conceptual works characterized by their deployment of the object that conform, even critically, to the conditions of representation dictated by art institutions (107). Inexplicably, this leaves out the theoretical elaboration of his own suggestion that language is the foundational condition of any institutionality.

Among philosophical inquiries into the nature of language, speech-act theory stands out in its recognition of the dependence of the efficacy of utterances on their social and institutional setting. As John Searle argued in his essay "What Is an Institution?": "If you presuppose language, you have already presupposed institutions . . . [I]nstead of presupposing language and analyzing institution, we have to analyze the role of language in the constitution of institutions" (2005:2). These comments, made in one of his late essays, don't come as a sudden and belated recognition of the dependence of speech acts on their institutional setting; rather, they highlight the importance that the social and conventional framework of a certain kind of statement held in speech act theory from the very beginning. J. L. Austin's 1955 Harvard lectures are loaded with numerous references to the performative speech act's dependence on "appropriate circumstances" and "accepted conventional procedures," the condition that probably gets its fullest elaboration in his notion of "total [speech act] situation" (1962:13, 27, 52). In order to accomplish an act *in* saying something, that act has to be integrated into a network of social arrangements sensitive to the institutional placement of utterances: rituals such as a wedding ceremony have different efficaciousness when performed on a theater stage and when performed in a church. The "circumstances," "procedures," and "situations" that establish validity of performative utterances are structured by social agreements, or rules, that enable language to act.

In his elaboration of speech act theory, Searle distinguishes between two basic categories of rules, which he names "regulative" and "constitutive." Both are concerned not only with language but also with behavior, linguistic or otherwise: whereas the former "regulate . . . existing forms of behavior," the latter "create or define new forms of behavior" (1969:33). And further, while regulative rules are imperative ("Do *X*"), constitutive are contextual: "*X* counts as *Y* in context of *C*" (35). This formula is one of the key insights of Searle's contributions to speech act theory, and it resurfaces in a number of his works, including the ones in which he discusses linguistic foundations of institutions. In fact, he sees it as the defining feature of all social institutions. In that sense, Searle's late work offers further institutional elaboration to his early examination of the rule-based nature of speech acts. In "What Is an Institution?" he parses out the distinctions between communality and institutionality. A collective is not an institution, but it could become a first step in its formation. According to Searle, in human societies, "cooperative behavior" takes the form of "collective intentionality," which should not be mistaken for just any indication of intention, but instead represents a "directedness of the mind" expressed in "beliefs, hopes, fears, and desires" (6). It provides a foundation for social facts, which he defines as "any fact involving the collective intentionality of two or more agents" (6). The social fact, that specifically human form of collectivity, is not yet an institution. In order to become one, it needs a mechanism for "assignment of functions" to objects or persons, which is not based only on their "physical structure," but on a "collective assignment of a certain *status*": "The object or person performs its function only in virtue of collective acceptance by the community that the object or person has the requisite status" (7). The recognition of the conventional nature of status is the requisite step from social to institutional fact. Social efficacy is contingent upon contextuality, and that is where Searle's old formula of constitutive rules comes into play. In fact, it is nested at the very center of Searle's definition of institution:

> An institutional fact is any fact that has the logical structure *X counts as Y in C*, where the *Y* term assigns a status function and (with few exceptions) the status function carries a deontology. An institution is any system of constitutive rules of the form *X counts as Y in C*. Once an institution becomes established, it then provides a structure within which one can create institutional facts. (2005:10)

One key feature of Searle's idea of the institution is its circularity; the other is its capacity to generate power, indicated here in his reference to deontology. He develops it in his next step:

> Human institutions are, above all, *enabling*, because they create power, but it is a special kind of power. It is the power that is marked by such terms as: rights, duties, obligations, authorizations, permissions, empowerments, requirements, and certifications. I call all of these *deontic powers*. (10)

Areas of overlap between institutions and apparatuses are broad. Certainly, they both participate in ideological operations. Searle goes as far as using the same metaphor for status functions and institutions that Althusser uses for ideology: that of social glue (9, 18, 19). However, the key difference between institutions and apparatuses is that the former, the way Searle conceives of them, don't participate in the process of subjectivation. One can gain access to an institution only insofar as one has been already summoned into subjecthood by apparatuses.

In order to earn its name, institutional critique has to engage precisely with these enabling and power-generating properties of institutions. That is to say, in order to become critical, art needs to examine its own deontic status: what it is and is not authorized and permitted to do; what it is required to accomplish; and the systems of certification, or rather, legitimization, that endow it with the status of art. Historically, institutional critique has been doing precisely that, as suggested in Blake Stimson's recognition that "institutional critique preserved the institution of art in the context of 1968's broad disavowal of institutionality by holding it accountable to its founding ideals" (2009:31). In other words, institutional critique has never transgressed the deontic boundaries of institutions to raise questions of the constitution of the artist as subject. Stimson's remark reads as a more or less direct comment on Andrea Fraser's assertions in her 2005 landmark essay "From the Critique of Institutions to an Institution of Critique." Speaking of Hans Haacke, one of the founding figures of institutional critique, Fraser claims that "anyone familiar with his work should recognize that, far from trying to tear down the museum, Haacke's project has been an attempt to *defend* the institution of art from instrumentalization by political and economic interests" (2009:415). In the end, it turns out that the circular nature of institutions determines the nature of its critique: in order to be able to offer critique, art has to be recognized by institutions. Discourses of contemporary art, such as art history, art criticism, and artists themselves, often seem at pains to show that from its inception, institutional critique has been treading carefully the boundary between institutions and apparatuses. Fraser approaches the limit of subjectivation when she asserts, in her conclusion, "It's not a question about being against the institution: We are the institution. It's a question of what kind of institution we are, what kind of values we institutionalize, what form of practices we reward, and what kind of rewards we aspire to. Because the institution of art is internalized, embodied, and performed by individuals, these are the questions that institutional critique demands we ask, above all, of ourselves" (416). It appears that the art of institutional critique consists of stepping on the dangerous line that separates institutions from apparatuses while being careful not to obliterate and erase that very same boundary. If an artist happens to wipe out that line, the institutional language makes sure that this gesture of erasure stays outside of its legitimizing operations. That leaves the question whether the critique of apparatuses is at all possible, and if it is, at what cost.

CONVERSATION PIECES

In his article "On Practice," published in the first issue of the journal *The Fox*, Mel Ramsden, a member of the New York branch of the conceptual art collective Art & Language, offered a pointed criticism of the contemporary art scene. He quipped: "To dwell perennially on an institutional critique without addressing specific problems within the institutions is to generalize and sloganize" (1975b:69). In the second issue, which came out in the fall of the same year, he published a review: "'City Arts Workshop—People Art in New York City' by Eva Cockroft and James D. Cockroft (Left-Curve, Summer 1975)." In his commentary on this article, which dealt with politicized murals on the Lower East Side, Ramsden again invoked the same concept he deployed in "On Practice," calling for a "critique" of "institutional mystifications" (1975a:40). Alexander Alberro, the editor of *Institutional Critique: An Anthology of Artists' Writings*, identifies these two instances as the first mentions in print of the phrase "institutional critique" (2009:8). How significant is it that, even though the practice of institutional critique started in the late 1960s in the works of artists such as Adrian Piper, Marcel Broodthaers, and Mierle Laderman Ukeles, the phrase that gave the name to an artistic strategy was first printed in the premiere issue of journal *The Fox*? Quite, as it turns out, especially if we consider Buchloh's historical framing of his object-centered reconsideration of conceptual art. Published in March 1975, the first issue of *The Fox* is situated just at the outside edge of the temporal frame that Buchloh gives to conceptual art ("roughly" from 1965 to 1975) and, more important, outside of the "stylistic homogenization" to which he relegates the activities of the curator Seth Siegelaub and "the authoritarian quests for orthodoxy by the English Art & Language group" (107).[5] In "From the Critique of Institutions to an Institution of Critique," which often has been read as a manifesto of the second generation of institutional critique, Fraser mentions the "possibility" that she is "the first person to put the term [institutional critique] in print" (2009:410). This can be read as the admission of her unfamiliarity with Ramsden's work, which in itself speaks to the pervasiveness of the efforts to downplay the legacy of Art & Language, and especially its New York wing (ALNY), from the institution of art history, and to do this with the wholehearted participation of critics, such as Buchloh, who identify with the Left.[6] This exclusion can be seen as an unwillingness and inability on the part of representatives of institutional critique to engage in the critique of the apparatus.

In "On Practice," Ramsden gets straight to the point: "It seems there is today a gelling of political, economic and administrative processes within a massive overarching apparatus of control over all aspects of everyday life—which might begin to give us some idea of the kind of thing we're up against" (1975b:72). Even while he gives a name (in print) to institutional critique, the substance of Ramsden's argument asks for an engagement with ideology. And that engagement can take place only within the apparatus. As Althusser warned, ISAs are "not only the *stake*, but the *site* of class struggle, and often of bitter forms of class struggle" (1971:140). As much as New York Art & Language attempted to establish a critical distance from the art industry, it was bound to it through its vital ties with Joseph Kosuth. So, for members of ALNY, the primary site of ideological struggle was his loft on Bond Street between Lafayette and the Bowery in SoHo.

An established artist at the time he started collaborating with the original Art & Language group based in the United Kingdom (ALUK), Kosuth helped the New York group to forge ties with their British "cousins," hosted meetings in his studio, and bankrolled the first issue of *The Fox*. ALNY was not a mere extension, or even less a replica, of its "transatlantic counterparts."[7] The art historian and ALUK member Charles Harrison observed that "the tendency in 'English' work was for priority to be accorded in the last instance to the organizing potential of formal and logical systems, and for the materials and persons thus organized to be treated as relatively incidental"; conversely, "The tendency in New York was for priority to be accorded to the composition of a working community and to the nature of its concerns" (1991:99). The members of the group were primarily concerned with their own positioning in relation to the art industry, strategies of collaboration within the group, and their interpersonal relationships. There was no formal admission process to the group. Instead, membership was established through participation. As Michael Corris explained in a dialogue with Sezgin Boynik, the editor of the journal *Rab-Rab*, one would join the group by collaborating with other members, which amounted to the future members of ALNY submitting texts to the ALUK journal *Art-Language* and collaborating on exhibitions such as *Index 001* (or *Documenta Index*), presented at Documenta 5 in Kassel in 1972 (2017:12). The members of the New York group saw exhibitions and "essayistic practice" as secondary in relation to the interactions within the group. The art historian Christopher Gilbert points out that "the conversational community that the group formed was not just an essential framework for work but was often indistinguishable from the work itself" (2004:326). In effect, if British Art & Language eliminated the art object in favor of linguistic material, ALNY shifted the emphasis from textual to dialogic practice. The group *was* the work.

Over the course of the group's short and turbulent existence (~1972–1976), three distinct projects came from this ongoing conversational practice. The first was developed through the process of "annotations" that eight members of the group conducted from January to June 1973.[8] The process started with the members of the group composing page-long statements, photocopying them in Kosuth's loft, and then circulating the copies among themselves. Each member of the group would choose one or more texts to "annotate," which lead to repetition of the process of copying and distributing the statement, which they referred to as a "blurt," the word used to, as Gilbert explains, "indicate their not necessarily logical character" (2007:84). The group would meet weekly in Kosuth's loft to discuss the blurts. After a period of six months, they indexed and compiled over four hundred of these annotations. In Corris's account of this process, a "number of 'clusters' began to emerge, and with those clusters, a sense of discursive 'space' in which themes and interests were fleshed out."[9] In the next phase, Ramsden and Corris devised an "index," or "retrieval device that would make the themes explicit" and establish links between individual annotations described by two connecting functions, "&" and "→".[10] Here the arrow stands for "conjunction" in the narrower sense of "implication"; and the ampersand for "concatenation," or a conjunction in a wider sense.[11] This process of creation, selection, and indexing resulted in a ninety-two-page booklet, *Blurting in Art & Language*, published in the fall of 1973. In his introduction, Corris explained that the purpose of the logical operations indicated by signs "&" and "→" was "not only to make the readings 'interesting,' but to make the readings problematic" (1973:1).[12] The point is, as he went on to explain, that "after reading a given blurt you have to ask yourself 'How do I go on?', 'Do I in fact go on?'" (1). In a way, the answer came in the second dialogic project.

Three members of the annotations venture, Ian Burn, Mel Ramsden, and Terry Smith, went on to record a series of conversational sessions, held in May,June, and July 1974. These recordings were the source of the second publication based on ALNY's dialogic practice, comprising an entire issue of *Art-Language* (vol. 3, no. 1, September 1974), to which the title *Draft for an Anti-textbook* was given. Published transcripts didn't include the names of speakers, so that the text appears as a series of paragraphs, different in length, that come from a unified collective voice. As the conversationalists put it humbly in their introduction, "Transformations from 'talk' to 'prose' [were], to some extent, dialogically cosmetic" (1974:1). Another "cosmetic" intervention was the division of "prose" into thirty-nine chapters, which ranged from

"Somewhere to Begin" to "What Are We Doing in Language" to "Leftish Critique." Some of them read as a theoretical preamble to the third and final conversational project, which concurred with the collapse of ALNY.

CONCEPTUAL THEATER

The last publication that came from the conversational practice of ALNY was also a transcript. The conversations, which included fourteen members of the group, were recorded during the meetings that took place in February and early March 1976, at the loft of artists Carole Condé and Karl Beveridge, located at 49 East First Street (Condé 2022). Edited transcripts of these conversations constituted the lead article in the third and final issue of *The Fox*, published in May 1976. Like the previous two publications that emerged from the group's conversational practice, "The Lumpen-Headache," as the article was titled, had a conspicuous conceptual framing. The meticulously edited transcript was divided into three parts, each representing a separate thematic unit. These three sections cohere into a larger narrative arc, with a beginning, middle, and end, so that the discussion takes the recognizable form of a dramatic text. In another similarity with the previous publications, "The Lumpen-Headache" came with an introduction, signed "Peter Benchley." The author of the introduction informs the reader that there were seven meetings, or "struggle sessions" as they were referred to by the members of the group, and that he selected the first and the last two for publication, thus giving the published transcript its three-part structure (1976:3). Having already referred to the participants in the struggle sessions as "characters," Benchley concludes the introduction with "one final point" concerning the names used in the transcript. Since "certain individuals did not want their names used," it was his decision to replace them with "appropriate genus, species, or trivial name of a freshwater tropical fish" (3). So the participants in the conversation were concealed behind pseudonyms "Albifrons," "Badis Badis," "Bellica," "Ciarius," and so on.

A closer inspection of this choice of aquatic fauna reveals that these "freshwater tropical fish" commonly populate aquariums. The choice of pseudonyms is all but random: it is an ironic reference to Benchley's characterization of the source of "struggle" in these "sessions," which comes from the social position of its participants. According to him, they are the members of "surplus intelligentsia" who, despite their progressive political positions, end up forced "to make a contract with the capitalist entrepreneur and become a 'unit' in the labor market. Such an individual is no longer bourgeois and not proletarian, they are, in other words, a kind of *lumpen-bourgeoisie*" (2). "The Lumpen-Headache" depicts the drama of artistic intelligentsia insulated from the rest of the society, swimming around in circles like exotic fish trapped in a living-room aquarium. In accord with the piscatorial theme of the piece, the editor of the struggle sessions transcripts adopted the name of the author of *Jaws*, the summer blockbuster novel of 1976. In a final theatrical turn, before the third issue of *The Fox* went into distribution, someone stamped on the journal's inner cover of roughly half of the print run the inscription "THE LUMPEN-HEADACHE Dramatis Personae," followed by the cast list of all fourteen conversation participants, in alphabetical order of their pseudonyms:

Albifrons	Christine Kozlov
Badis Badis	Carole Condé
Bellica	Andrew Menard
Clarius	Alex Hay
Hypostomus	Preston Heller
Jaculator	Jill Breakstone
Jarbua	Sarah Charlesworth
Metae	Nigel Lendon
Multifasciata	Karl Beveridge
Oscellatus	Joseph Kosuth
Pongo-Pongo	Mel Ramsden
Punkay	Michael Corris
Puntius Stigma	Ian Burn
Ramirezi	Mayo Thompson[13]

"The Lumpen-Headache" is based on dialogic practice typical of ALNY, and it reads as a documentary drama that details the implosion of the group. Commentators, historians, and the former members of ALNY agree that the artistic, political, and ideological issues that were straining relationships within the group coalesced around the faction consisting of Kosuth and Sarah Charlesworth, who was his partner at the time.[14] Gilbert references the members of ALNY who spoke of "deep ideological differences which had existed between Kosuth, Charlesworth, and the rest of the group, most significantly, the continuing fact of Kosuth's independent career and a perceived ideological incoherence that accompanied Charlesworth's embrace of socialism" (2004:336). Indeed, if the drama centered on this fracture at the center of the group, the true stakes were ideological.

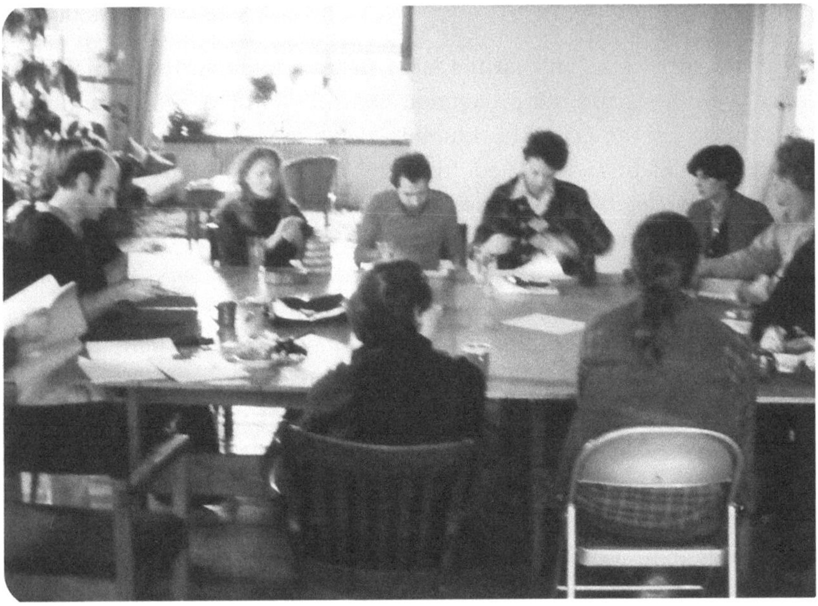

Figure 8. Meeting at Condé and Beveridge loft, February or March 1976. From left to right: Ian Burn, Christine Kozloff, Michael Corris, Mayo Thompson, Jill Breakstone, (from back) Mel Ramsden, Preston Heller. Photo courtesy of Carole Condé.

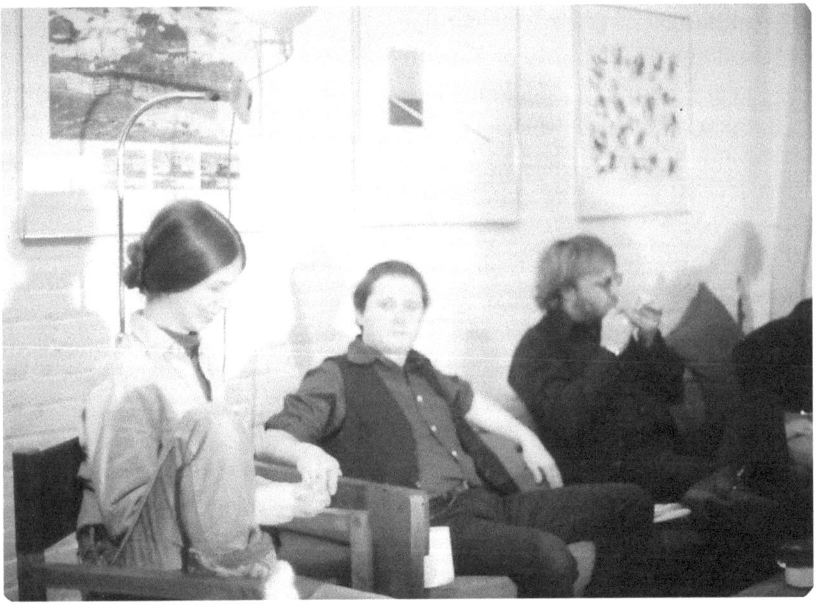

Figure 9. Meeting at Condé and Beveridge loft, February or March 1976. From left to right: Carole Condé, Mel Ramsden, Joseph Kosuth. Photo courtesy of Carole Condé.

After all, the struggle sessions were taking place in New York, in the very jaws of the apparatus of modern art.

From the outset, it is clear that the participants in the struggle sessions mean business. In this "drama," there is no need for a lengthy exposition. Jarbua (Sarah Charlesworth): "I'm not interested in working for a dictatorship of the proletariat. I am interested in working for a society that would be truly egalitarian which has a whole different basis of social relations" (Benchley 1976:4). Ramirezi (Mayo Thompson) positions himself on the radical wing of the ideological spectrum within this leftist circle: "I am 'for' the dictatorship of the proletariat, on the grounds that it's an historical necessity, its implementation at every level is needed to overthrow the state. The power of it is that it organizes the social relations" (9). The group members adopt a range of positions between these two extremes, with the majority closer to the latter.

If the first act of "The Lumpen-Headache" introduces personal disagreements, the second act focuses on ideological differences. Right at the get-go, the microphone is in the hands of the radical Left. Ramirezi/Thompson opens the salvo with a monologue about "socialist process," and Ian Burn (Puntius Stigma) follows by characterizing the group as "laissez-faire" with its penchant for "arguments" in favor of "'the rights of individuals' against a [fear of a] sort of 'group council,'" and pointing to "the existing hierarchy within the group in terms of work put out under just 'Art & Language.' To a certain extent credit would accrue to those already established, thus reinforcing the hierarchy" (12). Now all eyes are turning to whichever side of the table Oscellatus (Kosuth) and his ally Jarbua (Charlesworth) are seated. He attempts to maneuver out of the corner by pointing to ALNY's rift with the United Kingdom group and suggesting they abandon the name "Art & Language" altogether (15). As the pressure of the argument that favors the group over the individual increases, he diverts further in that seemingly radical direction. Having acknowledged that the group is "going through a Maoist stage," he suggests that they go all the way: "Unless we really start all over again, it's still just a radical reform of the old art group and if it's a new situation let's make it a *really* new situation. The only other way out of this is a political party. We will all belong to the party" (17). But Bellica, Ramirezi, Puntius Stigma, Pongo-Pongo, and others from the radical wing are not taking the bait. Earlier in the discussion, someone has already mentioned the need for "principles of unity," and as in a good Chekhovian drama, this political weapon will go off with a bang at the top of the third act.

The beginning of the third part of "The Lumpen-Headache" marks the moment when this specific political tactic entered ALNY's artistic practice. An abbreviated policy, the principles of unity was a tactical tool used in intraparty struggles during the Cultural Revolution in China, and from there it entered Maoist movements worldwide. Anti-revisionist communist groups in the United States were no exception. In the New York area, the growth of ALNY coincided with the political transformation of the Congress of Afrikan People into the Revolutionary Communist League (Marx-Lenin–Mao Tse-tung Thought). In an effort to establish a mass cultural organization, RCL (M-L-M) initiated the Anti-Imperialist Cultural Union (AICU), which in the winter of 1975 reached out to radical art groups in SoHo, such as the Photography Collective, the Marxist Literary Circle, and Artists Meeting for Cultural Change, in which several members of ALNY were active. Black nationalist organizations used the principles of unity in maneuvering to the political left and establishing their position there: the Black Women's United Front, which was instrumental for the transformation of the Congress of Afrikan People to RCL (M-L-M), adopted its principles of unity in October 1975 (Woodard 1999:182); that winter, RCL (M-L-M) chairman Amiri Baraka invoked the "principles of unity" in his campaign against the Revolutionary Communist League and Puerto Rican Revolutionary Worker's Organization (1976:4); and by the time of the struggle sessions, the AICU had already drafted its own version of the principles of unity, which were published in the first issue of *Main Trend*, one of the successor journals that emerged after the collapse of *The Fox* (1978:31).[15]

In a takedown of ALNY, which they published in *Art-Language* after the New York group had dissolved, the members of ALUK described the "principles of unity" as "pieces of truistic, crystalline, utilitarian, social-optimalist, fideistic over-simplifications, idealisations and worthless except as a testing ground for 'fitness' for the steering committee" (Art & Language 1977b:78). The AICU steering committee consisted of two members of RCL (M-L-M), an organizer from the Marxist Literary Circle, one independent artist, and one member of ALNY (78). The ALNY representative was Andrew Menard, and his familiarity with procedures that the AICU used to resolve its internal struggles made him the most likely to introduce the idea of principles of unity in ALNY's fateful group discussions in February and March 1976. Presented at the start of the third act of the struggle sessions drama, these principles stipulated that (1) all work "made public," including "exhibitions, published articles, teaching," should be "presented under the collective name"; that (2) "all work which is 'made public' has to be struggled over and accepted by the general body. This will set up a framework for self-criticism/criticism of work"; and, crucially, that (3) "working 'publically' in an individualistic manner will be considered as self-disqualification from this process" (1976:20). There follow three more "provisos," as the group also called these principles of unity, but they were far less consequential than the first three, which aimed to expose Kosuth's and Charlesworth's position as proponents of an individualistic approach to artistic production and the hypocrisy of their adoption of radical-left ideas. After the provisos, Pongo-Pongo (Ramsden) suggests that "a splinter group" supporting these stipulations should adopt the name "(Provisional) Art & Language," a maneuver that would effectively formalize the expurgation of Kosuth and Charlesworth from the group (21). In one last attempt, Kosuth tried to offer a list of principles to essentially counter the principles of unity, and in fact got everyone to agree about the group's "commitment to socialism" (32). But it was too late. The blade was already on its way down: all that was left was to go through the mechanics of the "roll call" in the final moments of the struggle session, which exposed the deep ideological fissure that separated him and Charlesworth from the rest of the group. The final stage direction of "The Lumpen-Headache" reads: "[Hallucinatory silence follows . . .]" (37). Somewhat unexpectedly, this piece of political theater ended on a note of a Beckettian drama.

Even as he maintains that the personal relationships and the ideological positions of individuals were at the center of conflict, Gilbert observes that "the particular wording of the provisions [was] far from arbitrary" (336). That pertains in particular to "self-criticism/criticism" in the second proviso. This introduces another procedure from the arsenal of the Cultural Revolution to "the West Broadway So-Ho-viet," as the British "cousins" ironically dubbed the New York Art & Language group (1977b:79). The practice of self-criticism was an instrument of party discipline devised by the Russian Bolsheviks. The Chinese Communist Party adopted it in the 1940s, and during the Cultural Revolution the practice was transformed into a mass public procedure. Lowell Dittmer offers a useful synopsis of this political ritual as practiced by the Party:

> The original institution of criticism and self-criticism was premised upon solidarity ("unity") among all participants . . . , which had been disturbed by an offence committed by one of them. To induce remorse in the offender, he is isolated from the others and criticized; he then confesses and solicits forgiveness from the others. In so doing he affirms that he has indeed committed the acts of which he is accused, but denies that he is "in" them; his appeal for forgiveness

> is a demonstration that he transcends his acts and his past and is not identical with them. In accepting his self-criticism and granting forgiveness, the others in turn acknowledge that their earlier criticism was partly incorrect or incomplete. The process is resolved in the externalization of the offence and the reintegration of the offender into a group newly purified and united by this emotional opening and surrender on the part of both the person criticized and his critics. (1973:722)

In routinized versions of criticism/self-criticism practiced in American Maoist organizations there is not a trace left of these cathartic denouements. A primer for AICU meetings from the early months of 1978 features "criticism/self-criticism" as the last item on the agenda, stating that it should "begin sharply at 2 ½ hours after opening of the meeting, so that total time of the meeting never exceeds 3hrs" ("Some Proposals" 1978:1). A partial transcript from one of the meetings held a few months later features an example of a rote recitation of self-criticism/criticism by "J. Byrron": "I criticize myself for subcoming [*sic*] to liberalism in the interest of false unity during this period. . . . However, I more severely criticize both David and Preston for liquidating their practice in the workshop at this critical moment. . . . I less severely criticize both Chryssa and Craig for periods of subjective antagonism to my leadership during this struggle" ("In Response" 1978:3).[16] It is hard to imagine how this ritual of ideological penitence would work in "self-criticism/criticism of work" stipulated in the ALNY principles of unity, and there is no trace of it in "The Lumpen-Headache." There is, however, a great deal of mutual personal accusation and defensiveness. If the group identified conversational practice as their primary artistic work, then self-criticism becomes an intensely reflexive undertaking. In short, from an ossified party rite, ALNY transforms self-criticism into criticism of the self. That points to the key difference between critique of institutions and critique of ideological apparatuses.

THE UPROAR

The introduction of principles of unity didn't bring anything new to the drama of "The Lumpen-Headache." Rather, the principles of unity represented a tactical positioning of a program that had been operational in the group from the very beginning of the struggle sessions and that had, in fact, preceded them. Already in the second act, Punkay (Corris) outlines this program. Recapping the sessions that were omitted from the published version of the drama, he asserts that the group has recognized that it "has long passed the point of being an art-group" and that it has "long gone toward being a socialist instrument, a party" (1976:13). There is an inherent danger in this, and he warns that the group should "stop couching" itself "exclusively in institutional terms" (13). There is more to Punkay/Corris's intervention than an attempt to preempt Oscellatus/Kosuth's maneuver of turning this art collective into a political party. He continues:

> I'll just iterate some practical points about supporting re-education along socialist lines. Group criticism of work; Group resolve to go on conversationally—and I'm doing this in increasing order of difficulty or approachability—collective work; expansion of publications and public activities, including teaching workshops; a move towards "thematic" gallery shows; a move toward the collectivization of income; a move toward non-participation in cultural institutions such as museums, and in general I guess an eventual withdrawal from the market and bourgeois art history. (13)

This is not a program for an action-critique of institutions, either. Gilbert's account of the editorial procedure at *The Fox* suggests that the journal itself was an extension of the group's conversational practice. The editors, who also wrote the majority of the articles, circulated their contributions "like the earlier 'blurts,' for everybody's comment before they were published" (2004:332). As a result, a number of articles were in conversation with one another. For example, Ramsden's call for institutional critique received further elaboration in articles by other editors and members of the group, such as Ian Burn's "Pricing Works of Art" in the first issue, or Andrew Menard and Ron White's "Media Madness" and Adrian Piper's "A Proposal for Pricing Works of Art" in the second. Seen in that light, "The Lumpen-Headache" is a final demonstration of the ALNY conversational practice as a critical undertaking much more rigorous and far-reaching than the work of the first generation of institutional critique from the late 1960s (Hans Haacke, Daniel Buren) that preceded it, as well as that of the second generation of institutional critique from the 1980s (Andrea Fraser) that came after this group's demise.

Going back to where we left Ramsden's "On Practice," we see that in the same gesture of calling for institutional critique, he also points beyond it: "Part of the drive for the disassembling of institutions is to escape from the institutions' topicalizations and sanctioned problems" (1975b:71). If artists are going to engage in a critique of museums, galleries, art journals, and critics, they can't do that from an imaginary outside: "Institutional dismantling now also involves dismantling myself; I am part of the problem, which is why I mentioned materialism before—the institutions are not just contingent" (71). If, as Alberro contends, Ramsden was indeed the first to put in print the phrase "institutional critique," the substance of his argument did not stop at the critique of art institutions. He clearly recognizes that the assessors and bureaucrats of art—museums and galleries, criticism and scholarship—are just peripheral elements of the apparatus. At its core is the artist as subject: "Perhaps paradoxically, there may now be opportunity for oppositional alternatives. How might they be initiated? For myself, one way may be to *acknowledge* that the capitalist apparatus has been internalized and that 'disassembling its relations means disassembling myself'" (72).[17] What Ramsden is pointing to is not a loss of the self, but the undoing of the ideologically constituted subject. So, here it is, the dreaded desubjectification. What might it look like? The subjectless discourse that Ramsden calls for is not that of science, *pace* Althusser, but of art. And in further distinction from Althusser, he recognizes that the dismantling of the subject requires a collectivity different from the political party, even, or perhaps especially, the one that claims to be established on "scientific" principles. The title of Ramsden's article, "On Practice," references one of Mao Zedong's key texts. And if Kosuth had read it carefully, he would not have proposed the transformation of ALNY into a political party. The faction of ALNY to which Ramsden belonged entered the "struggle sessions" with a clear idea that the party was *not* the kind of assembly required for the critical work of disassembling of the subject.

Throughout "The Lumpen-Headache," the dialogue is punctuated by textual interventions that depict nonlinguistic reactions. Some of them belong to the commonplace repertoire of theatrical stage directions, such as "[laughter]" and "[applause]," and others point directly to the source of the transcript: "[pause in the tape]" (1976:32). Most of these descriptors are conventional, and they don't seem to express the intentions of "Peter Benchley." However, as the intensity of the discussion increases, certain stage directions start appearing more frequently, and gradually begin to dominate all other stage directions. For example, the beginning of Corris/Punkay's monologue, cited above, is interrupted with "[uproar, some applause]" (13). Toward the end of the second part of the monologue, the

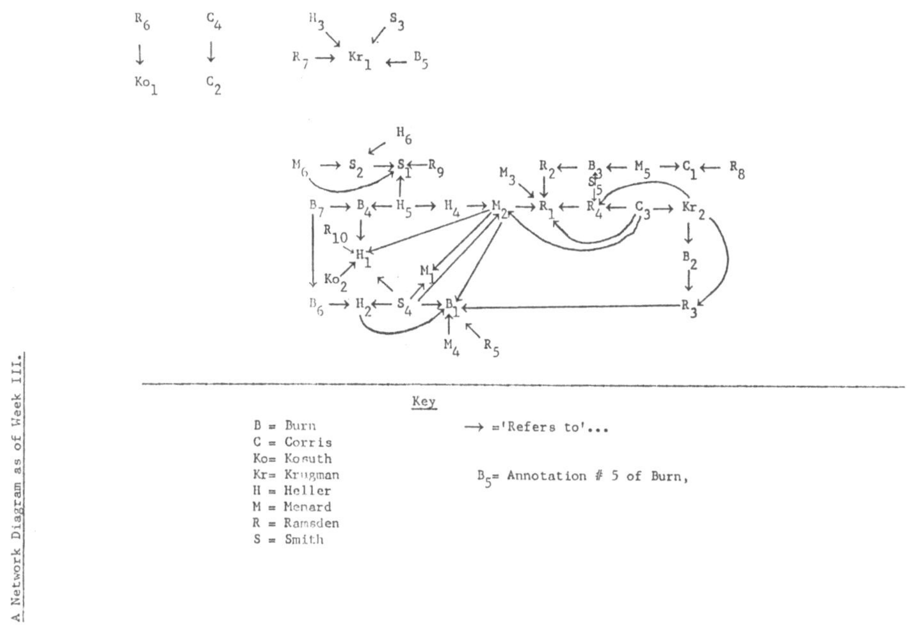

Figure 10. Michael Corris, *A Network Diagram as of Week III*, 1973, 8.5 × 11 inches, typescript and ink on paper. © 1995 Michael Corris.

"uproars" become more frequent, sometimes breaking in after each line delivered by sparring speakers (19). As the showdown between the group and Kosuth/Oscellatus reaches its climax in a sharp exchange between Oscellatus and Punkay, responses from the group threaten to overwhelm the dialogue. "[Uproar, uproar]" is followed by repeated instances of "[pandemonium]," as if the first stage direction is no longer sufficient to capture the intensity of the moment (35). Finally, the roll call concludes with "[uproar and pandemonium]" (36). It turns out that these breakouts from dialogue play a similar role as "→" and "&" (conjunction and concatenation, respectively) in *Blurting in Art & Language*: they are openings or passages that establish connections not between blurts or segments of conversations, but between entire conversational pieces that the group performed from 1973 to 1976.

In the introduction to *Blurting in Art & Language,* Corris speaks of the "Handbook," the final published product of the annotation process, as a "projection" of the relationships among eight individuals who were involved in the process of annotation, not a "reconstruction" of these relationships (1973:8). As much as the intricate organization of "annotating" tried to resist the linearity of a printed text, it still had to succumb to syntactical rules of writing, thus producing an incomplete mapping of the group. Hence, Corris resorted to making "sociograms" of the relationships among the eight artists involved in the blurting to complete the map (Figure 10).

Figures in Corris's diagram face or follow one another; they establish series and concatenations; and they make straight lines and sharp turns, so that if they confront one another, they may depart in a different direction. Corris suggests that the "conversational noise" that runs through the process of annotating introduces the notion of an audience, which means "projecting our own uncertainties" (1973:9). These moments when syntactical chains break down are instances in which the reader is asked to make a decision rather than to passively follow the text; each of these points is marked with the symbol "→" or "&." By disrupting the textual order, these symbols make visible the "anomalies and inconsistencies" that the annotators associate with the "pandemonium" (9). If in "The Lumpen-Headache" pandemonium was associated with theatrical outbursts of "conversational," or rather argumentative, "noise," and if in *Blurting in Art & Language* it helped forge a path through annotations, in *Draft for an Anti-textbook* it helped the group define some of the central tenets of their practice.

In the parlance of ALNY, "pandemonium" designates that state of affairs which is on the other side of certainty and determinism. Already in one of the first sections of *Draft for an Anti-textbook*, the conversationalists point out that "there's no epistemology that allows for uncertainty," so "what A&L has done is start by going into a wider and more refutable position . . . and here we get the origin of the whole 'wilful [*sic*] pandemonium' talk . . . and so the 'logical' connection between meaning and certainty is rejected" (Burn et al. 1974:10). They return to the idea of willful pandemonium in one of the last sections of the *Anti-textbook* to clarify that they are not trying to establish a "new order." Pandemonium, after all, is based on ideas of the inconsistent and the aleatoric, in which ALNY recognizes its proximity with Dada (36). Willful pandemonium is not an idea or an objective ("new order"), but a state: "From an institutional vantage point, this might be called 'chaos' . . . but from a personal vantage, is it really?" (104). Of course not. From a personal perspective, it is an individual in the state of "uproar."

> Part of the current problem for us is the confusion of the static body of authenticated truths in a series of propositions (which we don't

> have) with the "uproar"—or our "existing in the truth"—which more closely approximates the present goings-on.—But can you "communicate" uproar?—or is that a contradiction?—You exist in uproar, you experience uproar . . . or, in a Sartrean sense, you "exist" uproar . . . it's a contextual condition.—Does pandemonium have any "external" sense whatsoever? (58)

Just as "pandemonium" is not reducible to a literary allegory of chaos (such as Milton's capital of hell), so the "uproar" is not the state of alarm and upheaval. They both capture the nature and meaning of ALNY's conversational practice: "I don't particularly see that the uncertainty/uproar is reflected in the surface of conversation, but more in respect to points of reference that I accept, the sorts of contingencies I see operating between those points, and those points and me" (65). In other words, they are inseparable from the idea of "sharedness of language" or the creation of "languaged environments." Both of them are linguistic forms of the "sociality" that is at the very center of ALNY's artistic practice. It would be an oversimplification to say that the work of ALNY exhausted itself in conversational practice. This practice was just a medium, no different than canvas, clay, video camera, or performance the group used to carry out its actual work, which was aimed at a meticulous and unsparing dismantling of the ideological apparatus of art.

The conversational practice is not characterized by a firm and preordained progression of ideas. Instead, it is a process punctuated by breakdowns, collapses, interruptions, and pauses, all in the service of its ultimate goal of the production of knowledge through the process of desubjectification. "The classical notion of knowledge is equated with certainty," proclaim Burn/Ramsden/Smith in the *Anti-textbook* (1974:34). The basic condition for this "disassembling of the self" is sociality. "So when I carry on about indeterminism, uncertainty, pandemonium, and so on, stuff which is meant to bring the questions closer to sociality, then you can see how frail is the whole shibboleth of certainty (knowledge)" (34). And further, they tie the production of knowledge and the idea of certainty to individuality: "This is where the sociality stuff comes out a bit stronger . . . it's not a matter of knowing they are your experiences and not mine, it's a situation of *not knowing*" (54). Characterized by uncertainty and non-knowledge, sociality does not figure as the scene of the subject, but as its other. This raises a question: Does the individual inform social relations in which she engages, or the other way around? The *Anti-textbook* makes a clear distinction between the practice of sociality and other similar ideas fashionable in the art world of the day. One of the most pervasive was "collaboration."

Burn/Ramsden/Smith observe that "the problem with collaboration was the '*we* speak with one voice' implication; sociality might be more like '*I* speak with many voices' . . . sociality would be the inverse of collaboration" (54). And another one is "inclusion":

> You could view sociality as "the gaining access to" (a projection of) a "we" or an "our" . . . provided this becomes a matter of intimacy (possibility), not constraint. It takes on the character of including others—I might say then that a condition of sociality is that it is an "inclusive" notion of individual (or self), in contrast to any "exclusive" notion of individual—one that defines itself negatively, in respect of what it won't admit. (56)

Ideas such as "collaboration" and "inclusion" don't go far enough in capturing the idea of the "individual self" as the "convenient social fiction it generally is" (56). So the trio moves to the discussion of institutions, specifically, the interpersonal relationships in a corporation.

QUEER AS KIERKEGAARD

For ALNY, "bureaucracy" and "corporation" were the epitome of the capitalist constitution of the individual and the society. Bureaucratic relationships are determined by regulations, which are knowable and discoverable; and a corporation is that kind of social unit which is organized by profits. Here individuals are made to cohere, paradoxically, through competition. The main product of this kind of social institution is the individual as subject. And vice versa, the individual responds to the call of interpellation in order to be recognized as the subject in this kind of social organization. This is where one of the key distinctions between institutions and ideological apparatuses is located. If institutions contain and hold power, ideological apparatuses allow the power to flow through them: they are its conduits. The ideological apparatus is the kind of institution that makes the self legible to the state, and at the same time helps the self to enter the social relations organized by the state. Ideological apparatuses attach themselves to and insert themselves into interpersonal relationships in order to organize, shape, and direct them. They do that by privileging interests, which direct the process of subjectification. Ideology is not "in" apparatuses, and apparatuses don't produce ideologies. They come together in interests, which then determine behaviors of individuals. No individual responds to interpellation out of mere curiosity and abundance of choice. The individual is compelled to respond as subject.

Burn, Ramsden, and Smith are perfectly aware that bureaucratic institutions such as museums, political parties, and corporations are complex manifestations of fundamental forms of institutionalization that take place in and through language. The only segment of the *Anti-textbook* that explicitly addresses processes of institutionalization is segment 13, "Institutional Serenity," which is in its entirety dedicated to the discussion of John Searle's *Speech Acts*. The three interlocutors have already brought up Searle, placing his insight about speech acts as institutional performances in relation to his "instinctive conservatism," which is evident in *The Campus War*, the book in which he discusses the free speech movement at UC Berkeley (Burn et al. 1974:12). They have also brought up his idea of an "ideal speaker" (in their view, the world of "ideal speakers" and "ideal listeners" resembles a Broadway musical) and related it to the Greenbergian idea of an "ideal artist" (13, 28). If this "ideality" is, in effect, the main source of "institutional serenity," it is so because it is an expression of the rule-bound nature of speech acts. In building his speech-act theory on the idea of illocution, or doing through speaking, Searle unquestioningly follows J. L. Austin's idea of a "total speech act," according to which the "felicity" or "success" of a speech act depends more on "the total situation" than on the speaker ([1962] 1975:52). For the "word" to become one's "bond," the speech act needs to be performed under socially sanctioned circumstances. As Searle himself points out, the difference between speech-act theory and linguistics is that the former is not interested in language as structure, but in language as a "rule-governed form of behavior" (1969:41). Hence the institutional formula: "*X* counts as *Y* in context *C*." The rules cannot be anideological. In fact, rules are the elements of the apparatus that integrate speech acts into the fabric of ideology while at the same time giving them their ideological content.

The participants in the *Anti-textbook* conversations complain that it is Searle's "approach" that "bugs" them: "You start with little bits and try to work out to the context; but in doing that context is pretty much left dangling everywhere" (Burn et al. 1974:32). In that, their critique of Searle is similar to Jacques Derrida's a few years later, in which he famously pointed to the most glaring example of con-textuality, that of writing, as the blind spot of Searle's theory, raising the question of the possibility of "tracing" and "retracing" of an act or an event ([1977] 1988:6). However, the members of ALNY are not interested in subverting the hierarchies of language, but in exposing the social order inscribed in Searle's speech act theory. The main target of their criticism is the ideological content of what he presents as a theory of natural language. They move swiftly from summarizing Searle's theory to pointing out its ideological undertow:

> Speech-acts are entirely rule-governed forms of behavior; motor-body acts are likewise; as are desires, etc.; all thinking is rule-governed; natural processes are law-regulated; interaction between these is similarly rule-based; and everything else in this and any other possible world will eventually be able to be shown to be behaving according to rules of the kind already given. Of course, it's not stimulus-response behaviorism. And of course, much liberal chatter may be heard about the enormous "freedoms" which these rules "sanction" and "encourage." The monomaniac scientism is obvious enough. (1974:33)

In insisting that what distinguishes the act of promising from the act of fishing is that the former is "a matter of convention—as opposed to strategy, technique, procedure, or natural fact," Searle presupposes an agent, or a subject, as always already constituted by this linguistic institution (1969:37). Strategies, techniques, and procedures are not unique to human agents; conventions are. These social agreements are the very conditions of performativity: the citationality of speech acts is based on the rule-bound nature of language and its constitutive relation to the subject. This is one of key aspects of Judith Butler's understanding of performativity. As she points out in *Excitable Speech,* "The force of the speech act is separable from its meaning, and illocutionary force is secured through convention" (1997a:24). In a move somewhat analogous to the critique of Searle's speech-act theory outlined in the *Anti-textbook,* Maurizio Lazzarato bases his critique of Butler's idea of performativity precisely on the structure of "obligation" and "response," which are the basis of this citationality. He counters her argument about the possibility of performativity coming from infelicitous response by suggesting that "acting differently when addressed concerns all enunciations and not only performatives" (2014:179). Taking into consideration that the status of the subject is the indispensable condition for accomplishing a performative utterance, Lazzarato posits a number of different modes of action and response that, while coming from the subject, are "starting from the asignifying, unnameable, untellable," or in other words, from "the non-discursive in subjectivity" (180). Since "Grammatical intelligibility is a necessary but not sufficient condition of the verbal exchange," even if the interpellation includes much more than performative utterances and their underlying rules, intelligibility of the subject is still the sine qua non of performativity. Even when the subject is "bad," as both Althusser and Butler recognize, it is positioned in relation to a certain normative understanding of subjectivity. It may offer a hyperbolic or parodic discursive or gestural response to the constitutive call of the rules, but it still responds as a discrete, coherent, discursively constituted individual. As the purview of the individual, this non-discursivity is radically different from ALNY's "uproar."

ALNY's pursuit of sociality is based on the recognition that the critique of the apparatus can come only from that kind of institutionality which is constituted through intentionality that is not collective but mutual, and that is not based on the internalization of rules but instead questions the very nature of the interior as the defining property of a discrete self. They suggest that an effective critique of the apparatus can come only from an institution that is not the site of the constitution of the ideological subject, but its dismantling. The group of artists that went by the name of ALNY was not an institution; nor was it an anti-institution. It was not a shadow institution, and it was certainly not, as we have seen, a cooperative or a gathering. It was in proximity to the institution of art, but at the same time fiercely opposed it and guarded its independence from the art world. The prefix "counter" probably captures best this form of institutionality. As Derrida writes in his reflections on Jean Genet:

> The word "*contre*," counter or against, can equally and at the same time mark both opposition, contrariety, contradiction and proximity, near-contact. One can be "against" the person next to us, the one who is "right against" us, whom we touch or with whom we are in contact. The word "*contre*" possesses these two inseparable meanings of proximity and vis-à-vis, on the one hand, and opposition, on the other. (2004:18)

The group designated this counter-institutionality as *sociality*.

An alternative to performativity, sociality is not a mere aspiration toward collectivity, collaboration, or inclusion, but a strategy for disassembling the unitary subject. ALNY is not advocating schizo-procedures but rather the reconsideration of the relation between the self and the society. To "disassemble" oneself means, first and foremost, to wrangle oneself out from social arrangements stipulated and regulated by the apparatus. This "disassembly" of the subject does not presume its disintegration; on the contrary, it promotes a reassembly brought about through the establishment of relationships outside of, and opposed to, the dictates of the ideological apparatus. Crucially, the demand for disassembling the self is based on the recognition that the individual *is* an *assembly*. In its rejection of the subject as a unitary individual, sociality creates a pause in the ideological apparatus. It opens a lacuna: "Sociality is an integral feature of personal existence . . . not just being-in-a-world, but at the same time being-in-that-world-with-others" (Burn et al. 1974:57). This mode of social existence troubles existing social institutions because it presupposes an idea of the individual that is unrecognizable to them.

The "uproar" and the "pandemonium" are the forms of sociality that are unrecognizable to institutions; they are nondiscursive and extralinguistic enunciations of the fundamental unintelligibility of the non-unitary individual to ideological apparatuses. Instead of resorting to the ideals of collective action and social utopianism, the conversationalists of ALNY invoke them in opposition to these ideals: "Even Kierkegaard is queer on that point since the terms of his argument are the 'individual' and 'the crowd' . . . and the crowd is untruth while truth is inwardness." They go on to quote from Kierkegaard's *Concerning My Work as an Author*: "The crowd is, in fact, composed of individuals; it must therefore be in every man's power to become what he is, an individual. From becoming an individual, no-one, no one at all is excluded, except he who excludes himself by becoming a crowd" (1974:58). Uproar and pandemonium are the work of the individual who is the crowd. It is in these performances that the crowd of three, eight, or fourteen members of ALNY makes an exit, however *provisional*, from the apparatus. These are the instances in which the disassembled subjects generate sociality. The sociality of ALNY is not in any of their pointed exchanges, in their maneuvering, in their principles of unity and counter-principles of unity, in their blurts and diversions, or in any properties of the dramatic apparatus that captured the dynamics of the group. Quite to the contrary, it is located in the moments of the breakdown of this apparatus, marked with "[pandemonium]" and "[uproar and pandemonium]." If the principal artwork of ALNY was the critique of the apparatus, then, paradoxically, the collapse of the group should not register as a failure but as a full realization of the opening of the rupture within the ideological apparatus of art.

The principled adherence of "(Provisional) Art & Language" to the critique of the apparatus to its final conclusion, even at the price of the group's demise, is significant, and it exceeds the bounds of the critique of institutions in the 1970s. The idea of the disassembling the self offers a radical answer to the perennial question of "what comes after the subject."[18] At the same time, the radical idea of the individual as a crowd offers an alternative route to that of interpellation, which, as some Althusser's critics observed, condemns the subject to passivity.[19]

One of the most productive criticisms of the Althusserian subject came from the linguistic perspective, in Michel Pêcheux's book published only a few years after Althusser's ISA essay, *Language, Semantics, and Ideology*. According to Pêcheux, ideological interpellation "makes palpable the superstructural link" between "the *repressive* state apparatus . . . *and* the *ideological* state apparatuses," which is to say, "the link between the 'subject in law' . . . *and* the ideological subject" ([1975] 1982:105). In his analysis of Althusser's "theoretical theater" of interpellation, Pêcheux emphasizes the role of identification in the process of subject formation. The subject is identified as such by the state power, and in return identifies with the form imposed on it. Therefore, the central drama of the "theoretical theater" is that of "reduplication." Pêcheux suggests that "interpellation necessarily presupposes a *reduplication* constitutive of the subject of discourse" and emphasizes that "this *reduplication* corresponds exactly" to what he calls the "preconstructed" status of interpellation: "the 'always already' there of the ideological interpellation that supplies-imposes 'reality' and its 'meaning' in the form of universality" (156). In Althusser's ISA article, Pêcheux recognizes two "modalities" of this reduplication. The first one involves a "superimposition" of "*the subject of enunciation and the universal subject*," characteristic of the "good subject" who "freely" and "spontaneously" reflects the Subject (i.e., God in religion) (157). Althusser recognized that this is not always the case, leaving open the possibility of the "bad subject," which Pêcheux recognizes as the second modality of reduplication. Here the process of identification works in the opposite direction: "The subject, a 'bad subject,' a 'trouble-maker,' *counteridentifies* with the discursive formation imposed on him" (157). Pêcheux recognizes that the processes of both direct identification and counter-identification belong to the same operation, predicated on the passivity of the subject. Namely, both of them belong to what he calls "interdiscourse," or the discourse in which "subject-effect is constituted-reproduced as an *interior* without an *exterior*," which is his way of explaining one of Althusser's dicta: there is no outside to ideology (114). The interdiscourse "*continues to determine the subject identification or counter-identification with a discursive formation in which he is supplied with evidentness of meaning, whether he accepts it or rejects it*" (158). It is this "evidentness" that Althusser identifies as "obviousness" in which ideology finds its most secure shelter.

That is all clear. However, Pêcheux offers a third option, that of *disiden-*

tification, or "of the *taking up of a non-subjective position*" (158). He emphasizes that this modality doesn't amount to a "*desubjectification of the subject*" or an "abolition of the subject form" but instead "constitutes a *working* (transformation-displacement) *of the subject-form* and not just its abolition" (159). In addition to direct and counter-identification, then, Pêcheux offers an additional option of opposing ("dis") identification with the subjectivity imposed on the individual in the process of interpellation. José Esteban Muñoz took this modality from the strictly proletarian class politics that Pêcheux assigned to it and introduced it into the queer politics of minoritarian subjects in the United States. In his generative reading, Muñoz suggested that "to disidentify is to read oneself and one's own life narrative in a moment, object, or subject that is not culturally coded to 'connect' with the disidentifying subject" (1999:12). Muñoz's approach to Pêcheux is disidentificatory in its own right in that he insists on the utopian dimension of the modality he proposes. Namely, he suggests that "disidentificatory performances and readings require an active kernel of utopian possibility," and further claims that "although utopianism has become the bad object of much contemporary political thinking, we nonetheless need to hold on to and even *risk* utopianism if we are to engage in the labor of making a queerworld" (25). It is this seed of utopian possibility that emerges from ALNY's reworking of the idea of subjecthood.

However marginal in relation to the mainstream political theory and the main currents in criticism and art, it offers a glimpse of a possibility, however distant, of a different kind of politics and a different subject. This possibility offers a radical answer to the question of the revolutionary subject, that stumbling block of all twentieth-century revolutions. As many critics of real socialism recognized, the political revolutions such as those in Russia, Yugoslavia, and China never managed to resolve the problem of the bourgeois formation of the subject. It was, in fact, the deep cause of the ultimate demise of each one of them. The idea that the revolutionary subject, or the revolutionary class, consisted of individuals interpellated as subjects always resulted in an insoluble internal contradiction. The reason for that is that interpellation is an ideological operation inseparable from the historical form of the capitalist state. The all too easy and pervasive bourgeoisification of the members of proletarian class led, by rule, to the erosion of its class consciousness and of the revolutionary subject itself. One of the key takeaways of the self-defeats of the twentieth-century revolutions is that the revolutionary subject is not a simple collection of individuals who belong to the same social class. There can be no revolutionary subject without the revolutionarization of the very idea of the subject. A political revolution that preserves the bourgeois subject sets itself up on the road to impasses such as those of totalitarianism and the cult of personality, which undermined the twentieth-century revolutionary projects. ALNY's idea of the "uproar" allows for another reading of disidentification: not only in the sense of opposition, as in dis-agreement, but in the sense of granularization, as in dis-assembly and also dis-persion. The collectivity that ALNY envisioned is an assembly made possible by the transformation of the unitary subject and its replacement by the subject as a form of sociality. As the idea of the "individual as a crowd" suggests, this assembly-self is not, and can never be, uniform and militaristic. A social revolution can break new historical ground only on the condition, and the risk of, breaking the unitary subject.[20]

SIX | Strategy without a Subject

THE ARTIST VANISHES

> He was his own cancellation.
> —Vladimir Nabokov, *Pale Fire* (1962)

On 23 March 1987 at 6:30 p.m. in a small movie theater on the third floor of Centre Georges Pompidou in Paris, French artist Philippe Thomas performed *Pour un art de société. Conférence de Philippe Thomas* (For a Social Art. A Lecture by Philippe Thomas). The script, printed before the premiere, stipulates a general ambience "exactly the same as that which usually precedes" a talk, like many others that are happening in this and other museums world over ([1987] 2014:13). "Remarks on the mise-en-scène" call for a simple setup: a table and chair at one end of a room ("which could be, indifferently, an auditorium, a concert hall, an art gallery") with rows of seats for the audience. The staging instructions also call for "a video camera placed in the middle of the spectators" for the purpose of "recording the evening" (13). As if anticipating that someone might doubt the existence of this performance, Thomas makes sure to script into his introductory stage directions a mechanical recording device that would supplement any human witnesses of this event.

As the audience enters the room, music is playing over the speakers, a detail that is, according to the script, an indication that the performance is already in progress. At one point, the lights are dimmed, signaling the start of the main action. Thomas, who was in the room all along, stands up from his seat and approaches the desk that faces the rows of chairs. A slender and balding man in his mid-thirties "clad in Yohji Yamamoto," he holds in his hand the text of the lecture (13). There is nothing excessive or spectacular in this performance: the artist, alone, sits at the desk and reads his prepared remarks. He interrupts his monologue with the slightest of actions, which would easily go unnoticed if the playscript didn't specify that their purpose is to indicate breaks between different parts of the lecture: "In order to insist on the distinction of what one might take as two different parts, it would be advisable at this juncture for Philippe Thomas to find an expediency, such as pouring himself a glass of water, or taking off his jacket under the pretext of being too hot" (19). There will be another "expediency" built into the script—"he could for example look at his wristwatch, and undo it to have it permanently in front of him, on the table" (25). Together they suggest a conventional three-act structure to this unconventional piece of conceptual theater. The lecture ends abruptly when someone from the audience interrupts the speaker. After an improvised exchange between the lecturer and the heckler, the performance ends. As they leave the room, the audience members receive copies of the transcript of the lecture, with a different title and different author from those printed on the invitation card and program they received as they entered the lecture room: "Philippe Thomas décline son identité" (Philippe Thomas Declines His Identity) by Daniel Bosser.

According to this logic, the performance *For a Social Art. A Lecture by Philippe Thomas* happened only once, in that small cinema at Centre Pompidou, on 23 March 1987. The conclusion of the performance marked its renaming and change of authorship. To underline this transformation of the work and the singularity of the initial performance, exactly one year later, on 23 March 1988 at Musée de Grenoble Thomas delivered the same lecture under the title *Philippe Thomas décline son identité*, by Daniel Bosser. Subsequent publications of the script bore those distinguishing marks: in posthumously published collection of texts associated with the artist, *Sur un lieu commun et autres textes* (1999), the script was published with the new title and author (Daniel Bosser), the practice that Antony Hudek followed in his English translation of *Philippe Thomas Declines His Identity* published in 2014 by the London-based press Occasional Papers.[1] Both French and English versions of the published script include the subtitle *An Exhibit in One Act and Three Sets* (*Une pièce à conviction en 1 acte et 3 tableaux*).

From Marcel Duchamp's signature "R. Mutt" on the urinal he submitted to the exhibition of the Society of Independent Artists in New York in 1917, the questioning of the figure of the artist and the deployment of artistic identity as an artistic medium have been standard features in the arsenal of modernist art. During the 1970s, a number of performance artists adopted these strategies to create works of extraordinary variety and breadth. They were especially prominent in feminist artists' explorations of the question of identity: one needs only think of Adrian Piper's *Mythic Being* series (1973–75), or Lynn Hershman Leeson's *Roberta Breitmore* project (1974–78), or multiple personas that Eleanor Antin created between

1972 and 1980, from "the King of Solano Beach" to the Black Ballets Russes dancer Eleanora Antinova, and Antin's "nurses" (Little Nurse Eleanor, Nurse Eleanor Nightingale).[2] The creation of alternative personalities was not limited to feminist and performance artists: one of most intriguing departures into this territory was the New Zealand conceptual filmmaker Darcy Lange, who had a parallel career as a Flamenco guitarist under the name of Paco Campana (see Vincente 2008).[3] The practice of devising alternative personas even entered art criticism: the art historian Carol Duncan published several well-regarded articles as the fictive art critic Cheryl Bernstein, and in addition to his well-known artist persona Patrick Ireland, Brian O'Doherty created the female persona Mary Josephson, art critic.[4] And there is more, as we are going to discover by the end of this chapter.

By devising their personas as temporal objects, artists (and critics) appropriated the very process of consumption. Like clothes one wears, one can also choose, don, and discard an identity. Artists "acquire" alternative personalities and dispose of them in a manner similar to consumers who "try on" (test) or get a taste of the merchandise before they make their decision to purchase. Provisional ownership is the privilege of the bourgeois subject. In the 1970s, artists often resorted to identity-based work in order to subvert, and in doing so to expose, the transactional nature of art industry: the *Mythic Being* and *Roberta Breitmore* are artworks that cannot be bought and sold. Thomas does precisely the opposite. In a series of interviews with Stéphane Wargnier in the spring of 1995, just months before he died of AIDS, Thomas offered a clear explication of his artistic method. Speaking of the process he devised in the 1980s, he affirmed that the "piece can never be produced or made unless someone is there to say 'I'll sign it.'" In other words, the "working framework" on which the piece depends is the one in which the artist's autograph is not sufficient, because "It depends on the collector's signature" (in Bernard et al. 2021:46). Thomas presents it in the following way: "Someone wrote a check and his work, produced in accordance with this method, could be seen displayed in the walls of a museum" (62). In adopting and strictly enforcing this procedure, Thomas shifts the purchase of the artwork from its traditional placement in the aftermath to the very center of the artistic process: it is no longer a mode of exchange of the work of art but the mode of its production. By staking his art on the act of acquisition and on the collector, Thomas makes a double intervention in the status of identity-based art. First, his work poses the question of what happens when the sale becomes final: no lemons, and no returns. And second, it is a *sale*: by making the figure of the collector an integral part of his artistic practice, Thomas departs from well-established practices such as appropriation art and institutional critique.

Thomas was not the first nor the last artist to make financial and transactional aspects of the art industry a defining aspect of art practice.[5] In her examination of self-sale in art, Emily Apter points to Andy Warhol's distinction between "art art" and "business art," and the ways in which he pursued the latter; as well as Dan Graham's project *Income (Outflow) Piece* (1969), in which the "work" consisted of the incorporation of the artist as a "business" and his transformation into a commodity (2005:31). Graham never completed this piece (i.e., he did not incorporate himself and sell stocks), but other works, such as Lee Lozano's *Investment* (1969), Les Levine's *Profit Systems I* (1969), and Robert Morris's *Money* (1969–1973), were finished, at least in conventional sense of being exhibited. The art historian Sophie Cras suggests that this specific subgroup of conceptual art that emerged in the late 1960s used transactional procedures to highlight the status of investment that the finance industry attached to contemporary art during that decade.[6] While art was increasingly seen as an investment, "Artists turned investment into art," and in doing so, as Cras observes, "they scrutinized their socioeconomic position as professionals working in a specific field while at the same time examining the idea that the worlds of art and finance are self-referential, each one closed upon itself" ([2018] 2019:128). Produced more than a decade later, Thomas's intervention in "business art" concerns the subjectivity of the artist, which is pointedly manifested in his spotlighting of the artist's signature as the meeting point of art and industry. Lozano, Levine, Morris, and others preserved their identities in transactional works they devised, and Warhol used his name to add value to art and nonart objects. Thomas, on the other hand, staked his artistic practice on the idea of hedging authorship to the ownership of the work of art.

This conceit raises a host of questions about symbolic, institutional, and legal procedures related to the proprietorship of artworks and their material and symbolic circulation, including but not limited to citational practices in scholarly works, such as the one I am writing right now. Indeed, whose name should I include in the list of cited works when I discuss the above-mentioned performance lecture: that of Philippe Thomas, the person who wrote and performed the piece, or Daniel Bosser, the collector to whom he ceded its authorship? Can authorship of creative acts circulate in the way commodities do? As Molly Nesbit pointed out, from the very inception of the legal regulation of intellectual property rights in France, the earliest of that kind in Europe, the "essence of the privilege" of authors was that they "retained the rights over the fruits of their labor even after their work was sold to somebody else" (1987:233). Now Thomas was giving up not only the rights to his work but also his name. The logical outcome of this schema was supposed to be the erasure of the name "Philippe Thomas" from the chronicles of contemporary art, however modest his trace might have been in the first place.[7]

SUBJECT OF DISCRETION

> I think, said Thomas, and this invisible, inexpressible, nonexistent Thomas I became meant that henceforth I was never there where I was, and there was not even anything mysterious about it. My existence became entirely of an absent person who, in every act I performed, produced the same act and did not perform it.
>
> —Maurice Blanchot, *Thomas the Obscure* (1941)

In the course of his relatively short artistic career that spanned seventeen years (~1978–1995), Thomas moved fluently across media, using painting, photography, installations, sculpture, performance, and video. Still, text stands out as the medium he used most frequently. Émeline Jaret cataloged eleven books, thirteen articles, and seven advertisements that he published during his lifetime, in addition to numerous drafts and unpublished writings, which are now held at the Bibliothèque Kandinsky, Centre Pompidou (2016:46). From 1981 to 1988, he produced a series of textual works, each of them acting as an episode in a larger narrative that centers on the idea of authorship. The (initial) title of the performance at the Pompidou Centre, *Pour un art de société* (For an Art of Society), refers to the general idea that Thomas attached to the braided series of projects from this period. The "art of society" is not the same as the "social work of art," in the sense that emerged a decade later. In deploying "society," the artist keeps in play multiple meanings this word holds in French: its ordinary sense of the public or a collective order, but also a board game (*a jeu de société*) and, importantly, a company or a business establishment (the meaning reflected in the name of the French banking conglomerate Société Générale).

The first episode in this series is the manuscript exhibited in 1981 at the Ghislain Mollet-Viéville Gallery in Paris; the text was presented as anonymous, supposedly found by accident by the author of the exhibition, Philippe Thomas. The following year, Museum für Kultur, located in Berlin, published a booklet entitled *Frage der Präsentation* (A Question of Presentation), which included a German version of this unsigned text and an introduction by the translator, Detlef Carl. The chain continues with the article "Philippe Thomas: Sujet à discrétion," signed by Michel Tourner-eau, published in 1985, in the third issue of the Paris-based journal *Public*. This article, whose title can be read to mean either "subject to your discretion" or "unlimited subject," starts with the discussion of the exhibition of the found manuscript in 1981 and its analysis in *Frage der Präsentation*, and ends with an invitation to the person who orchestrated these artistic and textual productions to present himself publicly. The 1987 Pompidou Centre performance is a response to this challenge. The following year, with the piece *Pour un art de société (maquette pour campagne d'information et de publicité)* (For an Art of Society [Model for an Information and Advertising Campaign]), the "society" series gives way to Thomas's project centered on the art agency *les ready-made appartiennent à tout le monde®*, (readymades belong to everyone®), which he worked on during the early 1990s.[8]

The most prominent in this series is probably *Sujet à discretion*, which refers to both the above-mentioned article and the installation included in the exhibition *Les immatériaux* that Jean-François Lyotard curated at the Centre Georges Pompidou in 1985. *Sujet à discrétion* points to Thomas's interest in literature and his attempts to integrate art and fiction. His propensity to address the works of high modernism is reflected in his invocations of Vladimir Nabokov, first in the epigraph for "Philippe Thomas: Sujet à discretion," and then in the title of his exhibition *Feux pâles* (Musée d'art contemporain de Bordeaux, December 1990–March 1991), titled after Nabokov's novel *Pale Fire*. The other authors and novels he often invoked in his writings and in his works carried direct references to his name: one is Jean Cocteau's short novel *Thomas the Impostor* (1929) and the other Maurice Blanchot's *Thomas the Obscure* (1941). *Sujet à discrétion* takes the opening sentence of the latter novel, "Thomas sat down and looked at the sea" as its conceptual foundation ([1941] 1973:7). This installation consists of three identical color photographs of the calm sea under clear sky, with the blue line of the horizon bisecting the image. The labels attached to them offer a clear outline of his artistic strategy.

As Thomas explains, "What the photograph asks is that we read it as a gaze cast on the sea" (in Bernard et al. 2021:46). The first image is, as he puts it, "virginal," and is presented as a photograph of the seascape. That changes in the second image, to which he appended the label (which plays on the sentence from Blanchot's novel) "Philippe Thomas: Autoportrait (vue de l'esprit)" (Philippe Thomas, Self-Portrait [Mind's Eye View]). The third image is "left open for a transaction with a collector" (46). It carries

Figure 11. Claire Burrus, Subject to Discretion, 1985. © Claire Burrus, Paris; Jan Mot, Brussels.

the signature of the person who acquired it, Lidewij Edelkoort. This final step is necessary for the completion of the work. Only once there is a signatory different from Thomas does the artist consider the work complete and ready to enter the art "world."

With the performance *For a Social Art. A Lecture by Philippe Thomas,* the artist transposes the spatial structure of *Sujet à discrétion* into a temporal dimension. The author makes sure to take advantage of all available conventions that commonly accompany these kinds of events. The performance-lecture was announced with an invitation card that read "Following Michael Tournereau, who issued him a summons (in *Public* no. 3, 1985), after the exhibition *Fictionnalisme* which paid homage to him . . . Philippe Thomas strays, for the first time, from the withdrawal that he seemed to abide by. . . . A speech act is in itself an event" (in Jaret 2014:n.p.). This preamble can be seen as a neutral phase of performance, insofar as it was in the state of pure potentiality, an event that had not happened yet. The performance itself, with Thomas delivering the lecture, takes the place of the "self-portrait." Finally, the tagging of the name Daniel Bosser to the script marks the completion of the performance. This passage of performance into documentation opens the possibility of exploring other conventions specific to the media in which these documents (transcript, video) are produced.

In the published version of the performance script, the introductory "Remarks on the Mise en Scène" is followed by a single-page stage direction, which concludes with a quotation from Benjamin Buchloh's article published in *Artforum*: "The essential feature of modernist art is to criticize itself from within" (in Bosser 2014:13). The French edition of the script features both the English text of the Buchloh quotation and the French translation: "Le trait essentiele de l'art modern ou moderniste est de se critiquer lui-même de l'intérieur" (in Vaillant 1999:98).[9] It turns out that this formulation, as cited in the script, is nowhere to be found in any of Buchloh's texts published in *Artforum* prior to the date of the 1987 lecture. The statement that comes closest to it is part of a longer sentence in Buchloh's article on appropriation art, "Allegorical Procedures: Appropriation and Montage in Contemporary Art," published in the March 1982 issue of *Artforum*. The segment that corresponds to Thomas's epigraph is italicized: "Simultaneously, however, a different range of aesthetic positions has been developed by this new generation of artists which continues and expands *one of the essential features of Modernism—its impulse to criticize itself from within,* to question its institutionalization, its reception, and its audience" (1982:50). In the first sentence of his lecture-performance, Thomas already engages in a dual appropriation of Buchloh's text: he paraphrases a fragment of his sentence, thus defying the literary convention that the epigraph should be an exact quotation, and at the same time performs an act of translation, which, as Emily Apter points out, represents "a unique case of authorized plagiarism or legal appropriationism," that is to say, a site of the legal suspension of authorial ownership (2008:93). Like the epigraph itself, the gesture announces the internal split that runs through *Philippe Thomas Declines His Identity* as well as through other texts in the series that started with the found manuscript.

At the outset of his presentation, Thomas explains the idea expressed in the epigraph by suggesting that "it is THE SAME that must at once present itself to criticism (to posit itself as object) and to take on all its functions, as subject" (in Bosser 2014:16). This "reversibility of the referential relation" mirrors the very situation of Thomas's performance, in which the author is the same as the character that he represents. In this way, Thomas sets up a *mise en abyme* that widens and expands as the evening progresses. This whole discussion—that is to say, this whole enactment—concerns the status of artistic (re)presentation, the question that informs the series of works of which it is an integral part (*Frage der Präsentation*, etc.). So, when Thomas proclaims, "The exhibition—or more generally, the formative force of the logos—is like the Platonic *aletheia*: it only reveals—or leads to the stable, tangible 'truth' of being [*l'étant*]—in so far as it itself evades the very ORDER of this revelation," he is referring both to the general idea of the truth of representation as disclosure, and to the particular instance (the lecture) in which this idea is presented (18). He continues:

> And when Frege notes that the concept, in order to be the denotation of the grammatical subject, must first let an object "go proxy for it," he is saying nothing else, out of the sole necessity of this very substitution and the inevitable recourse to MIMESIS as the imperative order of an infinite displacement. (18)

In "Philippe Thomas: Subject to Discretion," the author similarly distinguishes between "direct imitation (dramatic mode) and diegetic imitation (narrative mode)" (Tournereau in Vaillant 1999:52). The central tension of both "Subject to Discretion" and *Philippe Thomas Declines His Identity* consists in setting these two modes against one another. Both texts, as well as *Frage der Präsentation*, appear as dense theoretical treatises stacked with citations from philosophers that range from the above-mentioned Frege to Jacques Derrida, Jean-Luc Nancy, Philippe Lacoue-Labarthe and to French linguists such as Émile Benveniste, Antoine Compagnon, and Oswald

Ducrot. As the essay, in the case of "Subject to Discretion," or the performance, in the case of *Philippe Thomas Declines His Identity*, unfolds, it becomes clear that the author's goal is to present them as thoroughly theoretical texts. Seen as conceptual artworks, they appear as an exaggeration and literalization of Joseph Kosuth's "Art after Philosophy."[10]

The tension, then, comes from the double nature of the scholarly article that is also a work of art. On the one hand, Thomas conceives of his theoretical text as self-referential to the point of tautology: it can "denote nothing other than the meaning or the signs—EXCLUSIVELY—of which it is given as a reproduction" (1999:52). In his acts of textual production, the artist dislocates this kind of writing from its proper place into the space of narration, or "fiction" (52). In *Philippe Thomas Declines His Identity* the theoretical discourse, which stands for a self-referential reality, is inserted into a narrative mode that is entirely structured by the "expediences" of performance. Paradoxically, the performer, who is physically present, becomes the property of fiction, and that which is purely conventional, the text, comes to occupy the place of the real. The relation between them is, as Thomas declares at the top of the lecture, the relation between the subject and the object. This internal split extends to the other productions from this series: the original text and translation in *Frage der Präsentation*, the theoretical text and artistic context in "Philippe Thomas: Subject to Discretion," the images and labels in the installation *Subject to Discretion*, and the author and the character in *Philippe Thomas Declines His Identity*. The last piece in the series stages most dramatically and explicitly the uncoupling between the (authorial) "I" and the "subject." This separation can reach its completion only outside of the confinement of the work, and it takes place through the radical transformation of the idea of authorship. By ceding authorship to the collector, the maker of the work becomes a character in its narrative. If the collector occupies the position of the real, then the author joins the artwork's fiction.

COLLECTOR'S ART

> There is no document of culture which is not at the same time a document of barbarism.
>
> —Walter Benjamin (1937)

Reflecting on Thomas's work from the perspective of the late 1990s, the art historian Patricia Falguières observed that "the whole thing began as a free-market fable . . . of the eighties where political economy had become the science of reality, and the production of wealth the only form of production allowed—on condition that one is able to transcend the opposition of work and property in *management*" (2000:49). Buchloh identifies this period with hyper-commercialization of art dominated by a new class of art patrons and collectors:

> At best, the rapidly expanding class of gallery- and museumgoers would define themselves as competent consumers of contemporary art, as the spectatorial strata disseminating the new culture of total affirmation, operating in institutional and commercial intersections where advertising and the circulation of commodities of art take place (frenetically active at the openings of gallery and museum exhibitions, as well as within the travelling circuits of biennials, auctions, art fairs, and so on). In short, what had emerged in the 1980s was a new public and a new apparatus of culturalindustrial [*sic*] production heretofore unknown to, and unthinkable at any earlier moment in the history of modernity. (2012:255)

By the time Buchloh wrote these lines, the new "spectatorial strata" had fully taken hold of the global art industry, harnessing it for their own purposes. In the introduction to the thematic issue of the journal *Texte zur Kunst* on the new art-collecting class, the editors—Sven Beckstette, Beatrice von Bismarck, and Isabelle Graw—also point to the 1980s as the period of emergence of "a new generation of collectors" who were "utilizing its art possessions in a targeted way as a means to assert its own power and economic interests" (2011:6). This new class of celebrity collectors include tycoons from the "new" Eastern Europe such as the Russian oil magnate Roman Abramovich and his partner Daria Zhukova and the Ukrainian steel mogul Victor Pinchuk, but also French fashion baron François Pinault, the UK financier Steven A. Cohen, and many others.[11] In the same issue of *Texte zur Kunst*, Niklas Maak observed that this new breed of collectors was transforming the very status or art and of art institutions. Whereas "in the old system, public museums and their curators wrote art history" so that "their collections were regarded as the gold standard for an artist's career," in the "new system . . . private collectors and gallerists . . . have divorced themselves from the major public museums and exhibition halls and established a mutually stabilizing network of international private exhibition halls in which a small number of recurrent characters dominate the scene" (2011:48). It turns out that, to a large degree, Thomas had anticipated this new art ecology in which the collectors were acquiring not only the artworks but, quite literally, the artists, and in doing so assuming a certain level of authorship.

Andrea Fraser's radicalization of transactional art can be seen as a critical response to the elevated status of the new art industry elites. While in her earlier work on institutional critique she focused on the museum, in her 2003 video *Untitled* she turned the spotlight on the relationship of the collector and the artist. In a quite unmetaphorical gesture, this video shows her transaction with an unnamed collector, where the "work" consists of their sexual encounter.[12] Whereas the pioneers of transactional art from the late 1960s kept a safe and ironic distance from the marketplace, Fraser places her body in its midst and in doing so subjects herself to enormous personal pressure and risk. After *Untitled*, she moved in her exploration of the role of the collectors, and more generally of the impact of financial and political power on art institutions, toward work that is data driven. In "L'1%, C'est moi," her contribution to the "Collectors" issue of *Texte zur Kunst*, institutional critique takes the form of an analysis that, with all of its graphs and lists, could easily come from social science.[13] This research shows unambiguously that "art prices do not go up as a society as a whole becomes wealthier, but only when income inequality increases" (2011:118). Contrary to the popular belief, "art booms" are not the signs of general social prosperity, but quite the opposite, of sharp rises of wealth inequality. Fraser's conclusion is disheartening: "What has been good for the art world has been disastrous for the world" (122). If this claim sounds familiar, that is because it resonates with one of Walter Benjamin's most memorable aphorisms.

It should not come as a surprise that the Benjamin quip I used as the epigraph for this subsection comes from his essay on an art collector ([1937] 2002:267). Eduard Fuchs, the owner of a large collection of erotica and an expert on caricature, is a far cry from art collectors Christian Boros, Julia Stoschek, and other representatives of the "new Bourgeoisie," which *Texte zur Kunst* presents as the breeding ground for the new type of collectors in Western Europe. Benjamin's essay has a surprising capacity to throw light on one aspect of the "old Bourgeoisie" that gets lost even in the sharpest critiques on the new crop of celebrity collectors. As he suggests in the title of his essay, "Eduard Fuchs, Collector and Historian," the focus on collecting brings materialist emphasis to art history, which results in the recognition that traditional cultural history has been "conjured by false consciousness" (267). In an important sequence that starts with a startling observation about "spiritualism woven into [bourgeois] revolutions," Benjamin pursues a series of connections: from "spiritualism" to the morality from which this spiritualism is "spun," to its "keystone" in conscience, which "stands under the sign of altruism"; being held up as a model to underclasses, altruism conceals "bourgeois interests" (277). These ideas and attitudes constitute an ideological order insofar as they inform behaviors:

> Considerations that focus more on the conscious interests of individuals than on the behavior which is imposed on their class—imposed often unconsciously and as a result of that class's position in the production process—lead to an overestimation of conscious elements in the formation of ideology. (278)

Following this line of argumentation, Benjamin offers a correction to the classical Marxist position about ideology as "false conscience," an idea that anticipates Althusser's thesis about the material nature of ideology.[14] Benjamin had a clear understanding of what makes ideological operations possible:

> An apparatus of judicial and administrative bureaucracies intervenes between the rulers of economic life and the exploited. The members of these bureaucracies no longer function as fully responsible moral subjects, and their "sense of duty" is nothing but the unconscious expression of this deformation. (278)

The operations of "judicial and administrative bureaucracies" was one of the areas that Thomas engaged in his exploration of the formation and potential dispersion of the artist as subject. In 1990–91 he mounted the exhibition *Feux pâles*, named after Nabokov's novel *Pale Fire*, at the Musée d'art contemporain de Bordeaux. Among items included in the catalog was an interview with Althusserian jurist and philosopher of law Bernard Edelman. One of the interviewer's queries seems to put to a test Thomas's artistic strategy:

> Imagine that an author, to express himself in an original way, undertakes to construct a fiction that he would like to inscribe in the reality of the world, instead of limiting it to a book or a painting. If he decides to attribute his authorship to others who, as such, will become actors, if not characters . . . how will the law react? (in Vaillant 1999:255)

The answer is not encouraging at all:

> Very bad! The law cannot accept on the one hand that personality can be sold, and on the other hand that human beings can become the "slaves" of an invisible author. It is in a way a reversal of what is generally called a ghost writer contract. For the law, the ghost writer is the one who sells his authorship. Here, the ghost writer would be the assignee of this quality since he would be the creator's slave. From a strictly legal point of view, this thing would therefore be, by definition, considered as null and void. (256)[15]

Edelman goes on to explain that certain properties are not the subject of economic exchange, such as one's citizenship, one's liberty, one's body, or, as it were, one's authorship. Nevertheless, in the catalog, the interview is signed with the name of the collector Jacques Salomon.

OVER-APPROPRIATION

> We're immersed in singular but agreed conditions where fiction and reality are mixed up!
>
> —Jean Brolly et al., "Fictionalism, a Material Proof" (1985)

Thomas takes the exhibition *Fictionnalisme: Une pièce à conviction* (Fictionalism), presented at the gallery Claire Burrus in Paris from the end of November 1985 to mid-January 1986, as the defining statement of his "art of society" period in the 1980s.[16] The centerpiece of this exhibit was a group portrait, *Hommage à Philippe Thomas*, modeled after Henri Fantin-Latour's painting *Hommage à Delacroix* (1864).

In this "manifesto photograph," as Thomas refers to it, a group of people occupy the same positions as the personages in Fantin-Latour's painting. In the nineteenth-century painting, the group of eleven persons includes luminaries such as Charles Baudelaire, Édouard Manet, and James Whistler; in the photograph that number is reduced to seven people from Thomas's inner professional circle of gallerists, artists, and collectors (Jean Brolly, Georges Bully, Herman Daled, Lidewij Edelkoort, Françoise Epstein, Dominique Païni, and Michel Tournereau). While in Fantin-Latour's painting, Delacroix is depicted in a framed portrait hanging behind the group of ten men arranged in front and around it, in the photograph modeled on

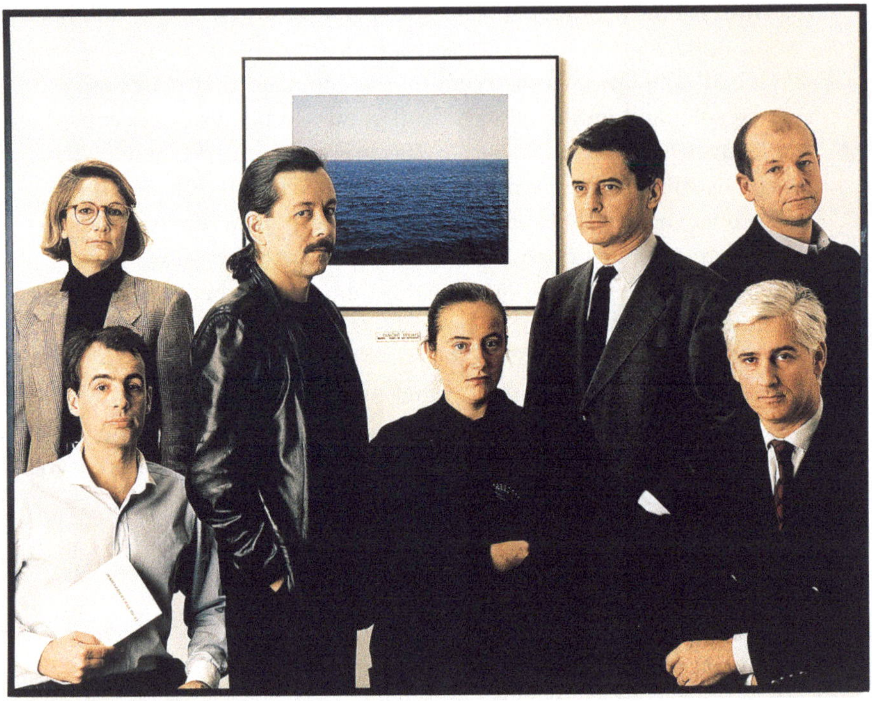

Figure 12. Homage to Philippe Thomas: group self-portrait, 1985. © Claire Burrus, Paris; Jan Mot, Brussels.

this painting, the picture within the picture is another photograph, *Philippe Thomas: Self-Portrait (Mind's Eye View)*, which the artist used as the central panel in the triptych *Subject to Discretion*. That is not the only self-referential detail in this composition: the person seated in the lower left holds the booklet entitled *Frage der Präsentation*. Thomas points out that both the label underneath the seascape and the title of the booklet are printed backward, "as if they were reflected in a mirror." If that opens the possibility, as he suggests, of reading "the entire image as the gaze of these seven figures as they look at themselves in a mirror," then it also suggests that the photograph captures the gaze of his own "mind's eye," coming from the "self-portrait" behind them (in Bernard et al. 2021:73). This suggests that there are two processes unfolding in *Homage to Philippe Thomas*.

First, this photograph is a "manifesto" only insofar as it exceeds its status as an image and acquires the significance of an event. The very act of gathering these seven personalities, their being together, and their agreement to pose for the camera is more significant than the photograph itself (which, after all, is just a piece of evidence of that event). Thomas conceived of *Fictionalism* not as a document of the assembly of a certain number of people, but as manifestation of a movement. In short, he conceived "Fictionalism" as yet another art-historical ism, such as futurism. Second, the group portrait is a collection of collectors. What the photograph mirrors, quite literally, is the artist seen not as a discrete individual—the subject—but as an assemblage of persons, statements, images, and relationships among these persons, and between them and other persons, statements, images, objects . . . In other words, this homage is dedicated not to a historical person, but to a certain conception of authorship and of the subject. It is one of the rare attempts at presenting, through artistic means, the idea of the self as a crowd (see the previous chapter). In the same gesture, it discloses and indicts the whole set of social operations that invalidate, prevent, and contain this understanding of the self. That idea of selfhood is precisely the region in which those "judicial and administrative bureaucracies" intervene. These interventions become particularly discernible in moments of radical political, social, and technological change. The reason Thomas invited Edelman to participate in *Feux pâles* is his groundbreaking work on legal responses to challenges posed by new technologies of reproduction that emerged with the rise of industrial societies in the West, such as photography and film.

In his book *Ownership of the Image*, Edelman shows that Western, and specifically French, legal statutes define the idea of the legal subject in terms of property. Here, the key term is "the subject in law," which he describes as "the general and abstract expression of the human person" based on the idea of ownership, that is, on "the *general capacity* of man to belong to himself and therefore to acquire." Therefore, "The freedom to acquire is the juridical consequence of the free ownership of oneself" ([1973] 1979:29). That suggests that the juridical ideology establishes the concept of the subject in law in relation to the "object in law" as that which has commodity-potential, or that which can be bought and sold, and is, as such, the subject of commerce and of contractual agreements.[17] The emergence of the new media such as photograph, cinematograph, and phonograph called for a revision and expansion of the legal code regulating and protecting the rights of the author. There was an imperative for the legal system to create a completely new juridical logic that could address ownership of representations of objects in law that have been already constituted through the process of appropriation (from nature, but also from labor). The question it faced was, who is the proper owner of mechanically produced images of a building or a tract of land, the subject in law who owns this real estate, or the maker of images who makes an impression of them? In response, the jurists came up with the concept of "over-appropriation," which, according to Edelman, "designates creation as property" and the "creator as the subject in law" (39). Using evidence from law archives, he shows the ways in which the power of the capital forced legal institutions to attach singular authorship to complex art forms that involve collective creative effort. The law of the capital demands the presence of an author who would carry legal responsibility for the work. Therefore, "The cinema work has its 'author,' *even if the author is not a subject but a process.* . . . The law will state what we would never have hoped it could state—*the true creative subject is capital*" (57). The judicial apparatus comes to inform, to some degree, the very idea of the subject in law: "This statement will be incarnated in the very ideology of the subject. Capital becomes the very person it interpellates. Capital assumes the mask of the subject, it is animated, it speaks and its signs contracts" (57). And in order to do so, it has to have a name attached to it: "Capital provides the name so that the name relates back to capital" (59). While the process of interpellation is still the motor of the apparatus, the "theoretical theater" that Althusser conjured limits and distorts the operations of that apparatus. So, as it turns out, in his interpellation of the apparatus, Althusser reduces and misrepresents it in the same way capital narrows and adapts for its own purposes the notion of the author.

This is one of the most overlooked aspects of the "death of the author" debate initiated with Roland Barthes's eponymous article published in 1967 in issues 5–6 of the experimental magazine *Aspen*.[18] In "What Is an Author," his presumed response to Barthes published two years later, Michel Foucault somewhat surprisingly engages with the ideas from the Althusserian Left. That engagement is most explicit in his allusion to ideology in the final pages of the essay. He suggests that the name of the author is not just any proper name, but a designation that brings together a certain number of works and endows them with coherence and homogeneity. "Unlike other proper names," the name of the author "seems always to be present, marking off the edges of the text, revealing, or at least characterizing, its mode of being" ([1969] 1998:211). At the same time, this designation is not a pure sign: it is endowed with biography, which comes with certain physiological, psychological, and social properties. Therefore, if the author is equally irreducible to a biological person and a linguistic sign, then the very placement of this complex figure outside of discourse and its reduction to pure soma is a fiction in its own right. The author is not a producer or a source of discourse, but its "function," and as such exemplifies the position of the subject. The author, like the subject, is an "ideological product," or better yet, an effect of ideology: "When a historically given function is represented in a figure that inverts it, one has an ideological production. The author is therefore the ideological figure by which one marks the manner in which we fear the proliferation of meaning" (222). The author's function is that of a material referent of texts. However fictional itself, this figure becomes a "functional principle" that "our culture" invented with the purpose to impede and prevent "the free circulation, the free manipulation, the free composition, decomposition, and recomposition of fiction" (221). In other words, the author is there to regulate discourse, to circumscribe and channel its circulation. But, what kind of discourse, or better yet, what part of discourse, is Foucault referring to when he speaks of fiction?

In May and June 1966, Foucault published in quick succession two articles about authors who could not be more different from one another, Jules Verne and Maurice Blanchot. In the first one, entitled "Behind the Fable," Foucault proposes that "fiction" is distinct from "fable": if the latter consists of the things said, the former is the "narrative system" or the discursive apparatus that reflects the narrator's relationship to narration (1998:137). Unlike everyday, extra-fictional, speech, the "work" is determined by the relation between "the speaking subject, his discourse, and what he tells," which is established in the "very act of speaking" (137). What is told is inseparable from the teller and the way of telling. While the fable is always concerned with itself, its fiction reaches outward through the figure of the author. If it is through the fiction that the fable engages the reader, then also through fiction it can reveal its narrative constraints. Foucault observes that "the discourse of the author, interrupting his narrative and lifting his eyes from the text to appeal to the reader," a narrative strategy that literature discovered in the eighteenth century, "all but disappeared" by the time Verne emerged on the literary scene in the middle of the nineteenth century (138). The very opposite of this gimmicky self-actualization of the speaking subject is its concealment behind the discourse, the strategy that seems to reach its pinnacle during the time of Foucault's writing. If, early on, this self-erasure was made possible by an evocation of reality, fiction soon renounced those outward layers of illusion, relying only on the dissembling power of language:

> The fictitious is never in things or in people, but in the impossible verisimilitude of what lies between them: encounters, the proximity of what is most distant, the absolute dissimulation in our very midst. Therefore, fiction consists not in showing the invisible, but in showing the extent to which the invisibility of the visible is invisible. (1990:24)

Because of that, Foucault claims, the fictitious "bears a profound relation to space; understood in this way, space is to fiction what the negative is to reflection" (24). And it is in this space of fiction, with which Foucault invokes Blanchot's "space of literature," that the speaking subject gets submerged and eventually disappears. The adventurous tales for adolescents, as much as the self-reflective prose barely disturbed by narration, open the possibility of the negative space of the author's self-abolition.

The catalog text *Fictionnalisme: Une pièce á conviction* is presented in the form of a "transcript" of a dialogue between two spectators at the private opening of the show:

> "Would there be any pleasure in reading if every sentence of the book had to be understood through a unique relationship—of identity!—with their author? If that were the case . . ."
> "Of course, there would be . . . no narrator, no character, no story . . ."
> "No potential fiction!"
> ". . ." (2000:31)

Here the emphasis should fall on the last line, which appears empty. This lacuna does not indicate a simple disappearance of the speaker, who stands in for the author. Instead, it can be read to designate the falling of the subject outside of the space of legibility constituted by the apparatus conceived in a certain kind of way: as a linear, projective, unidirectional "theater." It is precisely the opening of these kinds of lacunae that calls for the massive reconceptualization of the apparatus.

SUBJECT AT LARGE

> The history of art, instead of being a meta-narrative, as it usually is, could become the internal subject matter of the work. The question is: What would be the meta-narrative of the work whose internal subject matter is history of art?
> —Walter Benjamin, "On Copy" (2013)

Examining Thomas's notebooks from the early period of his work, Émeline Jaret observed his repeated use of the word *dispositif* in relation to the project entitled *AB*. For example, in a note jotted in 1978, he writes: "The mind itself would have to attach itself to 'a form'—*dispositif*—which prolongs it, rather than an organ of its body, or the body itself" (in Jaret 2015:47). It seems that, most commonly, he used this term to depict the relation between physical objects and mental processes. While in his textual works from this period such as *Spenserm* (1978) and *Sans titre* (1979), Thomas explored the placement of words and letters on the page, in *AB*, which he developed through a series of six exhibits that took place between 1978 and 1980, he expanded that idea to the relation between the physical space of the gallery and the symbolic space outlined by the work. At first, this inscription was quite literal: he started by using adhesive tape to guide the beholder's spatial perception of the exhibition space, but in the next step he removed that flimsy material and attempted to (re)structure the gallery through deployment of minimal linguistic interventions. Jaret observes that he used only letters "A" and "B" to indicate the path between certain points in the gallery, associating it "with the convention that determines the reading from left to right, the process that endows a sequence of letters with meaning" (48). In this way, Thomas situated his work at the intersection between geometric, linguistic, and architectural rules of intelligibility that help beholders orient themselves in space. Jaret reports that in the course of its successive installations, *AB* "integrates into its *dispositif* the surrounding space and the incidents that take place in it," including the spectators (49). Indeed, one of the central features of Thomas's *dispositif* is the encounter between spectators and the work, which, for him, exceeds the simple relation of beholding. The *dispositif*, as he conceives it, does not and cannot exist independently of the spectator. Instead, it emerges through and as an engagement of the experiencer's—be it a reader or a beholder—mental and physical habits.

Jaret points out that *AB* is Thomas's only work that he described as a *dispositif*, and that in the notes on his other works he replaced this word with "project," "fiction," and even "story." No less important is her observation that nowhere in his notes does he refer to Michel Foucault and his work on the idea of the *dispositif*, some of which preceded *AB* by only a couple of years (59). Even while Thomas abandons the term *dispositif*, it continues to resonate throughout his work. And furthermore, this deployment of one of the key concepts from this period of Foucault's work not only calls attention to the intersections between his philosophy and certain contemporaneous artistic practices but, even more significantly, highlights the importance that Foucault's work on aesthetics (literature, visual arts) held in the development of his research on the genealogy of power and, specifically, on the critique of neoliberalism he started developing in the final phase of his work.

Staying outside the debates that surrounded Althusser in the 1970s, Foucault engaged the idea of the apparatus more rigorously than many of the structuralist Marxist's supporters or detractors. In his reference to ideological "inversion," which he makes in the concluding paragraphs of "What Is an Author?," Foucault all but invokes the effects of the camera obscura. In doing so, he seems to adopt, almost without interventions, the classical Marxian notion of ideology. Only a couple of years later, in the final lecture of the seminar he held at the Collège de France in the academic year 1972–73, subsequently published under the title *Punitive Society*, he offers a critique of Althusser without mentioning him by name. Foucault's main objection concerns the separation of state apparatuses as repressive and ideological: "Power is not caught in this alternative of either being exercised purely and simply through violent imposition, or hiding itself and getting itself accepted by holding the wordy discourse of ideology" ([2013] 2015:233). He situates this criticism within a more general reformulation of the idea of ideology in terms of a power-knowledge relationship: "Every point at which a power is exercised is, at the same time, a site of formation, not of ideology, but of knowledge (*savoir*); and, on the other hand, every knowledge formed enables and assures the exercise of power. In other words, there is no opposition between what is done and what is said, between the silence of force and the prattle of ideology" (233). And we should add, not only between what is done and said but also where it is done or said, to whom and by whom, and using what tool, weapon, discourse, device . . . What Foucault calls for is a microanalysis of apparatuses and their operations, which he offers in his discussion of the police and penal systems scattered throughout the seminar, and on which he expanded much more systematically two years later in *Discipline and Punish* (*Surveiller et punir*; 1975).

Both in this inaugural work of his research on the genealogy of power and in lectures that led up to it, Foucault maintained that apparatuses are not "isolated edifices" but are instead deeply integrated not only into the structure of the society but into the life of each individual. *Discipline and Punish* surveys a massive change from the sovereign power, exemplified in the description of the nauseating spectacle of public torture of the regicide Robert-François Damiens in the opening pages of the book, to the disciplinary power epitomized by prison, which acquired its paradigmatic architectural form in Jeremy Bentham's plan for the panopticon with its obscure central tower and cells along the perimeter of the structure, floodlit by windows on the external wall. Disciplinary power organizes zones of visibility designed with the explicit purpose of imposing regimens upon bodies: the prison, the military barracks, the school, the factory. In these zones of exposure to the disciplinary gaze, power gains "the ability to penetrate into men's behavior" ([1975] 1995:204).

Disciplinary power produced specific kinds of performances—structured, discrete, repeatable, and transferable—and did that so pervasively and thoroughly that no other kind of performance could contend with them. Under this regime of power, performance becomes behavior solidified through its incorporation in the apparatus (*appareil*). These are behaviors behaved twice, thrice, and an infinite number of times. While not reducible to apparatuses, performances are inseparable from them: they populate these visibilities and in doing so expose the body to the gaze.

The *dispositif* renders conceptually visible the systems that have existed, all along, next to, in addition to, and in the shadow of apparatuses of interpellation. This "rendering visible" has a significant aesthetic dimension, and it is here that Thomas's and Foucault's thinking and deployment of the idea of *dispositif* are in close proximity. Thomas describes his works from the later 1970s as perceptual traps. Specifically, in his plans to use the adhesive tape in gallery installations, he notes that his aim is "to trap the gaze. Make [the reader] dissatisfied, 'frustrated' with his power, and confronted with a *gesture* he can only *imagine*; reconstruct it, in its result, mentally" (in Jaret 2015:55). And, more specifically, he stipulates: "If the *dispositifs* I put in place are 'traps,' we must—perhaps—make sure that they will take their prey, that is to say that the spectator will enter them" (57). Thomas describes his spatial/literary gallery arrangements in terms identical to the ones that Foucault uses to depict René Magritte's integration of the visual with the discursive in his works such *This Is Not a Pipe* (*Ceci n'est pas une pipe*, 1929). According to Foucault, in this painting, the calligram constitutes "the most perfect trap" ([1973] 1983:22). Thomas's gallery installation works in exactly the same way as the calligram: in both cases, the deployment of linguistic and visual signs results in an assemblage that subverts procedures of both reading and viewing. In Magritte's calligrams, the image literalizes the text, and conversely, the text symbolizes the image. What is caught in this double snare is the reader/viewer, who is suspended between two orders of signs, neither one of which produces a definitive meaning. The calligram, like the arabesque (and the situation, both discussed in chapter 4), is both text and image, movement and stasis, concept and object, and it involves the processes of resemblance and differentiation, regulation and discord, negation and affirmation. Considered next to Thomas's notes for *AB*, Foucault's discussion of the calligram in Magritte's paintings seems to anticipate and prepare his departure from the Althusserian idea of the apparatus (*appareil*). Starting in the mid-1970s, the *dispositif* emerges in Foucault's work as an expanded, spatialized and temporalized, and fully operational societal calligram.

While Foucault used the term *dispositif* throughout *Discipline and Punish,* he seems to have done so with greater frequency in the section on panopticism. In his next major work, *La volonté de savoir. Histoire de la sexualité, I* (*The History of Sexuality,* vol. 1, *An Introduction*) on which he started working, as the legend goes, the very same day he sent to the publisher the finished manuscript of *Discipline and Punish, dispositif* comes to occupy a more prominent place. As in his previous book, Foucault here uses both *appareil* and *dispositif,* but not interchangeably. To a greater degree than before, in the first volume of *The History of Sexuality* he underscores lexically the difference between *appareil* (device, instrument) and *dispositif* (ensemble, mechanism). Sometimes they appear in the same paragraph, but they designate different phenomena. For example, in the subsection entitled "The Uniformity of the Apparatus" ("L'unité du dispositif"), Foucault notes that power relies on certain "devices [*appareils*] and institutions," and generally, he reserves the term *appareil* for his references to the state apparatus. While he settles for these conventional uses of *appareil,* he is careful to outline the range of meanings he wants to cover with *dispositif,* the concept he places prominently in the title of the key chapter of the book, "Le dispositif de sexualité" (in English translation, this chapter title has been rendered, most unfortunately, as "The Deployment of Sexuality"). He does that by setting up a distinction between two kinds of *dispositif,* the "*dispositif* of alliance" and the "*dispositif* of sexuality."

The former, which is ahistorical and transcultural, appears close to the Althusserian *appareil,* while the latter is fully historical and specific to Western Europe and distinct from ideological apparatuses. Whereas the *dispositif* of alliance developed in "every society" as the system of marriage, kinship, and inheritance, regarding the *dispositif* of sexuality Foucault observes that, starting in the eighteenth century, "Western societies created and deployed a new apparatus [*un nouveau dispositif*] which was superimposed on the first one," that is, on the *dispositif* of alliance ([1976] 1978:106). There follows a series of juxtapositions that establish an affinity between the apparatus of alliance and the apertures at work in disciplinary regimes. Therefore, while the *dispositif* of alliance "is built around a system of rules defining the permitted and the forbidden, the licit and the illicit," the *dispositif* of sexuality "operates according to mobile, polymorphous, and contingent techniques of power" (106). Further, the former strives to "reproduce the interplay of relations and maintain the law that governs them," while the latter "engenders a continual extension of areas and forms of control." And it goes from there: the first establishes "the link between partners and definite statutes," while the second "is concerned with the sensations of the body, the quality of pleasures, and the nature of impressions." And finally, whereas the first one is "firmly tied to the economy due to the role it can play in the transmission and circulation of wealth," the second "is linked to the economy through numerous and subtle relays, the main of which . . . is the body—the body that produces and consumes" (107). Foucault concludes this mini-treatise on the *dispositif* of sexuality by asserting that its "reason for being" is "not in reproducing itself, but in proliferating, innovating, annexing, creating, and penetrating bodies in an increasingly detailed way, and in controlling the populations in an increasingly comprehensive way" (107). Clearly, the idea of *dispositif* pertains not only to sexuality but to a number of other social mechanisms that started emerging in the West around the turn of the eighteen century. In his sprawling interview published in the journal *Ornicar?* on the occasion of the publication the first volume of *The History of Sexuality*, Foucault underscores his usage of the word *dispositif* to designate a complex interplay of discourses with nondiscursive formations, describing it as a "thoroughly heterogeneous ensemble consisting of discourses, institutions, architectural forms, regulatory decisions, laws, administrative measures, scientific statements, philosophical, moral and philosophic propositions" ([1977] 1980:194).[19] The decisive property of this assemblage is its "strategic nature," which makes it possible to think of "general apparatuses" (*dispositifs ensemble*) in terms of "*a strategy without a subject*" (202, emphasis added). Here, Foucault departs decisively from Althusser's "little theoretical theater," which, as we have seen, centers on the process of subjectivation. Foucault's "strategy without a subject" resembles the central property of Thomas's "method," which is, as per Tournereau, based on the idea of a "missing 'I,'" the fact that makes it receptive to "all the characters of the first person pronoun" (1999:56). It is in relation to this aspect of Thomas's de-authorial *strategy* that the title of essay credited to Tournereau can be read as "subject at large." And not only the essay but also the installation with which it shares the title.

While formally identical, the three images of the seascape are infinitely different (Figure 11). The difference doesn't stem only from different designations and titles attached to them (from "neutral" to "self-portrait," to "authorial") but also from the very content of these images that appear as copies of one another. Here, "a strategy without a subject" seems to affirm Walter Benjamin's thesis about the epistemic excess of the copy in relation to its source: "The copy contains both the idea of its model and its own idea: the idea of being a copy. Paradoxically—but it seems true—this results in the copy being multilayered and more complex with regard to its meanings in relation to the original!" (2013:17). This epistemic surplus of the copy in relation to the original, with which it is formally identical, seems to stand in reverse proportion to the condition of authorship that is attached to them. In his seminal essay "On Copy," Walter Benjamin underscores the status of the copy as inseparable from the evacuation of the authorial "I": "If 'author' is defined as an exceptional and unique individual, able to express himself or herself in a way no one else can, then only an author could produce the unique and exceptional work we call an original. The maker of a copy could not be an author. Furthermore, in a copy we still see only the original and its author, while the maker of the copy completely disappears" (22). Thomas's method makes this erasure the condition for the production of the work so that, in another paradox, this empty center begins to generate multiple authors. This strategy transforms and expands Walter Benjamin's hypothesis about copies rendering the author anonymous.

"On Copy" was included in the book *Recent Writings* credited to Walter Benjamin and published by Vancouver-based art press New Documents. The note included on the inside back cover offers a few details about the author of this book. I copy it here in full:

> Walter Benjamin was an influential philosopher and art theoretician, best known for his 1936 essay "The Work of Art in the Age of Mechanical Reproduction." In 1986—many years after his tragic death—Walter Benjamin reappeared in public with the lecture "Mondrian '63–'96" organized by the Marxist center in Ljubljana. In recent years, Mr. Benjamin has been an associate of the Museum of American Art in Berlin, giving interviews and publishing articles on art, originality, museums, and art history. (2013:n.p.)

This note has been included in the entry on this book in WorldCat, the largest and most commonly used library database in the English-speaking world. The WorldCat page also features a color photograph of a young man in light-colored suit, standing in front of an audience, with several canvases of Mondrian-style geometrical abstractions on the wall behind him (according to some witness accounts, these were copies of Mondrian's paintings [see Gržinić 2000:78–85]). Presumably, the photograph is from the lecture mentioned in "About the Author," dispelling any possibility of a conflation between this lecturer and the author of the essays such as the one I cited earlier ("Eduard Fuchs, Collector and Historian"). Still, under the category "author," the WorldCat entry lists "Benjamin, Walter; 1892–1940."[20] The publication of *Recent Writings* was followed by speculations about the identity of its author, which fundamentally missed the point of Walter Benjamin's book (see, for example, Wetzler 2014; and Gollner 2014). Walter Benjamin, *Recent Writings*, is not an art-historical hoax, and art criticism is not a detective game. This book appears as an integral part of a larger meta-performance that aims to render observable the outer limits of the *dispositif* of art. There is no performance art "in itself," just as there is no sex or art "in itself." If, as Foucault suggests, "sex" is "a complex idea that was formed inside the *dispositif* of sexuality," and if, as Walter Benjamin asserts, art is "a notion defined by the story called art history," it would follow that performance art implies a *dispositif* that does not simply supersede apparatuses of interpellation (see Foucault [1976] 1978:152 and Benjamin 2013:144). It is contingent on them, expands and complements them, while at the same time calling them into question.

Each in their own way, Daniel Bosser et al. and Walter Benjamin demonstrate that, once put into circulation, the author function reveals the basic operations of the apparatus of art. Better than many others, the apparatuses of art show their vital dependence on an author endowed with material existence (*bios*/life, and its narrative, biography) not only to limit the dangerous and cancerous proliferation of fictions it produces, but also to provide those fictions with a material reality. In other words, the artist is the material of the apparatus. The biggest fear of the apparatus of art is the fictionalization of the artist as its sole anchor in the real. The only way for artists to demonstrate the materiality of the apparatus is to fictionalize themselves. The two lectures, the one in Beaubourg and the other in Cankarjev Dom ("the Marxist center in Ljubljana"), clearly indicate that, paradoxically, this self-fictionalization requires a material demonstration of the author function, or performance. What that risky maneuver reveals are the limits of the apparatus. That exposure of the ideological apparatus of art is already a crack on its smooth, seemingly impenetrable, material surface.

SEVEN | Performance Art Histories and the *Dispositif* of Ideology

1. REPERFORMANCE

On the winter solstice 1975, British-Canadian artist Clive Robertson executed a twenty-one-hour performance, *The Sculptured Politics of Joseph Beuys*, at the Parachute Center for Cultural Affairs in Calgary, Canada. The first twenty hours and forty minutes were closed to the public. The audience joined Robertson for the last twenty minutes, during which he performed a segment entitled "How to Explain Pictures to a Dead Hare." It was a recreation of the famous action Joseph Beuys had performed ten years earlier, on 26 November 1965, during the opening of his exhibition at the Galerie Schmela in Düsseldorf. Documentation of the Calgary recreation, consisting of photographs and Robertson's writings published the following year in the San Francisco–based alternative art magazine *La Mamelle*, depicts some of the basic features of the performance: the gallery floor was painted blue and had a wood stud standing vertically in the foreground; a photograph shows that there was a tape recorder on the floor next to the beam, a music stand to the left, a replica of Beuys's 1964 installation *Fat Chair* in the back of the room, and a cymbal hanging from the ceiling close to the center; a dead hare lay in the foreground, with the artist prostrated on the floor a few feet behind it. Another photograph shows a corner of the gallery space with a refrigerator surrounded by a tiny wall made of clay on the gallery floor; the only item in the fridge was a black plastic bag filled with snow (*La Mamelle* 1976:n.p.).[1] In photographs published in the *La Mamelle* portfolio, Robertson appears dressed in the signature Beuys outfit: a felt hat, a pocketed vest, and a white button-down shirt. Unlike Beuys, who plastered his face with honey and gold leaves, Robertson used fat and bronze; and unlike Beuys, who spoke inaudibly to his dead hare while cradling it in his arms, Robertson used a tape machine to play a "German voice . . . reading statements from and texts about Beuys" as he picked up and held the dead hare (1976:n.p.).[2] After some twenty minutes, he left the room, leaving the audience behind.[3]

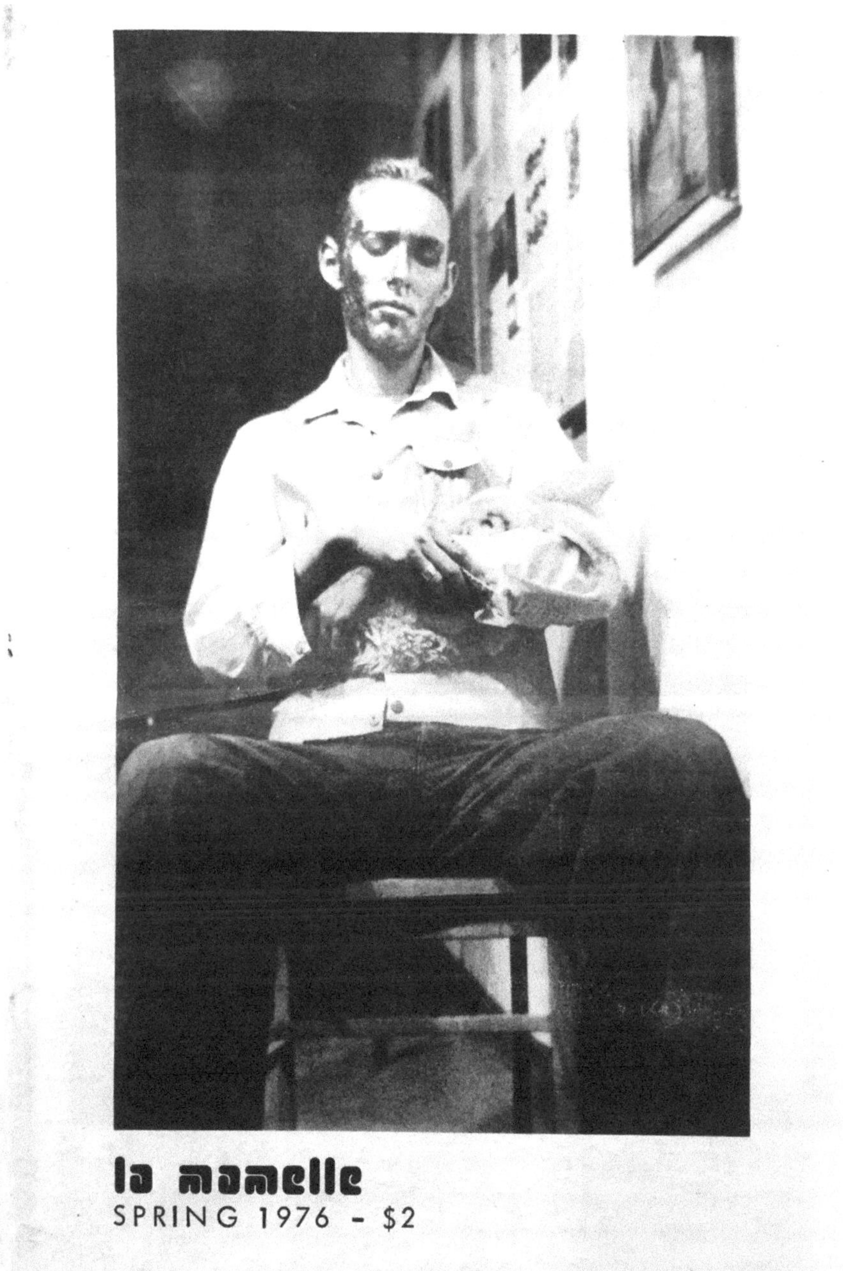

Figure 13. Clive Robertson: *How to Explain Pictures to a Dead Hare, La Mamelle,* 1976

This "examination of the actions of Joseph Beuys through re-enactment and reconstruction," as Robertson later described it, was part of his larger art project, which he called "identity transfer" (1979:133). Robertson envisioned this strategy of performance-making as being analogous to other public loan services, such as book and video libraries and "image banks" (1976:n.p.).[4] He developed the concept for this "sociological art" while working on reenactments of Fluxus events with the artist group W.O.R.K.S. in 1972–73 and based its whole premise on the idea of "art legends" such as the "legend of Duchamp, the legend of Klein, the legend of Beuys and recently near legend of Chris Burden" (1976:n.p.). In an interview with Peggy Gale on the occasion of the Fifth Network / Cinquième Réseau conference on video art in Toronto, Robertson spoke about his "painstaking preparation" for this performance, from the process of his "discovery" of Beuys's action through research, to physical preparation of the space, to "detailed planning of tasks for each of the 21 hours," to the action in front of gallery audience (in Gale 1979:5). He concluded that he had "failed in attempting to make a genuine transference; it was too difficult to overcome the difference between myself as a person and Beuys as a person" (5). Robertson's "How to Explain Pictures to a Dead Hare" was not a performance of, but about, Joseph Beuys. The structure and procedures involved in the process of the artist's work resemble a scholarly project rather than an ad hoc performance: from the artist's archival research, to his conceptualization of the piece, to the twenty-plus hours of solitary work, to the final presentation, it comes across as a performance essay.

Robertson's strategy of reenactment and reconstruction almost literalizes Althusser's thesis from his ISAs article about actions "inserted" into practices (1971:158). In 1965, Beuys's *How to Explain Pictures to a Dead Hare* was billed as an "action"; Robertson's 1975 "How to Explain Pictures to a Dead Hare" was a practice. There is no room for irony here: Robertson inserts Beuys's *action* from Gallerie Schmela into his *practice*; that is to say, Beuys's performance becomes the *object* of (artistic) labor. However, that is not all. The principle of "identity transfer" suggests that this practice is not reducible to a simple replication. In his reflections on this performance Robertson asserted that for its duration he had given up his "freedom to a sort of determinism that society has tended to impose on me: art" (1976:n.p.). In a conversation with video artist Vera Frenkel published a couple of years later in the journal *Centerfold*, Robertson came to the conclusion that in his "Beuys projects" he was using the German artist not as a model or an icon but as a "framing device" (1978:27). This reconstruction of Beuys's performance went largely unnoticed by art institutions, and so did the art-making project of identity transfer.

Thirty years later, the art industry made a U-turn. Marina Abramović's 2005 show *7 Easy Pieces* at New York's Guggenheim Museum introduced the technique of "reenactment and reconstruction" as the principal method for the insertion of performance into art institutions. Not surprisingly, one of the seven pieces that she included in this show was Beuys's *How to Explain Pictures to a Dead Hare*.[5] Abramović's goal was not to take past performances as "frames" or containers of behavior, nor did she comment on the status of the artist as subject. As she stated in the introduction to the exhibition catalog, appropriately titled "Reenactments," her intention was to "open a discussion" about transmission of the ephemeral art of performance, which is to say, about the ways of reading and interpreting the extant documentation and its use for the retrieval of live acts; she was no less explicit about the second question she wanted to investigate, that of "preservation" of performance art and its display "in a museum after the event" (2007:10). Although she used procedures similar to Robertson's (archival research of sources, analysis of documents, etc.), she did not see her reenactments as performance essays, but as performance artifacts.

In an interview with the art historian Amelia Jones two years after the show, Abramović confessed that she saw herself as "an *archaeologist* really" (Abramović and Jones 2012:549). She noted that this "archaeological" approach was particularly prominent in her work on Beuys's piece, and that it was prompted by a simultaneous dearth and wealth of documentary source materials: on the one hand, there was a photograph of this performance that became iconic, thus overdetermining interpretations of other aspects of the piece; and on the other, there existed a number of films that the artist didn't authorize (551). She ended up using them nevertheless and simply repeated "the actual movements" while also adding "a few things" (552). Like Robertson, in her reenactments Abramović used a combination of repetition and interpretation; unlike him, she claimed that this procedure resulted in a reclamation of the "original" performance. Another key difference between these two reenactments was the role of the audience. There is almost no mention of spectators in the documentation of the Calgary performance published in *La Mamelle* or in Robertson's later discussions of this piece. It seems that, as was the custom with early performance art in the 1970s, the visitors came to the gallery, witnessed the performance, and left. An entirely different relationship between (re)performance and the audience developed in Abramović's Guggenheim show. Most of them came and left, but many came again and stayed longer than usual museumgoers. In the interview with Jones, Abramović pointed out that "an enormous number of young people came, who had only known the works from these bad photographs," adding that they wanted "to see something" and to "then reflect on it and have discussion." Repeat performances generated repeat audiences: "Because they had to spend so long time together they would say 'Oh, I'm going to lunch; let's have lunch together,' you know, go to lunch, come back, go to dinner, come back, so they start to have a relationship. Looking at this piece becomes an experience that is really so organic, so alive" (556). So, if on art-historical level reperformance claims to recapture the original act of performance, on the social level it strives to reestablish the organicity of communal relationships.

7 Easy Pieces was a clear indication that, at the beginning of the twenty-first century, leading institutions of modern art were finally ready to exhibit and collect, which is to say commodify, performance art. Abramović's comments about her show suggest that this internal transformation was informed, in part, by relational aesthetics of the 1990s and its repositioning of artworks as networks and museums as spaces for socialization (see Bourriaud [1998] 2002:18, 33). Five years later, Abramović's career retrospective *The Artist Is Present* in New York's Museum of Modern Art, curated by Klaus Biesenbach, took the effort of institutionalization of an art form with deeply anti-institutional roots to its logical conclusion. In addition to artifacts from performances, photographs, and videos, a group of twenty-nine young performers participated in reenactments of five performances from Abramović's four-decades-long career: *Imponderabilia* (1977), *Relation in Time* (1977), *Point of Contact* (1980), *Luminosity* (1997), and *Nude with Skeleton* (2002–5). While at the Guggenheim Abramović gave seven hour-long performances, this time she trained reenactors who performed in two-and-a-half-hour shifts (Abramović 2010:np). This continuous presence of live performances in MoMA galleries had the potential to generate moments of sociability similar to those that occurred at the Guggenheim. Still, the center of attention was not on the reenactors but on the performance Abramović created for this occasion and performed every day for the duration of the exhibition (14 March–31 May 2010) in the Donald B. and Catherine C. Marron Atrium. The performance eponymous with the exhibit (*The Artist Is Present*) was a variation of the performance series *Nightsea Crossing* she performed with her former partner and collaborator Ulay in the 1970s and 1980s. The setup for the MoMA performance consisted of an austere wooden table and two wooden chairs positioned under a square beam of light at the center of the atrium. This simple structure facilitated face-to-face encounters between the artist and audience members, who would sit across the table from her.[6] The artist was, as it were, present in the atrium exhibit seven hours daily (and ten on Fridays), and any audience member could join her for any amount of time. The rules of performance prohibited any physical or verbal interaction between the artist and the sitters.

In itself, this performance become a powerful generator of relationality not only between the artist and her visitors, but also among the museum visitors, who queued for long hours to join Abramović at the center of the atrium.[7] While MoMA's formidable PR campaign for this exhibition started with stories and images from the artist's extraordinary career, it quickly shifted to the visitors to the museum. The integral stage elements of *The Artist Is Present* were not only the table, chairs, and ushers who regulated the crowds and stage-managed the performance on a day-to-day basis but also stage lights in four corners of the space, photo and video cameras and their operators, computers and other equipment, and personnel who participated in documenting and broadcasting the performance. If the performance itself focused on the exchange of gazes between the artist and individual audience members, the museum apparatus transformed it into a spectacle of documentation and dissemination of the process of spectatorship. More important than any of Abramović's collaborators in front of the cameras was the one behind a specific camera: the photographer Marco Annelli, who was in charge of taking pictures of every spectator in the procession of those waiting to face the performer in *The Artist Is Present*, and selecting them for inclusion in a Flickr page linked to MoMA's website.

Photographs and video were no longer documentations of performance but inherent elements of the work. They seeped out of the auditorium through a daily live feed on MoMA's website, the Facebook page of the performance, where museum visitors could post their impressions and communicate with each other, and a Flickr page, where the museum posted daily the images of the sitters. The *New York Times*, which covered the exhibit extensively, reported that by the time the show closed, the live feed had almost eight hundred thousand visitors and the Flickr page had some six hundred thousand hits (in subsequent months and years these numbers steadily increased). Still, that was only a fraction of performance's online presence. Soon after it opened, a number of private blogs, Facebook pages, social media postings, and even an online video game dedicated to the exhibit popped up on the internet (Fisher 2012:163). In short, the artwork, in this case the performance, was no longer a meeting point or an interstice of personal interactions between spectators. Its nature as a network was not only metaphorical or personal: it was, more than anything else, digital.

The first decade and a half of the new millennium saw an upsurge of interest in performance art among art professionals and scholars; this once-marginalized art form reached a wider audience than ever. Abramović's exhibits in the Guggenheim and MoMA contributed significantly to this trend. The unprecedented attention that MoMA gave to online presentation of Abramović's exhibit serves as a reminder that this mainstreaming of performance art coincided with the rise of digital capitalism to the very top of the financial world. Shoshana Zuboff sees the first decade of the twenty-first century as the formative decade of surveillance capitalism. Her decision to take the moment of Apple's surpassing Exxon as the top corporation in market capitalization is largely symbolic, as there were other dates during that decade that could be taken as markers of that watershed moment: for example, in April 2010, as Abramović and her spectators sat facing each other and digital cameras, Facebook introduced the "Like" button as a communication tool among its users, which turned out to be one of this vast service's most popular and recognizable feature (Zuboff 2019:159). What went largely unobserved in the debates around presence and liveness in performance art swirling around *The Artist Is Present* was the degree to which the show accomplished the seamless integration of performance and digital media. If the central operation of surveillance capitalism consists in expropriating behavioral surplus, then the fair question to ask is What kind of behavior was produced and harvested in this exhibition? The simple answer is: none other than in any other museum show. The audience came, observed the artwork, and left. The difference is, obviously, in the artwork. The performance in MoMA's atrium placed the artist as the central artwork of the entire exhibition, giving all other artifacts (material residue from other performances, images and videos, and even live reenactments) the stamp of "presence." In the last analysis, what was harvested and appropriated in this exhibit was the performance apparatus itself. This operation marked performance with a stamp of permanence, while concealing the ideological basis of its durability and transferability. It was in this symbolic passage of performance to the other side that its apparatus came into full view.

THE ART OF CONDUCT

Abramović's MoMA exhibit does not conform perfectly to the fundamental principles of surveillance capitalism. Its relationship to it is ambiguous at best. On the one hand, taking digital shots of all participants in performance and posting them online appears to be the apotheosis of surveillance and especially of surveillance capitalism, if we consider that all of those images contributed directly to the symbolic capital of the institution that was collecting and exhibiting them. On the other, each one of Abramović's roughly fourteen hundred co-performers had to sign a release form for video and still images, which goes directly against the premise that "digital dispossession," that is, extraction of behavioral data obtained without users' knowledge and approval, represents the "original sin" of surveillance capitalism (Fisher 2012:167).[8] By the time *The Artist Is Present* rolled around, it was common for major art institutions to mount significant online presentations of their flagship exhibitions. In that sense, the entrance of performance in the global art industry, symbolized by Abramović's New York exhibits in 2005 and 2010, does not represent a shift in the paradigm of the apparatus. Instead, it brings fully into light the constitution of performance by different apparatuses. What places these exhibits and these performances at the intersection of the performance apparatus (*appareil*) and the most advanced form of capitalism is the supplanting (strictly in the sense of Hegelian *Aufhebung* as simultaneous overcoming and preservation) of the former by the latter. Disciplinary apparatuses are effective only insofar as they are complemented by apparatuses (*dispositifs*) for the production of subjectivities, which employ processes other than mechanisms based on interpellation, from the police summoning the passerby to the panoptic organization of visibilities and regimens.

In the corpus of Gilles Deleuze's writings on Foucault, two short texts published after Foucault's death stand out as a summary and continuation of his work on apparatuses. In "What Is a *Dispositif*?" he recognizes the "line of subjectivation" as one of three key dimensions of Foucaldian *dispositif*, the other two being "the line of knowledge" and "the line of force" ([1989] 2006:339). Deleuze emphasizes that "the Self" is distinct from power and knowledge: "It is a process of individuation that effects groups or people and eludes both established lines of force and constituted knowledge" (341). The processes of subjectivation always take place in apparatuses, which are not uniform in the production of this "surplus value." The production of subjectivities in apparatuses as Althusser conceives of them (*appareils* of the repressive state apparatus [RSA] and of ISAs) is based on a general principle of the radical asymmetry of power; the *dispositif* belongs to a different type of apparatus. *Dispositifs* don't interpellate individuals as subjects; instead, they channel, prompt, nudge, cajole, direct, assess, and advise. It is these modes of the production of subjectivities that determine the differences between historical formations in which they occupy dominant positions. While in "What is a *Dispositif*?" Deleuze mentions, in passing, apparatuses of sovereignty and discipline, in the second short article,

"Postscript on the Societies of Control" (1990), he elaborates in a greater detail on three paradigmatic apparatuses and the societies they help define. In addition to the first two models that were in existence since the beginning of modernity (RSA and ISAs), there is a third model that began to gain prominence over the previous two at the turn of the twentieth century. In both texts Deleuze credits William Burroughs with attaching the attribute of "control" to this new apparatus ([1989] 2006:346; 1992:4). In "Postscript," he highlights some of the distinctions between disciplinary and control apparatuses: whereas the first organize enclosures (factory), the second establish controls (corporations); and where the former set up *molds,* the latter are *modulations* (4). The difference Deleuze establishes is not so decisive when it comes to the production of subjectivities. Observing the bipolar nature of disciplinary societies—on one side is "the signature that designates the *individual,*" and on the other "the number or administrative numeration that indicates his or her position within the *mass*"—he suggests that Foucault identified the source of "this double charge in the pastoral power of the priest" (5). While Foucault indeed recognizes pastoral power as a model for a certain process of subjectivation, he did not attach it exclusively to disciplinary apparatuses.

At several points in the first volume of *The History of Sexuality,* Foucault indicates that the formation of *dispositifs* is predicated on a power relation that developed in the shadow of the sovereign and as distinct from disciplinary apparatuses. Instead of summoning the individual into a preconceived form of subjectivity, the procedures that came from this new power relation "took charge of men's existence," that is, of "men as living bodies" ([1976] 1978:89). Foucault is explicit and direct on that point: "one of the most significant aspects" of the entire history of the *dispositif* of sexuality is the mechanism of power that "had its beginnings in the technology of the 'flesh' in classical Christianity," which he defines as "the Christian pastoral" (113). The following year, in his lectures at the Collège de France for the academic year 1977–78, published under the title *Security, Territory, Population,* Foucault sets out to describe the genealogy of this kind of the apparatus. Here he argues that if disciplinary power "affects . . . subjects" as "bodies capable of performances, and of required performances," that does not mean that this is the only force that affects bodies, and that the compulsion by the disciplinary apparatus is the only, or the most effective, way of making bodies perform ([2004] 2007:21). Alongside disciplinary, there is, or rather there has been for a while, a different technology of power that constitutes the subject in a way that is radically different from the panoptic gaze. While this power also involves strategies of visibility, its function, form, and purpose differ significantly from the spectacle in sovereign forms of power and from the surveillance in disciplinary forms of power. Foucault ties this form of visibility to "pastoral power," which, as he argues, can be traced back to the early days of Christianity. If discipline molds behaviors into performances, pastoral power holds sway over them under the broad category of "conduct." Foucault makes sure to define this term as precisely as possible: "Conduct is the activity of conducting (*conduire*), of conduction (*la conduction*) . . . , but it is equally the way in which one conducts oneself (*se conduit*), lets oneself be conducted (*se laisse conduire*), is conducted (*est conduit*), and finally, in which one behaves (*se comporter*) as an effect of a form of conduct (*une conduit*) as the action of conducting or of conduction (*conduction*)" ([2004] 2007:193). His main focus is not on the formation of "pastoral power," but on the detachment of its techniques from religion, which took place in the course of the eighteenth century, as they were passed over to the art of government, thus forming a new form of power relation. Government by conduct acquires its most advanced form in neoliberal societies of the second half of the twentieth century.

With the category of conduct, Foucault is setting up an important epistemological distinction in relation to behavior. Behavior is neutral: it can be behavior of an animal, or of a human being, or of a mechanism; and it is a closed system, as the theory of behaviorism insisted. Conduct implies a relationship: being led and leading, being conducted and conducting; it allows not only a transfer of power but also its exchange: one cannot conduct without having been conducted. The category of behavior opens the Althusserian apparatus (*appareil*) to conceptual weakness that the *dispositif* doesn't allow for. Practices that are inherent in *dispositifs* are not behaviors, but conducts. While sovereign and disciplinary modes of power necessarily involve technologies of subjection, pastoral power is a technology of subjectivation, which brings together subjection and subject formation. The final outcome of this process is the modern subject: in an implicit retort to Althusser, Foucault asserts that the history of the pastorate is the history of the subject in the West (184). The emergence of *dispositifs* is inseparable from the formation of a new form of society, which Foucault defines in terms of "security," not of "control."[9] In a further distinction from Deleuze, who held that disciplinary apparatuses are "finished," Foucault insisted that the three regimes of apparatuses are not mutually exclusive. Sovereignty, discipline, and security do not necessarily pertain to successive historical periods, but describe different modalities of power. Instead of the sovereign spectacle or the disciplinary gaze, the main organizing principle of security societies is the government of conduct. According to Foucault, while "sovereignty capitalizes a territory" and discipline "addresses the essential problem of a hierarchical and functional distribution of elements,"

> Security will try to plan a milieu in terms of events or series of events or possible elements, of series that will have to be regulated within multivalent and transformable framework. The specific space of security refers then to a series of possible events; it refers to the temporal and the uncertain, which have to be inserted within a given space. ([2004] 2007:20)

Clearly, Althusser's notion of the apparatus is operative within sovereign and disciplinary modes of power. If disciplinary apparatuses, which are epitomized in Althusser's institutions and *appareils*, turn behaviors into (structured, discrete, etc.) performances, security apparatuses (*dispositifs*) let them spill over the "material givens" and allow them to find their own paths across a terrain that is no longer stratified according to a strictly hierarchical organization of power. It is in this sense that disciplinary societies are molds and security societies are modulations: if the letter *normalize*, the former *norm*. Disciplinary societies strive to erect the firmest possible barrier between the external empirical world and the unreliable interior region of the subject, which is rife with uncontrollable forces of desire and imagination. These societies thrive on positivism, and it is no wonder that Foucault took Bentham's plan for the panopticon as the paradigmatic apparatus of disciplinary societies. However, disciplinary order leaves unexplored vast riches of the interior, and this wealth is not only metaphorical but quite literal, in the economic sense of the word. This interior incessantly spills out over the walls of disciplinary apparatuses (*appareils*): the barracks, the factories, hospitals, schools. This requires apparatuses (*dispositifs*) of a different kind, the ones that are capable of taking into account fictions that incessantly flow out from the depths of the self. The *dispositif* gives solidity to that which is invisible and intangible in the production of subjectivities.

Although they use identical procedures, techniques, and even models, Robertson's and Abramović's reenactments belong to different orders of apparatuses. In Robertson's performances from the early 1970s, the "identity transfer" posits identity as a frame that lends a certain definitive and discrete form to the individual. The frame is mobile, and it establishes a form of communication between one subject and another, or one artist and another. Accordingly, this "transfer" appears as a hyperbolic staging of processes at work in disciplinary apparatuses.[10] In her recent work, Abramović uses performance to elicit certain forms of behavior, stimulate patterns of sociality, and introduce both of them into symbolic and economic circulation. She was never coy about what her intentions were when she argued for the inclusion of performance art into premier art venues and its full integration into global art circuits: it was to mainstream it, canonize its key works, and make performance artworks into branded products the same way many other art forms were in the past. As the result of this campaign to preserve and commodify past performances, in Amelia Jones's apt formulation, Abramović placed herself "at the forefront of an industrial-strength institutionalization of performance histories" (2011:19). As Lütticken recognized a few years earlier, "performance art has never been a threat to the spectacle," so "its integration in the spectacle as media performance comes as no surprise" (2005:171). In this context, the strict rules that Tino Sehgal imposed on recording of his museum performances is no more than "an ideological smokescreen for the spectacle's rather less cute archaisms" (173). It would be erroneous to take Abramović's museum extravaganzas from the first decade of the twenty-first century as a turning point in the history of performance art; rather, they were a sign that it had already entered the art apparatus, which has been fully incorporated into contemporary security society.

What was on display in MoMA's Donald B. and Catherine C. Marron Atrium between 14 March and 31 May 2010 (for a total of some 716 hours) was a veritable *dispositif* for the production of subjectivities. In this scale model of surveillance capitalism, the viewers lined up to enter the performance space as the space of subjectivation. The ones who attempted overt performances by putting on elaborate makeup, dressing up (or down), or departing in numerous ways from the rules set by the artist and implemented by the museum only highlighted the true performance of subjectivation that was taking place in the nonexceptional behaviors of the others. The thrill that the audience experienced and the tears they shed came in response to the spectacle of subjectivation through conduct that in this performance received an aestheticized form and was celebrated as such. The cost of the inclusion of performance in the mainstream art industry was its integration into a new power structure that took full advantage of its apparatus, thus stultifying whatever critical potential it had (or it thought it had). These are the conditions that the new generation of performance artists have to come to terms with in the wake of this industrialization of performance, its histories, and its apparatus. One such artist is Cassils, a Canadian born, US-based transgender artist.[11]

CASE 1: CARVING AND CUTTING

In early 2011, only months after the conclusion of Abramović's induction of performance into global art industry, Cassils entered a program of rigorous physical training. This is their description of the regimen:

> Over 23 weeks I built my body to its maximum capacity. I did this adhering to a strict bodybuilding regime constructed by master bodybuilding coach Charles Glass. David Kalick, a nutritionist specializing in diets for sports competition, designed a diet where I consumed the caloric intake of a 190-pound male athlete. I also took mild steroids for eight weeks of the training. (in Tsaconas 2016:199)

The goal of this strenuous regime of exercise and diet was to gain twenty-three pounds over a period of twenty-three weeks. This process of (re) shaping their own body was at the core of Cassils's art project *Cuts: A Traditional Sculpture* (2011). This work was in dialogue with Eleanor Antin's landmark 1972 performance *Carving: A Traditional Sculpture,* in which the artist lost ten pounds over the course of a five-week diet. *Cuts* was not a reperformance in Abramović's sense; nor was Cassils adopting an artist's identity as a "frame," as Robertson did in his Beuys projects in the 1970s. Instead of "retrieving" a past performance or engaging in "identity transfer," with *Cuts* Cassils started what became their standard practice of collaborating with the past performances and revisiting the works of artists such as Antin, Robert Kienholz, Harun Farocki, and, more recently, Carolee Schneemann and Piero Manzoni.

The title of Antin's performance refers, of course, to carving as the sculptural technique of form-making based on the elimination of layers of material. Commenting on her process, Antin suggested that she started with a decision to "make an academic sculpture," and ended up doing a "piece" using "the method of the Greek sculpture" (281). She situates *Carving* within art history by referencing, more or less explicitly, Kenneth Clark's *The Nude: A Study in Ideal Form,* which was, for decades after its publication in 1956, considered the standard scholarly work on the subject.[12] Positioning Antin's *Carving* (and other feminist works from the period) in relation to Clark's distinction between nakedness as "natural and 'bad'" and nudity as "ideal and 'good,'" Joanna Frueh suggests that "just as the classical Greek nude occludes women's bodies in this kind of aesthetically rigid form, so the socially correct beautiful body disciplines—and punishes—women, through frustration, guilt, anxiety, and competitiveness with other women" (1994:195). Almost forty years later, at the time Cassils engaged in the grueling process of making their performance, Antin's *Carving* was situated within the art-historical narrative that it once challenged. *Cuts: A Traditional Sculpture* appears almost as a point-by-point reversal of *Carving: A Traditional Sculpture*: whereas Antin's objective was to lose weight, mostly in fat, Cassils's goal was to add muscle mass; where the first accomplished her goal through passivity and deprivation of food, the second accomplished theirs through arduous activity and excessive consumption of (certain) foods; and while, in doing so, Antin consciously embodied prevailing cultural standards about femininity, Cassils forcefully rejected them. All of this is not to say that Cassils aimed to refute and criticize the work of Antin and other feminist artists from the 1970s. Quite the contrary: Cassils's return to Antin's piece is a historical recoil of sorts, a step back that helped Cassils spring forward with greater force. What Antin's and Cassils's performances have in common is the displacement of the main action from the gallery space into the artist's everyday life. In itself, that places significant emphasis on the documentation of the performance process.

Antin referred to the "carving piece" as her "naturalist autobiography" (1975:280). The performance itself encompasses a thirty-six-day excerpt from her life, documented in a series of photographs taken daily, showing her nude body from the front, back, and both profiles. This daily routine of dieting and photographing resulted in a portfolio of 148 photographs. As she put it in an interview she gave a few years later, lined up next to each other along the wall, the photographs show "about twenty running feet of nudity" in which "you can read the weight loss" (1975:280). In Antin's gallery shows, the photographs were not presented linearly, as "twenty feet of nudity," but as tableaux in which the photographs were organized in a grid-like fashion. The vertical columns consisted of four photographs taken daily, which were then placed next to each other, making the rows of eight pictures (Figure 14).

This kind of arrangement was quite common for that period. One need not go further than Carl Andre's floor arrangements of squares (e.g., his magnesium, zinc, lead, etc. squares, 1969), or Sol LeWitt's compositions of squares and cubes that follow the pattern of progressive variation (e.g., *Corner Piece #4*, 1976). Writing at the end of the decade, Rosalind Krauss proclaimed the grid as the hallmark of modernist art. She concluded that "as we have more and more extended experience of the grid, we have discovered that one of the most modernist things about it is its capacity to serve as a paradigm or model for the antidevelopmental, the antinarrative, the antihistorical" ([1978] 1986:22). In other words, the grid does not facilitate progression and transformation, but supervision and containment.

Building on Deleuze's and, primarily, Guattari's writings from the 1970s, Lazzarato recognizes two "power apparatuses" determining the process of subjectivation: social subjection and mechanic enslavement. The former has been the focus of Marxist scholars, including Althusser's theory of ISAs.

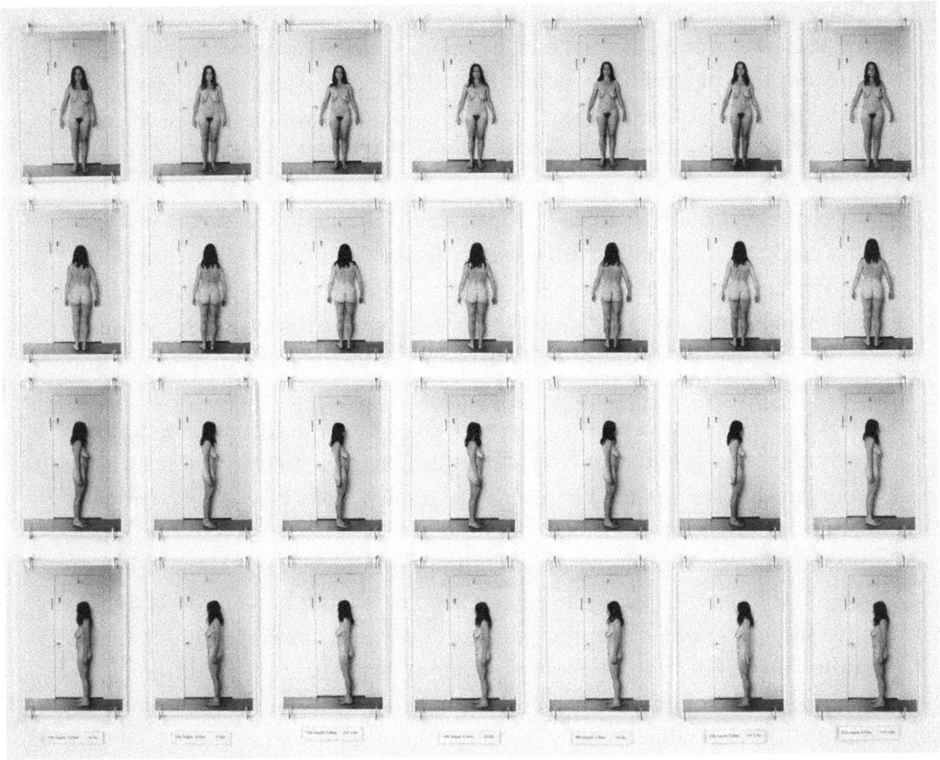

Figure 14. Eleanor Antin: *Carving: A Traditional Sculpture*, 1972

Pointing directly to Althusser's RSA and ISAs, Lazzarato suggests that machinic enslavement "does not operate through repression and ideology" (2014:38). Instead, it "activates *pre-personal, pre-cognitive,* and *preverbal* forces (perception, sense, affects, desire) as well as *suprapersonal* forces (machinic, linguistic, social, media, economic systems, etc.), which, beyond the subject and individual relations (intersubjectivity), multiply 'possibilities'" (31). He goes on to map these two "power apparatuses" onto two semiotic orders: whereas social subjection, as exemplified in theories of interpellation, mobilizes "signifying semiotics" or, simply put, language, machinic enslavement mobilizes types of asignifying semiotics "which do not involve consciousness and representations and do not have the subject as referent" (39). Lazzarato's list of examples of asignifying semiotics includes stock market indices, currency, mathematical equations, diagrams, computer languages, and national and corporate accounting. If there is a model of machinic enslavement in modern art, it is certainly the grid.

In her discussion of the works such as Hannah Wilke's *S.O.S. Stratification Object Series* (1974–82), featuring a grid of her photographic portraits "scarified" with her chewing gum sculptures that "variously read as vulva, womb, and tiny wounds" and Martha Wilson's *Breast Forms Permutated* (1972–2008), in which the artist presents a "grid of photographed breasts—naturally permutated," Frueh pointed out that feminist artists' response to their male colleagues' "interest in systems, permutations, and grids" was often playful and ironic (1994:192, 195). Indeed, compared to Wilke and Wilson, Antin comes across as deadpan. Her presentation of photographs of her body in neutral postures organized in a grid recalls the technique of biometry, which was prominent in policing and medicine, thus pointing directly to the power apparatus of machinic enslavement. That makes Cassils's decision to intervene in the arrangement of the photographic documentation of their performance even more significant. While pursuing the same routine of taking photographs daily, Cassils does not follow Antin's organizational principle of stacking four pictures in a single column and then sequencing them chronologically. Instead of a sequence of columns, they present the documentation of their performance in solid blocks of pictures, each block built of 5X5 photographs, capturing one of the four bodily positions (front, back, left, and right profiles, Figure 15).

The image does not appear to be caught between two oppositional pulls (vertical and horizontal), but rather fills out blocks of (pictorial) space, thus establishing a different, nonbiometric record of Cassils's sculpting process. In their work with grids, feminist artists such as Antin, Wilson, and Wilke expose the rigidity of the binary organization of gender. What the grid suspends in an uneasy equilibrium is the myth of the feminine as that which is passive and horizontal, and the masculine as that which is active and vertical. If in *Carving* Antin forces her body to comply with the gendered nature of this structure, in *Cuts* Cassils exposes the violence that the grid exerts on the bodies made to conform to it. In twenty-three weeks of training, they made their body push against the grid, distort, and rip through it. While rejecting the horizontal line of femininity, Cassils's doesn't comply with the vertical column of traditional masculinity, either. They cut across these categories and literally build the body that the grid-machine tries to enslave.

Instead of being limited to a sequence of photographs, the process of making *Cuts* generated an entire constellation of works in several different media, from performance, to video, print, and digital. Through this proliferation, Cassils undermines the economy at work in feminist grid-works of the 1970s. While Antin, Wilke, and Wilson positioned grids as final points of their performances, Cassils used the strenuous activity involved in *Cuts*

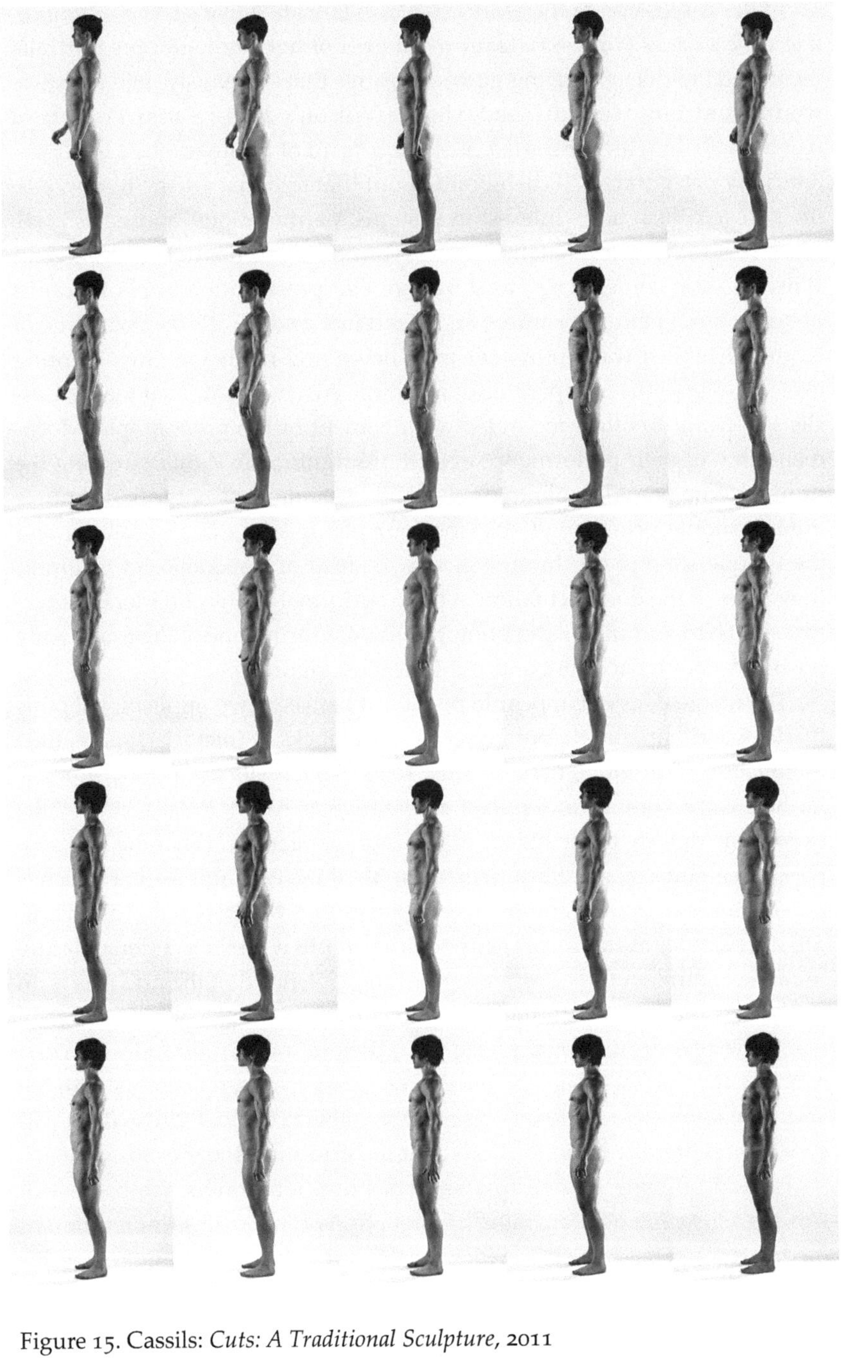

Figure 15. Cassils: *Cuts: A Traditional Sculpture*, 2011

to produce a number works, which included an homage to Linda Benglis's famous *Ad* in *Artforum*; the video *Fast Twitch // Slow Twitch* (2011); a zine called *Lady Face / Man Body* (2011), which was connected to a blog of the same name (ladyfacemanbody.com); and a series of collages, *Disfigured Pin-ups* (2011) (Cassils 2015:36). Further, *Cuts: The Traditional Sculpture* intersected with other performances Cassils was working on at that time: *Hard Times* (2011–13), in which Cassils poses on an elevated wooden plank, wearing a prosthetic mask, a blond wig, and a bikini tan; and *Tiresias* (2011), a durational piece in which they press their bare chest against an ice sculpture of a male torso that strikingly resembles classical Greek art, so that the body heat slowly melts this ideal of masculine strength until it crumbles. If in *Carving* Antin submitted to the principle of containment—containment of the body that is not allowed to expand and grow beyond certain aesthetic limits, but also disciplinary containment in a machinic procedure of capturing the body—in *Cuts* Cassils is on the move, cutting across media in a culture saturated with images.

One of Cassils's key accomplishments with *Cuts* was to demonstrate viscerally the cost and strain involved in the liberation, however temporary and transient, from the forces of machinic enslavement. In late July 2011, Cassils made the following entry in the diary record of their daily gym routines and calorie intake during their work on *Cuts*:

> I also felt like shit. I was so tired all the time from all the heavy lifting. My joints ached constantly, and my muscles became so tight that my girlfriend had to take my t-shirt off at night because I was no longer flexible enough to do so myself . . . injury was imminent, and though I managed to stop before it got too bad, it was just a matter of time before I was limping around with buckled knees like all the other bodybuilders. I stopped this project on July 27. On this day I stopped the creatine and the steroids. I stopped force-feeding myself, and I took two weeks off the weights. Within 14 days I had shed eight pounds of muscle. My skin grew thick as the testosterone withdrew from my system. My mood swung. (in Tsaconas 2016:204)

It seems that the way out from machinic enslavement is through machinic emancipation. This strategy also brings into question the other power apparatus, that of social subjection, which, as Lazzarato points out, assigns "an individual subjectivity, an identity, sex, profession" with the goal of procuring and distributing "place and roles within and for the social division of labor" (2014:24). All of these, and many other, facets of subjectivation work in unison, and in each of their performances Cassils questions any number of them at once. For them, "trans" pertains to more than one facet of subjectivity: surely transgender, but also transnational (their background in the Canadian system of funding and evaluating artists informs significantly their positioning vis-à-vis art institutions in the United States), and transprofessional (for a while, their day job as a personal trainer was running parallel to and in conjunction with their art projects).

In his work on trans-identities and practices, Jack Halberstam argues that a trans body challenges "many more binaries beyond male versus female," so that it "confronts rather than confirms common assumptions about the coherent and incoherent, material and immaterial, internal and external" (2018). Halberstam indicates this complexity of non-gender-binary orientation with an asterisk: "trans*." This expansion of trans-positionality opens new and productive approaches to a number of practices, especially in the arts, exemplified in Halberstam's powerful argument for trans* reading of Gordon Matta-Clark and the Anarchitecture group.[13] Still, Halberstam's insists on grounding this approach in the epistemology of the trans* corporeality as belonging to bodies that

> function not simply to provide an image of the non-normative against which normative bodies can be discerned, but rather bodies that are fragmentary and internally contradictory; bodies that remap gender and its relation to race, place, class and sexuality; bodies that are in pain; bodies that sound different from how they look, bodies that represent palimpsestic identities or a play of surfaces; bodies that must be split open and reorganized, opened up to chance and random signification. (2018)

While warning against an easy analogy between the incisions that Matta-Clark makes into architectural structures and the surgical cut in the trans* body, Halberstam points out that these interventions trouble conventional gendering of the architect and a built environment in terms of power that the patriarchy assigns to them. What makes Cassils's work exceptional is that in their trans-work, they bring into question the foundational role of the surgical cut for the trans* body. Having started working out in their mid-teens in an effort to overcome their childhood health issues, Cassils explains that in creating their gender-nonconforming identity they decided to use bodybuilding "as opposed to just surgery or hormones . . . because body building is such an incredible caricature of masculinity" (2019:127). This does not amount to some kind of noninvasive challenging of gendered norms for the body, but, quite the opposite, it is a more far-reaching incision into mechanisms fundamental for the constitution of identity (gender, political, racial, cultural, etc.).[14] The anarchitectural performances of cutting into built structures were prepared by the cut into the social world of art made by the Anarchitecture group. Like its exact contemporary Art & Language New York, this collective made that incision to remove the artist as a singular, coherent, and centered subject that formed the cornerstone of the art apparatus. In their interventions, Cassils makes tangible, that is, literally gives the body to that process of subjectivation which, as Deleuze suggests, reaches "the extreme edge of an apparatus" and marks "the passage from one apparatus to another" (2006:341). Deleuze names this process the "line of fracture." That is the *constitutional cut* of Cassils's work, and it is this fracture across and between apparatuses that *Cuts* makes visible.

Cassils is not subjectified as "artist," nor is their art a strategy for presenting a nonnormative subjectivity. They cut open the frontiers between apparatuses and obliterate distinctions between artistic media: an action transitions into a sculpture, into an installation, into an image, into a digital file, into a social intervention. (It is worth noting that the Anarchitecture artists shared this fluid movement across traditional media: from architecture, to performance, to food, to music . . .). As Amelia Jones observed in relation to Cassils's performance *Becoming an Image* (2012–15), this piece and its continuation in different media constitute a new "hybrid practice" and as such require a "new hybrid mode of analysis" (2015:21). What makes this practice hybrid is not only the use of different media but also the fracturing of the partitions that separate them. Cassils's practice doesn't belong to any of these media, but to an assemblage of ever-transforming artworks, or trans*formances. *Lady Face / Man Body*, *Disfigured Pinups*, and other pieces are not only byproducts or documentation of *Cuts* but the lines of fracture through which this work escapes the status assigned to performance art by the *dispositif* that was on display in MoMA in the spring of 2010.

CASE 2: POWERS (THAT BE)

Edward Kienholz's installation *Five Car Stud* (1969–72) depicts the torture and lynching of a Black man (maybe a wayward bluesman who made a wrong step on his precarious journey). In the thick of the night, there are five cars parked on a dirt patch. Four passenger vehicles are circled in the middle to form a small arena. Their lights are on, illuminating the scene in which five whites are brutalizing a young African American man. They are pressing his back to the ground. Two are holding his outstretched arms, the third is tugging on a thick rope tied to one of his ankles, and the fourth is squashing his ankle with his foot, while leaning on a shotgun. The fifth man has the Black man's pants pulled down, grabbing on his penis with his left hand, and pressing a knife to its base with the right one. Another man is standing guard, resting his right hand on an open door of the fifth car, a pickup truck parked slightly to the side, and holding a shotgun under his left am. It's impossible to take in the whole scene at a single glance and from a single point of view. A young white woman sits on the passenger side in the truck, covering her mouth with the palm of her right hand and using her left hand to lean on the seat—gestures of distress. The glove compartment in front of her is open, with a can of coke, a bottle of booze, some paper cups, and a pack of smokes resting on the open door. The final protagonist in this tableau is a bespectacled boy staring at the scene of castration through the windshield of one of the cars, an old Plymouth.

Dramatic and elaborate as it is, this installation is not a simple staging of the short news report that Kienholz read in 1969, which prompted him to make this piece; nor is it a variation on *5 Card Stud*, Henry Hathaway's 1968 movie about lynching in the Wild West, with which the installation resonates in many ways. Although it looks like an elaborate apparatus, Kienholz's piece shows just its dusty and empty shell, which makes it even more disturbing. A closer look reveals that the six white thugs have their faces covered with grotesque Halloween masks: a scary clown, a pale vampire, a face resembling the kid from the cover of *Mad* magazine . . . Rubber masks covering faces made of plastic? Representation of representation, concealment of concealment. As behavior, the apparatus is in the muscles, sinews, convictions, and beliefs of assailants; and it is in the pained body, in the mouth wide open in a silent scream, in saliva mixed with blood drooling from the victim's mouth, in the injury that draws life out from him. And furthermore, it is in ideas about race and violence that animate the bodies of the members of this lynch gang, and in the mechanisms that synchronized their actions with social institutions that gave them permission to act. Kienholz's elaborate representation of the ideological apparatus of whiteness has entered another apparatus, the apparatus (*dispositif*) of art, and quite literally disappeared within it: it was first shown in Documenta 5 in Cassel, which Harald Szeemann curated in 1972, and was briefly on view in Akademie der Künste in Berlin and Kunsthalle Düsseldorf before it vanished from view for full forty years in the storage of the Japanese collector who purchased it (McEvilley in Holm 2011:91).[15] It surfaced again in

2011 and was on view for the first time in the United States at Los Angeles County Museum of Art in 2012.

I first saw the photographs of Kienholz's installation a few years later in Cassils's studio during their residence at the Montalvo Arts Center in Northern California. Our conversation turned to Kienholz as Cassils was telling me about the piece *The Powers That Be (210 Kilometers)* they did in 2016 in Koupio, Finland, as the recipient of the ANTI Festival International Prize. They told me that the subtitle of the performance referred to the distance separating this Finnish town from the Russian border. What moved them to engage in a dialogue with *Five Car Stud* was the shocking realization about the lack of legal protections for the LGBTQI community in Russia, which meant it was always open season on its members. Cassils told me how they went to websites of ultranationalist and "religious" groups that promote violence against queer and trans people, and showed me a video these thugs made of beating a young gay man whom they met in an online chat group and arranged a date with under false pretenses. In that studio, the dusty shell of the apparatus suddenly filled up with bodies, blood, fear, and aggression. It was conjured by Cassils, their voice trembling as they were telling me about the unbearable cognitive dissonance they felt in the safety of Koupio and the real threat that hung over lives of queer people only a short drive from there. That unbearable conflict between safety and danger did not end at Finland's border with Russia. It was very much present in their adopted home of Los Angeles and elsewhere in the United States, where trans people are significantly more likely to suffer a violent death than any other group.

The cognitive clash that anguished Cassils brings back the question about the relationship between the RSA and ISAs. Althusser made a sharp distinction between them, to the point of singularizing the former and using the plural for the latter. That is because, according to him, the RSA is directly in the service of the state, while ISAs are relatively autonomous and include both state and private institutions and entities. While it might appear that Lazzarato's pairing of social subjection and machinic enslavement restates Althusser's RSA-ISAs coupling, it further questions and complicates them. This troubling of clearly differentiated *appareils* goes along libidinal lines, which Lazzarato takes from Félix Guattari. While he engaged with Althusser's ideas sporadically in his writings throughout the 1970s, Guattari addressed his notion of ideological apparatuses in the project Collective Equipment and Semiotic Subjugation, which he was working on in 1979 just before he embarked on *A Thousand Plateaus* with Deleuze, and which was published posthumously in 2011 under the title *Lignes de fuite:*

Pour un autre monde de possibles (*Lines of Flight: For Another World of Possibilities*). Here he directly states his disagreement with Althusser's separation of apparatuses into repressive and ideological. Guattari argues that "the State is everywhere and before being incarnated in repressive instruments, it functions in the libido. We really mean libido, because the movement of ideas, in this domain above all, cannot be separated from the metabolism of social unconscious" ([2011] 2016:100). *Five Car Stud* is a visual analysis of this integration of repression and ideology into a racial apparatus that is operative, persistent, and unceasing and that leaves in its path a trail of Black bodies. Guattari argues that "the economic base does not constitute an infrastructure that necessarily imposes itself on the libido and on ideas. Everything can become infrastructure!" (100). Mapping this libidinal landscape in painstaking detail, Kienholz's diorama captures the performance of *repellation* in its full force.

Critics and art historians tend to interpret Keinholz's installation as a narrative that captures in a single tableau a story about an interracial date violently interrupted by a gang of white men. (The husband of that distressed woman and his pals? Is it her son in the Plymouth? We can only guess.)[16] They don't lynch the man by hanging him from a tree, as racist mobs did in the South: they do that by castrating him. That is precisely where the libidinal currents of the apparatus come to the surface. In Kienholz's installation, the realistic representation breaks down in the Black man's body and more precisely, in the area just above his crotch. His torso is made of a metal receptacle filled with used motor oil. Plastic cubes with the letters *R, G, N, E, G, I* float in viscous liquid, and no matter how chance rearranges them, they spell one and only one word (so much for semiotic subjugation). The dark fluid in the victim's chest indicates racist essentialization of the body ("black blood") but also points to a surreptitious and violent affiliation that the lynch mob and their enablers establish between this body and the machinic assemblage that surrounds it. There are two socialities at work *Five Car Stud*: one consists of humans and the other of machines. The Black man is caught in the process of being valiantly expelled from the first to the second one. He is a laboring machine, a worker. It is this specific form of objectification with which the gang of white subjects repels him from entering the society they claim as their own, while at the same time integrating him into the apparatus of machinic enslavement.

For *The Powers That Be*, Cassils, like Keinholz, aims the headlights of parked vehicles to form a central arena, which is located in a parking garage, and not on a deserted country road. The space between the cars is filled with an audience, with Cassils performing alone in the middle. In *The*

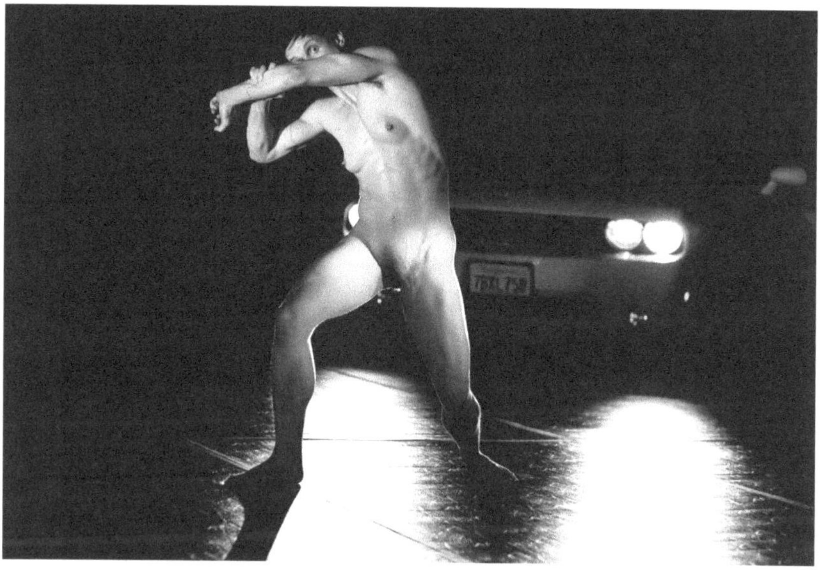

Figure 16. Cassils: *Powers That Be*, 2016

Powers That Be, they add two more technological layers to Kienholz's machinic assemblage made of cars and bodies. First, there is an audio soundtrack coming from stereos in the parked vehicles, consisting of static noise and samples from local radio stations, which audio artist Kadet Kuhne designed for this performance. In addition, Cassils invited audience members to record this live event with their phones and to upload pictures and videos to the performance website, thus adding a whole new layer of surveillance to the situation of the body caught in the headlights. The new set of digital machines added to the Keinholz-inspired cars have the capacity not only to project light but also to absorb and process it, organize it into images, and instantly transmit them to other locations. These micromachines are not powered by gas-gulping engines and have no moving parts. Battery-powered and digitally operated, they perform the basic function of surveillance capitalism: they extract behavioral information from the body and translate it into behavioral data, which they add to a vast repository of raw material available for further processing.

Cassils's body, illuminated by car headlights and captured by digital cameras, ends up being caught between two modes of capitalist production. Theirs is an alienated body mechanically repeating gestures without visible cause, purpose, or effect. Cassils's muscles twitch violently. Engaging an invisible adversary, their body gets slammed against the concrete floor, pushed against the wall, and then pressed down, hard; they fight back with their fists, but each attempt misses; they kick, but always get the air; they maneuver to avoid the opponent, but always get pinned down. Their pale, non-gender-conforming body charges into space and *the invisible hand* always strikes back. Or rather, invisible hands: this body is not contained by the grid of disciplines; instead, it is surrounded by the security milieu consisting of *dispositifs*. There is no hope of leaving the apparatus of gender, they seem to suggest, without stepping into the apparatus of race, and out of the apparatus of race without stepping into apparatus of class, or into apparatuses of art, urban stratification, and so on, ad infinitum. So, instead of searching for, or claiming, an impossible outside, Cassils exposes the charged frontiers between the apparatuses by squeezing their body in-between them and engaging in the ghost combat of invisible punches and visible injuries.

Cassils's performances always involve arduous training, and for *The Powers That Be* at the Broad Museum, they worked with Hollywood fight choreographer Mark Steger. The goal was not to create a performance art replica of screen violence; this shadow fight was not a staging of violence, but of power: of "powers that be," powers that are there, in bodies, in objects, in images, and in their midst—in the air, so to speak. In other words, Cassils doesn't stage repression in the apparatus of the state but, I would contend, the operations of powers at work in a *dispositif*. For, as Foucault proposes in volume 1 of *The History of Sexuality*, that methodological statement of his entire project on the genealogy of power, the *dispositif* concerns itself with "the investment of the body, its valorization, and the distributive management of its forces" ([1976] 1978:141). It coalesces through an interaction of forces, not through the impact that force exercises on its object. Deleuze drives this point in his book on Foucault: "Force is never singular but essentially exists in relation with other forces, such that any force is already a relation, that is to say power: force has no other object or subject than force" ([1986] 1988:70). Not surprisingly, in order to describe the new apparatus (*un nouveau dispositif*, [1976] 1978:106), Foucault needs to first establish the meanings and functions of power through a series of propositions. So, famously: power is not an object, "something that is acquired, seized, or shared," but something that is "exercised from innumerable points"; and "relations of power are not in a position of exteriority with respect to other types of relationships." Nor does power have a center: "Neither the caste that governs, nor the groups which control state apparatus [*appareil*], nor those who make the most important economic decisions direct the entire network of power that functions in a society." And indeed:

"Should it be said that one is always 'inside' power, there is no 'escaping' it, there is no absolute outside where it is concerned, because one is subject to the law in any case?" (94–95). Gradually, it becomes clear that Foucault seems to ascribe to power a number of characteristics that Althusser attributed to ideology.

If in "What Is an Author?" Foucault deployed a classical Marxist idea of ideology as false consciousness, by the time he wrote *History of Sexuality* there was room left only for ideology in the sense given to it by the eighteenth-century philosophers who coined the word—as the science of ideas.[17] Foucault summarizes this notion of ideology as "a theory of ideas, signs, and the individual genesis of sensations," and more importantly for his project, "a theory of the social composition of interests"; further, he suggests that the discourse of the Idéologues came together with other scientists, such as the Physiocrats and social economists, to form "concrete arrangements (*agencements concrets*) that would go on to make up the great technologies of power in the nineteenth century" (140). While Foucault still makes oblique references to Althusser—consider, for example, his remark about "spontaneous philosophy" (125)—his massive revision of the idea of the apparatus leaves almost no room for ideology in conventional Marxist sense. In fact, it can be said that the relation between power and the *dispositif* that Foucault proposes stands in reverse proportion to the relation between ideology and the apparatus (*appareil*) that Althusser outlines in his ISAs essay. Whereas, for Althusser, apparatuses are the instruments of ideology and are co-constitutive with it, power is intrinsic to *dispositifs*. Further, whereas in Althusser's *appareil* disciplines dictate the interpellative constitution of the subject, the *dispositif* facilitates strategies for organization and management of subjectivities, exemplified in the ideas of pastoral power and the government by conduct. Finally, if Althusser conflates ideology and power—all power is ideological, ideology is the nexus of power—Foucault sets them apart in order to render the apparatuses legible. This replacement of opaque apparatuses (*appareils*) with thoroughly rational and analyzable *dispositifs* comes at the cost of ideology.

And yet it would be incorrect to say that the *dispositifs* are an-ideological. Cassils's works belong to that corpus of performances which offer a powerful demonstration that the responses to bodies that are Black or queer or poor or foreign are always ideological. By placing their body at the cross section of headlights, gazes, and phone camera lenses, Cassils exposes the ideological organization of gazes in surveillance capitalism. In their trans*formances, the asterisk represents the site of conflict, resistance, disjunction between ideological apparatuses and seemingly nonideological *dispositifs*. If Kienholz's *5 Car Stud* stages the apparatus of racism as a gory diorama, *The Powers That Be* exposes the ways in which the *dispositif* of art aestheticizes, absorbs, and, ultimately, neutralizes these acts of ideological violence. On the one hand, the *dispositif* releases art of the burden of medium-specificity. It allows performance to claim all those institutional channels through which the artist's body enters the circulation of images, signs, and objects while maintaining the status of liveness, thus capitalizing on the presumption of authenticity that comes with it. On the other hand, the *dispositif* elicits resistances, which are no longer treated as anomalies to be eliminated. Instead, they are neutralized through their integration into the *dispositif*'s operations, which always leaves open the possibility of critique of the very idea of the *dispositif*.

In the lectures *Security, Territory, Population*, Foucault recognizes the importance of these resistances that emerge in opposition to the operations of pastoral power. He notes that this form of power elicits pushbacks expressed through the phenomena of "counter-conduct" as the "struggle against the processes implemented for conducing others" ([2004] 2007:201). These refusals to accept the government of conduct took the form of "behavior, which may be either strictly individual, or individual but serial, through contagion, as in the case of mysticism, for example, with the formation of groups that break up almost as soon as they are constituted" (204). While Foucault outlines, in broad strokes, the early forms of counter-conduct in relation to the techniques of pastoral power within religious institutions (asceticism, mysticism, eschatology, etc.), importantly, he returns to the idea of counter-conduct in his final lecture of the seminar to point out that counter-conduct did not disappear with the secularization of the pastoral power, while insisting on the difference between the forms of counter- or *mis-conduct* and the notion of dissidence (202). Unlike dissidence, which opposes power from without, counter-conduct is inherent to security apparatuses and as such subject to reintegration. In their performances, Cassils mobilizes this position of immanence to create art as counter-conduct. Working within and against the *dispositifs* of surveillance capitalism, Cassils exposes the complex operations of the concealment of ideology on which this form of power stakes its success and its very survival.

In an attempt to bring the discussion of the *dispositif* into the digital age, Giorgio Agamben establishes a part-biographical, part-etymological connection between Jean Hyppolite's *positivité* and Foucault's *dispositif* ([2006] 2009:3). As catchy as this association might appear, everything suggests that the opposite is the case: the defining characteristic of the *dispositif* is not its affinity with Hegelian positivity, but its capacity to absorb the negative. Agamben stays close to Foucault when he suggests that the *dispositif* is "anything that has in some way the capacity to capture, orient, determine, intercept, model, control, or secure the gesture, behaviors, opinions, or discourses of living beings" (14). But then he proceeds to qualify that "anything" as a tool: "It is clear that ever since Homo sapiens first appeared, there have been apparatuses; but we could say that today there is not even a single instant in which the life of individuals is not modeled, contaminated, or controlled by some apparatus" (15). Instead of attempting to offer an analysis of the digital *dispositif*, he gives up and plunges into technophobic rancor.

> He who lets himself be captured by the "cellular telephone" apparatus—whatever the intensity of the desire that has driven him—cannot acquire a new subjectivity, but only a number through which he can, eventually, be controlled. The spectator who spends his evenings in front of the television set only gets, in exchange for his desubjectification, the frustrated mask of the couch potato, or his inclusion in the calculation of viewership ratings. (21)[18]

Agamben published this essay in 2006, only months before Apple launched its first iPhone, which combined mobile phone, pocket computer, and miniature television. One can only imagine that he would declare it a perfect infernal machine. Agamben's association of desubjectification with a presumably Western individual who can afford a sofa and a TV only bespeaks the narrowness of his idea of the subject. As Alexander Weheliye shows in his critique of Agamben's philosophy of "bare life," the horror of desubjectification is inherent to racialized constitution of the subject (2014:39). What conceals these desubjectivizing processes is ideology, which is woven into the very fabric of pastoral power. And vice versa: it is only through the pastoral mode of power that ideology could ever become that cohesive force in the society that Althusser talks about.

When Maurizio Lazzarato claimed that neoliberalism construes the individual as an "entrepreneur of the self" and that (following Guattari) subjectivity has become its "number one target," he was still not taking into account the full effects of surveillance capitalism ([2009] 2017:33, 193). For example, he fails to include algorithms in his inventory of the instruments of machinic enslavement. What makes an apparatus (*appareil*) "machinic" and "enslaving" is its unidirectional flow of power. Asignifying semiotics "connect an organ, a system of perception, an intellectual activity, and so on, directly to a machine, procedures, and signs, bypassing representations of a subject" (Lazzarato 2014:40). In a multi-billion-dollar intervention, surveillance capitalism reversed this flow, showing that these processes can go in the opposite direction, too: an organ, system of perception, or intellectual activity can directly feed into a machine, and a machine can be responsive to it. This process reaches a new level of sophistication with large language models and AI technology. That is precisely what creates the illusion of "autonomous subjects" at the neoliberal core of surveillance capitalism. More radically, surveillance capitalism sees precisely these processes of subjectivization as instrumental for the production of raw material for extraction. Instead of looking actively for any gaps in the apparatus and creating mechanisms for their capture and closure, as disciplinary societies do, the production of subjectivity under conditions of surveillance capitalism involves the creation of lacunae as its own lines of flight. Surely these openings are temporary: surveillance capitalism will recognize and focus on them as a new area for extraction. To a certain degree, the apparatus of surveillance capitalism encourages this kind of counter-production. The central struggle in surveillance capitalism is over these openings, which are positioned, at least initially, in immanent opposition to the apparatus. The counter-behavior they generate is the raw behavioral material that surveillance capitalism exploits. By inviting audience members to take pictures and upload them onto the web, Cassils is directly engaging and challenging this operation of the apparatus of surveillance capitalism. In Cassils's trans*formances, the body channels contradictory impulses, performs uncontrollable behaviors, and materializes subjectivities difficult to absorb. In short, it works to generate *unextractable behaviors*.

CASE 3, 4, 5, . . .

Case 3: The signal strategy that Cassils deploys in performances is to insert their body between apparatuses (*dispositifs*) and in doing so create a three-dimensional impression, a negative as it were, that no apparatus can fully absorb. That reminder is what constitutes Cassils's performance art. They do that in *The Powers That Be* but even more explicitly in *Becoming an Image*, a performance in which they attack with their bare fists a two-thousand-pound block of clay. If in *The Artist Is Present* the unsuspecting spectators queued up to become an image, Cassils shows here that "image" has nothing light, ethereal, or passive about it. It is a hard imprint, which resists and pushes back. They assault the clay chunk of roughly human size in pitch darkness, illuminated only by the sudden flash from a camera. What is the labor of becoming an image: physically assailing a block of clay, or being assailed by the flash and the camera? These mediums capture the body in different ways: the latter produces light, highly mobile, easily disseminated images, a commodity that enters the markets of surveillance capitalism; and the former produces a formless pile of matter, a counter-commodity. On the one hand, glossy photographs from *Becoming an Image* are exhibited in Cassils's shows. From there, they move through diffuse currents of surveillance capitalism: they are posted on Cassils's website, they travel on their Instagram account, and they are printed in their monograph. I find them on the cover of Rachel Carroll's book *Transgender and Literary Imagination* (2018) and on the front page of of *GLQ: A Journal of Lesbian and Gay Studies* (26:4, 2020). On the other hand, Cassils would go on to use the bashed block of clay to cast a two-ton bronze sculpture, *The Resilience of the 20%*, a title that calls attention to the statistical increase of violence against trans people in a single year (2012). Then, in the spring of 2017 this sculpture became the main prop in the communal activist performance *Monument Push* that Cassils organized in Omaha, Nebraska, for which they worked with local activists to identify sites of "trauma, violence, celebration, resistance, and resilience" (Cassils 2020). They used these locations to establish the route along which a group of activists and artists pushed the sculpture. *Monument Push* went in a direction counter to that of surveillance capitalism.

Case 4: *Inextinguishable Fire* (2015), a performance referencing Harun Farocki's 1969 film of the same title, in which Cassils executes a full head-to-toe stunt burn.

Case 5: *Pissed* (2017), a two-hundred-day durational performance in response to the Trump administration's rollback of an Obama-era executive order that allowed transgender students to use bathrooms of their own choosing, during which the artist collected and stored their urine, presented in Ronald Feldman Gallery in New York in uniform plastic containers alongside a piss-filled glass cube that recalled Hans Haacke's *Condensation Cube* (1965).

Case 6: *Alchemic* (2017), a series of photo-performances done in collaboration with Robin Black.[19] Color photographs of Cassils's gold-painted body mounted onto polished Plexiglas surfaces placed on gallery walls in juxtaposition with containers filled with piss in *Pissed*. "Pairing the gilded body against the vat of urine [. . .] poses the questions: Whose lives are considered precious and valued and whose are deemed disposable?" (2019:24). The new gilded age of surveillance capitalism consumes the lives it constitutes as dispensable and unworthy. In their more recent art projects, Cassils stages a pushback against this consumption.

Case 7: *Houston Piss Drive* (2018), a collectively produced installation, with the same purpose and form, but done collectively.

Case 8: *Solution* (2018), the expansion of another work, this time *Tiresias*, into a collective action involving artists Fanaa, rafa esparza, and Keijaun Thomas . . .

This list goes on and on. The tendency is to expand from solo works to projects that include other artists and entire communities, while not giving up on high artistic standards, conceptual acuity, and political punch. Consider *In Plain Sight* (2020), a large-scale art project that Cassils organized together with rafa esparza that involved a group of eighty artists who were, according to Cassils's website, "united to create an artwork dedicated to the abolition of immigrant detention and the United States culture of incarceration" (Cassils 2020). It involved aerial paintings in blue skies above prisons that spelled out messages such as "Care not Cages" and "Shame #defundhate #xmap." The last phrase refers to online and Instagram components of this project, which garnered millions of hits. In this constellation of performances, installations, and actions, Cassils self-locates in a transitional position between performance history and the wider political action in the present, thus indicating the key difference between re- and trans*formance. Consider also *Human Measure* (2022, 2024), their first dance piece, which started as a dialogue with Yves Klein in a workshop they lead during their residency at Stanford in 2017. What started as an experiment with dance and martial arts grew into a powerful kinetic mediation on trans* visibility that slams down hard on the use of trans bodies as a political token in contemporary US politics, while not giving up an inch of cheerfulness and joy that can come only from an intense sociality. Uproar.

The creation of negativities, of counter-conducts, is not the goal; the production of unextractable behaviors and counter-collectivities is. As a highly public form of art, performance brings the struggle over their production into the open. When I say that Cassils, but also rafa esparza, Keijaun Thomas, and a number of other members of the new generation of performance artists, are placing their bodies between faultiness created by apparatuses, I have this struggle in mind. They counter the processes of desubjectification, which are far greater than those that Agamben could ever imagine, by inserting their practices into crevices of the security society and keeping them open, not allowing these openings to close on them. They work to usurp behaviors that surveillance capitalism sees as raw material for extraction. Production of new political and artistic collectivities does not only entail identifying and widening the ideological cracks in the smooth, rational facade of this society. These performance artists take a different approach to the *dispositif*: one not of distance and denial but of proximity and power. Not giving up on their position at the junction of apparatuses, they are not asking what surveillance capitalism dictates, imposes, or even "allows," but *what it desires*. Their strategy is clear: only insofar as we know what security society does not yet know about itself can we forge behaviors and collectivities that will disturb, distort, and transform its operations.

Postscript to Non-ideology

When they stated in the opening pages of *A Thousand Plateaus* that "there is no ideology and never has been," Deleuze and Guattari seem to have flagged the conclusion of the short period of intense debate about ideology, its operations, and its material existence ([1980] 1987:4). As it turned out, this period, which lasted from the late nineteen-sixties to the early nineteen-eighties, coincided with a number of social, political, and economic developments that affected the whole globe. The emergence of neoliberalism is one of them. If we take into account Daniel Bell's eulogy to ideology delivered in the late 1950s, it turns out that that the rise of neoliberalism took place during the brief period bookended by the proclamations of ideology's end and its nonexistence.

All of this is not to accuse Deleuze and Guattari's position of being close in any way to that of the neocon bunch. Rather, their claim about the nonexistence of ideology places them on the far end of the spectrum of its deniers. They didn't spend much time elaborating on their assertion. Instead, they went on to say, almost laconically: "All we talk about are multiplicities, lines, strata and segmentarities, lines of flight and intensities, machinic assemblages and their various types, bodies without organs and their construction and selection" (4). This suggests that the allegation of ideology's unreality rests on methodological procedures and theoretical foundations they established in the first volume of their *Capitalism and Schizophrenia* project. Still, in *Anti-Oedipus*, Deleuze and Guattari don't venture any definitive statements about ideology, nor do they return to it in any extensive way in the remaining five hundred pages of *A Thousand Plateaus*. Instead of engaging in an analysis of ideology, in their first book they specify the zones it occupies and mechanisms by which it operates. Proposing that unlike psychoanalysis, schizoanalysis aims "to analyze the specific nature of the libidinal investments in the economic and political spheres, and thereby to show how, in the subject who desires, desire can be made to desire its own repression," they uncouple desires from interests, which remain within the domain of ideology: "All of this"—libidinal investments, desiring subjects—"happens, not in ideology, but well beneath it" (105). While not disputing the existence of ideology, they go on to reiterate this point on several occasions throughout *Anti-Oedipus* (see, e.g., [1972] 1977:122, 345, etc.). How, then, did they change their minds and dismiss ideology altogether in the second volume of *Capitalism and Schizophrenia*?

There are numerous indications that apparatuses were a big part of the problem. In *Lines of Flight*, Guattari offers a critique of Althusser's separation of apparatuses into repressive and ideological almost identical to the one Foucault presented in his lectures at the Collège de France in 1972–73 (see Foucault [2013] 2015:233). However, Guattari takes his objections further and ends up offering an analysis that foreshadows the dismissal of ideology in *A Thousand Plateaus*:

> The fact that Louis Althusser detaches apparatus that arise from the private domain from what he calls "Repressive State Apparatuses" seems to be of the greatest interest, but we part company from him when he characterises the former as being fundamentally "ideological." The problematic that we have ourselves sought to outline, with collective assemblages of enunciation, diagrammatic machines and Collective equipment functions, has, on the contrary, led us to consider the existence of a continuity between the blatant forms of public repression and the innumerable "private" modes of internalisation of repression. ([2011] 2016:99–100)

But what is this internalization if not an ideological operation? Sensing that he is entering a contradiction, Guattari offers yet another justification of his argument:

> Althusser has made ideology too general a category, encompassing and confusing radically heterogeneous semiotic categories. In identifying it, following the classical tradition, with logos, he wanted to underline that it could not underline a productive force. And on this point we can only part company with him. (100)

The site of that internalization is the apparatus, through which ideology acquires its material existence. However, the apparatus, as Althusser conceives of it, doesn't suffice. Guattari suggests that the analysis of social assemblages should not be limited to "the visible parts of equipment such as schools, prisons, stages, etc." but should expand to "the fundamental element of their functioning" that "derives from their aptitude for capturing not just interests, but also individual and collective desires" (100). Guattari's active search for analyzable social entities of this kind is indicated in his shift from the notion of the "apparatus" to "equipment." This is not an accident, nor is it a question of mere semantics.

The phrase "collective equipment," which, remember, Guattari built into the very title of his manuscript, refers back to a recorded and published conversation he had with Deleuze and Foucault in the early 1970s. This debate—in which François Fourquet also participated—offers ample evidence of their attempt to give more precision and substance to generalities that plagued the theory of ideological apparatuses prevalent on the left at that time. The case in point is the discussion "Equipment of Power: Towns, Territories and Collective Equipment," published in 1973 in the special issue of the journal *Recherches*, "The Genealogy of Capital." The phrase "collective equipment" comes from the language of the French state bureaucracy, which used it to designate elements of public infrastructure such as highways and telephone companies and services such as education and law enforcement. Foucault takes the example of roadways to demonstrate the ways in which this kind of public property serves private capital. According to him, the key characteristics of collective equipment are the production of the means of production (roads provide access to mines and factories), the production of demand (access to markets), and the mutual adjustment of one to enhance the other ([1973] 1989:106). As he points out, the forms of collective equipment are instances in which the state becomes visible: they are the "elements" of its "crystallization" (106). Guattari's contribution to this conversation was to assert that "collective equipments, as such, are the social unconscious. There is no other kind. They all work on structures of representation. The collective equipment is only apprehended in the universe of representation" (109). It seems that here he is still in step with Althusser, if we take into consideration the deep ties between ideology and representation. But it is among the mechanisms of representation where he "part ways" with Althusser. Concepts such as RSA and ISA are not sufficient to capture the complex functioning of collective equipment; the concept of the *dispositif* is. This apparatus-form positions ideology between an individual's desire and the "crystallizations" of the state that Foucault brings up in conversation with Deleuze, Fourquet, and Guattari.

As we have seen, during the 1980s, on several occasions Deleuze returned to Foucault's work on the *dispositif* and used it to analyze the most recent permutation of capitalism. In "Postscript on the Societies of Control," he wrote that each "type of society" corresponds to the "type of machines" it produces and utilizes. So the old sovereign societies worked with simple pulleys and levers, and disciplinary societies devised energy-intensive machines. Consequently, while "nineteenth century capitalism is a capitalism of concentration" epitomized in the "factory as the space of enclosure," the computer is a new kind of machine typical for the societies of control ([1990] 1992:6). This machine positioned at the center of "a capitalism of higher order production" is no longer promoting concentration, but dispersion: "What it wants to sell is services and what it wants to buy is stocks. This is no longer a capitalism for production but for the product, which is to say, for being sold and marketed" (6). Therefore, "The family, the school, the army, the factory are no longer distinct analogical spaces that converge toward an owner—state or private power—but coded figures—deformable and transformable—of a single corporation that now has only stockholders" (6). Significantly, he adds that even art has left its "spaces of enclosure" to join this endlessly pliable space of dispersal. This looks very much like an anticipation of the form of capitalism that rose to prominence in the first decades of the new millennium.

However, surveillance capitalism corrected Deleuze on several points. First, it showed that capital's dispersive power is far greater than he anticipated: it targets not only family as an abstract social unit comparable to factory or school, but each individual personally, and this personalization extends from there to all those transformable codes, including art. Second, while characterized by monopolistic practices, surveillance capitalism is not driven by a single corporation but by a number of corporations that share a single logic based on the production and extraction of behavioral surplus. Finally, while benefiting from deregulation and flaunting the ideal of a "small state," the technologies that made surveillance capitalism possible—from the internet to GPS and beyond—were, as the economist Mariana Mazzucato shows (2015), made possible by that very state and its agencies. Surveillance capitalism does not do away with the state but harnesses it for its own purposes. I wrote this book during the time and in the society that saw a massive attack on the state by private interests. It is not just the Silicon Valley, California, and the United States that are going that way. Western liberal democracies are following suit. France today is not what it was when Guattari and Deleuze were writing about collective equipment, control societies, et cetera. The tactic of big business is clear: it is no longer partnering with the state, but taking control of state functions and with it, of great swaths of the society. The Aristotelian idea of *horror vacui* applies as much to society as to nature. Neither one tolerates vacuum: as soon a state institution withdraws and lets go of one of its functions, big business moves in and takes possession of the evacuated social space. The difference is that in a politically regulated space, individuals have at least some, however minimal, impact on the decision-making process. In corporations, they have none. The delusion of consumer power has carried over from industrial to surveillance capitalism, and many still believe that their purchase choices can make an impact on the business entities they engage with. As Serra spelled out on TV screens long time ago, in that economy they are the commodities, not consumers. Their power is exactly zero. Try living without internet access in the United States, and you will find out how powerful you are.

The alignment between the mode of production and the state is ideological. The very idea, which Guattari first put forward also in the 1980s, that subjectivity is the main product of this output, suggests that ISAs are back, if they were ever really gone. If the ideological production of nonknowledge during the Cold War took place under the shadow of the threat of nuclear disaster, this time around it is submerged in the processes labeled the Anthropocene. In their brisk critique of Bruno Latour's paradigm of the last (or the latest) geological formation, Éric Alliez and Maurizio Lazzarato invoke a familiar idea when they ask if "the Anthropocene" might be "the name of something other than the revelation of the 'geological force' of 'humanity,'" and asking if it might be "a possible definition of the 'false consciousness' of capitalist being, to which the *depoliticized* 'nature' of the Modernity of the Great Bifurcation (Nature/Culture, Subject/Object, etc.) should be referred?" (2016:348). Their answer is that the Anthropocene is a Capitalocene. The task, then, is not to repoliticize "nature" but to recognize that it has never been apolitical. The ideological operation of that depoliticization is on display in Foucault's analysis of security societies in their formative stage.

In the third lecture of *Security, Territory, Population* (1977–78) Foucault outlines that stage by elaborating on differences between apparatuses of discipline and security. They come across most clearly in their responses to a crisis, specifically to a smallpox epidemic. On the one hand, disciplinary mechanisms deploy the techniques of individualization and segregation: they treat the sick and keep them apart from the healthy. On the other hand, security apparatuses take the population as a whole and calculate the probability of morbidity and mortality.[1] Foucault effectively sums up the opposition between the two by saying that whereas discipline establishes norms (limitations of actions, circulation, etc.), security normalizes ([2004] 2007:62). Setting up of norms, or norming, necessarily calls for training, that is, the active shaping of behaviors into performances. The operation of normalization, on the other hand, "consists in establishing an interplay between those different distributions of normality" (63). What does that mean? If disciplines prohibit and mandate, then "the mechanisms of security" are connected to what Foucault, following eighteenth-century Physiocrats, calls "physical processes, which could be called natural processes, and which we could also call elements of reality" (63). Instead of the elimination of certain phenomena (contagion, crime, etc.), security mechanisms take the route of a "progressive self-cancelation of the phenomena by the phenomena themselves. In a way, they involve the delimitation of phenomena within acceptable limits, rather than the imposition of a law that says no to them" (66). But what happens when the delimitation exceeds all manageable limits? And what happens when *natural processes* become literally so: when nature begins the process of self-cancellation?

With all of their positivity and generality, security mechanisms appear utterly incapable of addressing this kind of crisis. The obstacle to their operations is not contained in the phenomena they are addressing, but in the very mechanisms that generated both disciplinary *appareils* and *dispositifs* of security. Gaston Bachelard spoke of epistemological obstacles to the production of scientific knowledge at the beginning of the nineteenth century. Now, as these obstacles penetrate much deeper through all segments of society, down to every individual, they become a great deal more unyielding, they last much longer, and they are engaged in the production of non-knowledge. In short, they show themselves to be thoroughly ideological. Althusser claimed that he had borrowed the idea of "epistemological break" from Bachelard when he used it to introduce his thesis about the scientific status of historical materialism (1969:168). His subsequent retraction of this position as "theoreticist" has somewhat obscured his claim about the Marxist critique of capitalism as an epistemological break. Now, decades after the demise of real socialism, which took the air out of debates about its possible historical and geographical trajectories in the future, it seems that "epistemological break" is acquiring a new meaning. The multiscalar problem that humanity is facing now—comprising ecological disaster, the question of the sustainability of a capitalist mode of production, the depletion of energy sources, environmental justice, colossal wealth and income inequalities, the rise of artificial intelligence, and many other crises—is not an apocalypse, but a deep epistemological break. Here it is important to remember Althusser's distinction between "essential section" (*coupe*) and "break" (*coupure*) in his analysis of historical time in *Reading Capital*. His coauthor of this book, Étienne Balibar, explains that in the "essential section" Althusser found "the possibility of 'reading' in the immediate of a *present* (or of an instant) the whole system of determinations of a historical phenomenon by the means of the social totality" (Balibar 1978:219). In other words, the climate crisis is not a sudden break, an abyss of an approaching catastrophe, but a fissure that capitalism introduced from the moment it entered the world-historical stage.

The return of the critique of ideology and its apparatuses is fueled by this conflict between capitalism as the mode of production and the carrying capacity of the planet it conquered. If ideology has been displaced by other concepts (power-knowledge, habitus, etc.) and its apparatuses dismissed, they became indispensable in current reckonings with the Capitalocene. I will offer a few random examples. We can start with the author of this unelegant term, Jason W. Moore, who clearly lays out an argument for the very idea of the Anthropocene as profoundly ideological. This ideological formation conceals, as they often do, the operations of an apparatus that has reached a planetary scale. Namely, according to Moore, the irresistible rise and spread of capitalism was fueled not only by its encounter with an innate and virgin "nature," but by its production of Nature as cheap and available in strictly capitalist terms: "Capitalism must commodify life/work but depends on the 'free ride' of uncommodified life/work to do so" (2015:192). Capitalism does not thrive on production of value, but on devaluation: only through its devaluation can behavior become a "natural" resource. The second example comes from insights based on the onus placed on human behavior in attempts to engage climate change. It permeates a vast majority eco- and climate change art produced in the past decade, and the art historian T. J. Demos summarizes the dilemma that this art presents as the choice either to "modify the world" or to "modify behavior" (2017:26). I will conclude with the call for the deployment of ideological apparatuses in efforts to slow down and even reverse the course of the climate change. Even in its heyday in the 1970s, the Althusserian concept of ideology did not reach a broader audience than it did in 2020 via Kim Stanley Robinson's instant cli-fi classic *The Ministry for the Future*. One of the early brief chapters in the fragmentary configuration of this immense novel features a familiar, yet uncredited, definition of ideology as "an imaginary relationship to a real situation" (2020:40). Robinson's contribution to the Althusserian legacy is to give ideology a non-pejorative meaning. If science, like philosophy or religion, is an ideological form, then, he suggests, its task is "to invent, improve, and put to use an ideology that explains in a coherent and useful way as much of the blooming buzzing inrush of the world as possible. What one would hope for in an ideology is clarity and explanatory breadth, and power" (40). Then he adds, to conclude this single page-long chapter, an acknowledgment of the status of his book as an ideological apparatus: "We leave the proof of this as an exercise to the reader."

If Althusser's question of *thinking the epistemological break* has been redefined as the supreme problem of *entering that break*, the performance apparatus appears better prepared for that venture than any security *dispositif*. That temporary fissure, that non-place of insecurity, is where impossible collectivities and unextractable behaviors are at home. This is not to say that early performance art invented these as activist strategies that can be used formulaically to address the mechanisms that are forcing the nature down the path of self-cancellation. Rather, they demonstrate that impossible collectivities and unextractable behaviors are co-constitutive with the cracks that open the paths for creation of strategies of performance-making that can respond effectively to apparatuses of the Capitalocene. It is my hope that *The Performance Apparatus* can aid the important work of making political performances capable of addressing the break that the world has already entered.

Notes

PREFACE

1. Another quite telling irony was that Bell's story about Tailhade and the waning of ideological violence was published at the very beginning of the decade marked by ideologically driven political violence without precedent in recent US history. That irony starts with McCarthyism and the "red scare" that was reaching its crest when he was publishing the articles featured in his book, and it came full circle with the publication of its follow-up, *The End of Ideology Debate* (1968), the volume edited by Chaim Waxman, which sported a dedication to the recently assassinated Martin Luther King Jr. and an eerie reference to Senator Robert F. Kennedy, who would soon suffer the same fate as Dr. King.

2. Elsaesser's phrase reads: "Cinema has many histories, only some of which belong to the movies" (2014:17).

3. Eva Cockroft (1974) published one of the earliest disclosures about CCF's funding sources. For a fuller exposé on this subject, see Saunders 1999 and 2000 (the same book was published under two different titles). More recently, Berlin's Haus der Kulturen der Welt hosted the exhibit *Parapolitics: Cultural Freedom and the Cold War*. This project was documented in an excellent catalog/book edited by Anselm Franke, Nida Ghouse, Paz Guevara, and Antonia Majaca (2021).

CHAPTER 1

1. See, for example, Felman [1983] 2003; Johnson 1977; and Sedgwick 2003.

2. For an inspired discussion of Austin's use of "etiolations," see Joy Brooke Fairfield's unpublished dissertation (2016).

3. She went on repeating her dubious argument about the "esthetics of performativity" in books and articles that followed *The Transformative Power of Performance* (Fischer-Lichte [2004] 2008). The further she went, the more hyperbolic her assertions became. In "Culture as Performance," an article in which she presented the activities of her Kulturen des Performativen research group, she went as far as claiming that "our research on performance and performativity can be regarded as a 'new' Enlightenment" (2009:10).

4. While Marx and Engels appear as signatories of this manuscript, Marx was recognized as its primary author.

5. Ricoeur holds that Althusser replaces Marx's idea of "reality" with "science" (1986:chs. 7–9).

6. Unless otherwise noted, all translations from French are by Jasminka Jakovljević and the author.

7. For more on Foucault's *dispositif,* see Chapter 6, "Strategy without a Subject."

8. He marks the second meaning by writing the first letter in uppercase: "Theory (with a capital T)" is a "general theory, that is, the Theory of practice in general" that produces "scientific truths." For example, "This Theory is the materialist *dialectic* which is none other than dialectical materialism" (Althusser 1969:168).

9. The French phrase *qui est à l'appareil,* meaning "who is there" or "who is speaking," fits perfectly this situation. While it is implied in Althusser's essay, he does not use this exact phrase.

10. Pathologization of certain uncategorizable behaviors is a standard way of forcing them into RSA or ISAs: carceral, medical, etc.

11. In the second half of the 1960s, Althusser's notion of theoretical practice attracted much more attention than his comments on ideology. The impact of this idea is evidenced in broad range of philosophical and political engagements, from the small journal *Theoretical Practice* (1971–73) published by a group of British radical political theorists to Jacques Derrida's 1976–77 seminars at École normale supérieure, published as *Theory and Practice.*

12. Walter Benjamin, Brecht's friend and interlocutor, developed his distinct idea of the apparatus later in the decade. In his detailed discussion of Benjamin's idea of the apparatus as one of the key elements of his inquiry into the historicity of perception, Antonio Somaini suggests that his use of "the term *Apparat* to indicate both the *sensory* and the *technical* apparatuses involved in different technically mediated experience . . . seems to indicate a certain predisposition by the human sensory organs, to the encounter with technology" (2016:11). For an insightful discussion of theatrical performance in Benjamin and Althusser, see Butler 2015.

13. As Bojana Cvejić observed in her own excellent discussion of dance and "theatrical apparatuses of representation," this could be seen as yet another of the "proverbial attempts of philosophy to usurp dance [or, in this case, theater] as a philosophical problem while ignoring the problems that dance poses itself" (2015:3).

14. In February 1956, only months before he died, Brecht went to Milan to see Strehler's production of his *Threepenny Opera,* which he described as "brilliant" (in Fuegi 1994:588). On Brecht's last days and his visit to Milan, see also Jakovljević et al. 2018:101.

15. Consider, for example Barthes's texts "Diderot, Brecht, Eisenstein"

([1973]) and "Mother Courage Blind" ([1955] 1972), and "Un réalisme épique" ([1959] 1967) and other essays by Bernard Dort.

16. Although Althusser never specifically commented on Brecht's early play *A Man's a Man* (1926), it seems inscribed all over the French philosopher's little theoretical theater. At the center of Brecht's play is Galy Gay, a common man, an everyman. Early on, he is described as "a man who can't say no," which brings to mind Althusser's subject who responds to the policeman's call nine out of ten times (Brecht 1977:11). In one of his ecstatic monologues, Gay offers a startling vision of the drama of interpellation as a farce: "But who am I? You see, I've forgotten. Last night when it was raining, I still knew. It did rain last night, didn't it? I beg you, when you look over here or in the direction this voice is coming from, please believe it's me. Speak to that point in space, call it Galy Gay, or something else, have pity, give me a piece of meat. Where it goes in, that's Galy Gay, and also where it comes out" (Brecht 1977:50). In the conclusion of the succeeding scene, Brecht offers quite an Althusserian summation of this reduction of the subject: "One man is no man. Until somebody calls out to him" (58).

17. Recently, film studies has seen a reinvigoration of interest in apparatus theory. See, for example, Elsaesser 2011.

18. The title of his article in the original is "Cinéma: Effets idéologiques produits par l'appareil de base" (Baudry 1970).

19. Baudry 1975. Translated into English as "The Apparatus" (Baudry 1976).

20. It was subsequently included in the book *Théorie d'ensemble* (1968), edited by Michel Foucault and including the essays by himself, Julia Kristeva, Philippe Sollers, Roland Barthes, Jacques Derrida, and others.

21. Major contributions to the theory of cinematic apparatus have been published in English in Rosen 1986; Cha 1980; and Lauretis and Heath 1980, which I discuss below. For a survey of the role of apparatus theory in cinema studies, see Allen 1995. Individual articles on the subject of cinematic apparatus are too numerable to be cited here. While interactions between cinematic apparatus theory and theater and performance studies would be interesting and could yield some revealing insights, that is not the main objective of this book.

22. The book consists of a proceedings from the conference "The Cinematic Apparatus," held in February 1978 at the University of Wisconsin–Milwaukee.

23. Phelan offers a pointed critique of the material aspects of the apparatus in *Mourning Sex: Performing Public Memories* (1997). Contributions of *Mourning Sex* have been largely overshadowed by the landmark essay "Ontology of Performance: Representation without Reproduction" from her previous book (1993). The field would benefit from a reconsideration of *Mourning Sex* from the apparatus theory perspective, among others. *The Performance Apparatus* does not continue her strain of psychoanalytic analysis of the apparatus but complements it from the perspective of the critique of ideology and its dispositifs.

24. Blau continued the exploration he initiated in this essay in *To All Appear-*

ances: Ideology and Performance (1992). Here Blau's discussions of Althusser are mostly limited to his book *For Marx*, while he curiously avoids any engagement with Althusser's idea of the apparatus.

25. The editors of Benjamin's *Selected Writings* explain that in this sentence from the second draft of "The Work of Art in the Age of Its Reproducibility," he alludes to "*Heinrich von Ofterdingen*, an unfinished novel by Novalis first published in 1802. Von Ofterdingen is a medieval poet in search of the mysterious Blue Flower, which bears the face of his 'unknown beloved'" (2002:130).

26. For excellent reproductions of Damiani's set drawings, see Morbio 2018.

27. Todosijević also adds that "these differences between a performance artist and a performing artist are" not only "of technical and stylistic," but also of "ideological nature" (1983:60). My translation from Serbian.

28. Gustave Flaubert captures this idea in his quip that "the artist in his work must be like God in creation, invisible and all-powerful; you can sense him everywhere, but you cannot see him" ([1857] 1997:247–248). Jacques Derrida's critique of "theological stage" in "The Theater of Cruelty and the Closure of Representation" is relevant here (1978:235).

29. OED Online, March 2022, https://www-oed-com.stanford.idm.oclc.org/view/Entry/17197?redirectedFrom=behaviour (accessed 15 March 2022).

CHAPTER 2

1. Similarly to those twenty-first-century people in Nottingham, "The Super Girls" had a rate of success 50 percent higher than male teams (44).

2. One of Pask's inventions in the 1950s was the Musicolor machine, which predated light shows used in entertainment venues. In the following decade, he wrote a proposal for a cybernetic theater and collaborated with the theater director Joan Littlewood and architect Cedric Price on their project for the Fun Palace in London, which was never completed.

3. This was a different apparatus, much closer to Michel Foucault's *dispositif* than Althusser's *appareil*. For more on Foucault's idea of *dispositif*, see Chapter 6, "Strategy without a Subject."

4. The diagram has been reproduced in Munder 2019:109.

5. The same year, Willats produced another diagram, *The Twin Towers*, featuring two structures identical to one in the first diagram, described as "Towers of ideological consciousness" (in Casser and Ziegler 2010:151).

6. Reproduced in Casser and Ziegler 2010:148–149. Willats's *Homeostat Drawing* is also available at http://stephenwillats.com/work/homeostat-drawing/

7. I had access to a Serbian translation of Barilli's article "Comportamento" published in the journal *Ideje* in 1979.

8. For more on the exhibit *Opera o comportamento*, see Barilli [1972] 2017. On the other side of the Adriatic, the art critic Ješa Denegri throughout the 1970s called attention to artists' behavior as an integral part of their work. For example, in a text for the New Art Practices exhibit in 1978, he wrote that what a

number of artists "had in common" was "a continuous change of behavior and action aimed at creating as much room for free manoeuvre as possible" ([1978] 2024:326). This is just one of his many references to the centrality of artists' behavior in reorientation of the arts in the 1970s.

9. For more on the formation of performance studies, see McKenzie 2001; Jackson 2004; and Harding and Rosenthal 2011.

10. The rationale for this integration of performance arts with the social sciences may have been not only scholarly but also economic. If the revolution in sciences and technology that took place during and after the Second World War was bankrolled by the federal government, the research in social sciences was supported by private institutions. In her excellently researched book about the university where I work, Rebecca Lowen discloses that "in the first fifteen years after World War II, private foundations provided substantial support for social science research, particularly research of a behavioral and scientistic bent. The end of the 1940s marks not the end of foundation support for the social sciences but rather the beginning of the Ford Foundation's massive program of patronage of the social sciences and, particularly, of the behavioral science" (1997:194). The Center for Advanced Study in the Behavioral Sciences at Stanford University, which I referenced in the preface to this book, was established in 1953 with generous help from the Ford Foundation (201). Humanities, and especially the arts, were left out of this bonanza, and Schechner was very much aware of it. In 1965, he published the article "Ford, Rockefeller, and Theater," a detailed analysis of subventions for theater from private foundations, in which he observes: "It is ironic that campuses have fostered several scientific revolutions while remaining stubborn tories in the arts" ([1965] 1969:31).

11. It was first published in Schechner 1974.

12. Stephen Bottoms (2003) recognizes the efficacy-entertainment dualism in gender politics of Schechner's publications from the early and mid-1960s, arguing that it informed ideological differences between traditional theater studies and the new discipline of performance studies.

13. This article was based on a talk that Schechner gave at the Wenner-Gren Symposium on Cultural Frames and Reflections in Stockholm, Sweden, in 1977. It was originally published in Schechner 1981.

14. That goes back to Max Reinhardt's festival performances and the emergence of film. In his book *The Democratic Surround: Multimedia & American Liberalism from World War II to the Psychedelic Sixties* (2013), Fred Turner provides important cultural context to theatrical environmentalism. For a razor-sharp dissection of participatory theater of the 1980s, see Fuchs 1996; and for a multifaceted account of immersive theater early in the twenty-first century, see Frieze 2016.

15. Serra's short video piece is, of course, available on YouTube (Serra 1973).

16. The statement issued on 31 May 2023 reads, in full: "Mitigating the risk of extinction from A.I. should be a global priority alongside other societal-scale risks, such as pandemics and nuclear war." This sentence is widely available on the internet, and it defies, like AI itself, citational practices commonly used in humanistic scholarship.

CHAPTER 3

1. Reed picks up this phrase from Amiri and Amina Baraka's *The Music: Reflections on Jazz and Blues* (2021:105). In his book, Reed offers insightful readings of Baraka's "phonographic poetry" from the 1960s and 1980s–1990s, which leaves his work on funk in the 1970s as a curious lacuna. Reed dedicates a paragraph to Baraka's work with the Advanced Workers on pp. 126–127.

2. Joe "Jio" Williams, telephone interview by the author, 15 August 2020; Joe Caposella, telephone interview by the author, 15 August 2020. Joe Caposella was Williams's friend who occasionally stepped in as the manager of Nbuda. On the record and on the Jazztage website he is listed as a vocalist. That was, as he explained, because the festival would not cover the costs for managers of visiting groups. As a testimony to the quality of the Advanced Workers / Nbuda, he cites the anecdote of Herbie Hancock's praise for the band during their rehearsal before the concert at the festival.

3. *Amiri Baraka & The Advance Workers*. The record is available on YouTube.

4. In her seminal *Liner Notes for the Revolution: The Intellectual Life of Black Feminist Sound*, Daphne Brooks calls for recognition of a Black feminist voices "distinct from the Black male radical tradition of writers like Douglass, Dunbar, Du Bois, and Johnson" (2021:89).

5. James R. Martel offers a valuable reading of this scene in Althusser and Fanon in *The Misinterpellated Subject* (2017).

6. Baraka refers to the doctrine of Kawaida that Maulana Karenga developed in the 1960s, which had at its center an elaborate behavioral apparatus that consisted of attitudes, regimens, and rituals. Simanga writes that the members of the organization were "disciplined, rising early in the morning, and expected to begin working by 7:00 am and work a 12-hour day [. . . They] were polite and serious, and they were in good shape from physical training and a lean diet devoid of meat but containing fruits, vegetables, and fish. They didn't drink, use drugs, or smoke" (2019:55). And further, "As a quasi-religious philosophy, the Doctrine of Kawaida also had various rituals to accompany its message. There was a wedding ceremony and a burial ceremony as well as process for naming children and other rituals" (56). Karenga developed a distinct personality cult, which Baraka took over for a period after he split from him in 1972. "An example of this," writes Simanga, "was the elevation of Baraka's birthday, October 7, as an organizational spiritual holiday" (86). When two years later he rejected Pan-Africanism, that entailed much more than a dietary change.

7. See his scathing report "Some Questions about the Sixth Pan-African Congress," also published in the pivotal year 1974.

8. While generally critical of Baraka, Jerry Gafio Watts is pointedly derisive about his poem collections from this period, *Hard Facts* (1972) and *Poetry for the Advanced* (1979). See Watts 2001.

9. I am quoting from the version of "Projective Verse" that LeRoi Jones/ Amiri Baraka's Totem Press published in 1959 as a stand-alone pamphlet.

10. After the February revolution, "Bolshevik" was appended to the name of the party: first, it was Russian Social Democratic Labor Party (Bolsheviks), and starting from March 1918, Russian Communist Party (Bolsheviks).

11. For an excellent discussion of Baraka's work on building Black cultural institutions in Harlem, see Elam 1997.

12. He continues: "Our sincerity was our ideology, a gestalt of our experience, an eclectic mixture of what we thought we knew and understood. What we wanted. Who we thought we were. It was messy" (Baraka 1984:318). Baraka was not the only leading figure of Black Arts Movement who recognized this need for ideology. Barbara Ann Teer, the founder of Black National Theater, also spoke about the movement's need for "a code of ethics. A value System. An ideology! Without a strong foundation, the house crumbles" (1971:58). Whereas this search for ideology led Baraka to the radical Left, Teer took the spiritual route: "Another reason we need an ideology, is that art must flow from an ideology. We are African people. And Africans are spirit people. So we must have an ideology that will help us develop a spirit culture" (in Russell 1971:58). This ideological vacuum was observed on a broader postcolonial landscape. As Adam Shatz reports in *The Rebel's Clinic: The Revolutionary Lives of Franz Fanon,* during his journey across newly liberated sub-Saharan states, Fanon noted in his diary that "the greatest obstacle to African independence was not 'colonialism and its derivatives' so much as the 'absence of ideology'" (2024:287).

13. Michael Corris, email to the author, 30 July 2020.

14. It seems that Baraka spoke to that effect at the Afro-Latin Cultural Festival held at SUNY Binghampton in late April 1975. Also speaking at this event, Cedric J. Robinson offered a polite but firm refutation of Baraka's position. See "The First Attack Is the Attack on Culture" (2019:69–74). A few years later, in *Black Marxism,* he wrote in regard to W. E. B. Du Bois's thesis about the crucial contribution of the formerly enslaved Black workers to the Civil War and the abolition of slavery: "The revolution had *caused* the formation of revolutionary consciousness and had not been caused by it. The revolution was spontaneous" (2000:238). And he applauded the assertion that C. L. R. James made in *Notes on Dialectics*: "*There is nothing more to organize*. . . . Organization as we know it is at an end. The task is to abolish organization. The task today is to call for, to teach, to illustrate, to develop spontaneity—the free creative activity of the proletariat" (283). *Black Marxism* can be read, in part, as an elaborate response to those radical Black movements that in the 1970s retreated to the positions of the orthodox party communism of Stalin and Mao.

15. Eshun's line reads: "In the mad science of the studio, mixadelics is science gone glad" (1998:146). Here the case in point is P-Funk and George Clinton's "Dr. Funkenstein."

CHAPTER 4

1. If not otherwise indicated, all translations from French are by Jasminka Jakovljević and the author.

2. This quotation comes from the new translation of *Hamburg Dramaturgy*, in which Wendy Arons and Sara Figal translate Lessing's *Zurüstungen* as "apparatus" (2019:253). In an earlier translation published by Dover, Helen Zimmern rendered this word as "artifice" (1962:200). Lessing uses *Zurüstungen* again a few lines later, which Zimmern translated as "display" and Arons and Figal again as "apparatus." In their translation, the letter also concludes with the invocation of "pomp and apparatus." In his third iteration of the "pomp and . . ." phrase, Lessing used the word *Verzierung*, which Zimmern translated as "decoration" (201). In their translation, Arons and Figal use the word "apparatus" in a sense that differs significantly from the range of meanings it has acquired in discussions of ideological state apparatuses.

3. See, for example, Young and Massey 1978 or, more recently, Ball 2020.

4. His other works include "Pensée vivante et perfection formelle" (his doctoral thesis, 1925), *L'abstraction sentimentale* (1925), *Avoir une âme* (1938), *L'ombre de Dieu* (1955), and the posthumously published *Vocabulaire d'esthéthique* (2004), one of his very few works that is still in print. *The Different Modes of Existence* and "Of the Mode of Existence of the Work to-Be-Made" are his only works that have been translated into English. They were published in a single volume long after they came out in French, together with a useful introduction by Bruno Latour and Isabelle Stangers.

5. That they have casually disregarded this book is suggested by its misdating both in their introduction (59) and the bibliography attached to it (90): in both of these instances, they provide 1959 as the date of its publication; actually, the "curious book" was published in 1950 and reissued in 1970.

6. While Souriau's theory of situations initially had some uptake in French and continental dramatic theory, it never evolved into a widely accepted method of dramaturgical analysis. In the 1960s, French scholar Paul Ginestier developed a theory of "dramatic geometry" reminiscent of Souriau's spatial vision of the dramatic situation; and in the early 1970s, Danish scholar Steen Jansen published an extensive essay on dramatic situations, drawing directly on Souriau's ideas. In Yugoslavia, a Serbian translation of *Les deux cent mille situations dramatiques* was published in 1982, and I first became familiar with this version during my undergraduate studies in dramaturgy at the drama schools in Skopje and Belgrade.

7. Unless otherwise indicated, all translations from Souriau's *Les deux cent mille situations dramatiques* are by Erik Butler and Kimberly Jannarone.

8. Using completely different sources, French anthropologist André Leroi-Gourhan performed a similar recovery of spatial and gestural symbolization as an alternative to the culture of the line ([1964] 1993).

9. Translated from French by Jasminka Jakovljević and the author.

10. *Réique* is Souriau's neologism made from the Latin *res* (thing).

11. In his influential book *Abstraction and Empathy* (1908), Wilhelm Worringer argued that abstraction was central to aesthetic experience of ancient Near Eastern cultures. He takes the art of ancient Egypt as his primary example of this primary abstraction.

CHAPTER 5

1. In French, *institutions* and *appareils*, respectively.

2. Paul Ricoeur offers a different interpretation of Althusser's terminological choices. He suggests that "apparatus" belongs to the same linguistic pool as "superstructure" and "infrastructure." "It is not by chance that Althusser's term is apparatus and not institution, because an apparatus is more mechanical. An apparatus is something which functions, and therefore it has a more conceptual kinship with structures and reproduction, with structural language in general. All these functions are anonymous and can exist and go on by themselves" (Ricoeur 1986:134).

3. Rancière's article was based on the course he taught at Université de Paris VIII/Vincennes in 1969, which exactly overlaps with the time Althusser was working on his ISA essay. It was first published in Argentina in 1970 and in France in 1973 in the journal *L'homme et la société*, and was included, a year later, in the book *La leçon d'Althusser*.

4. The thesis of his "Aesthetic of Administration" essay I quoted above is a rephrasing of his characterization of "the present moment" in *Art & Ideology*: "The access that artists have to the actual apparatus of ideological production is at very best that of a parasite who mimics and excels in the strategies of consciousness industry" (Buchloh 1984:6). In this catalog essay, Buchloh uses Althusser's discussion of ISAs as his main theoretical frame.

5. Buchloh's exclusion of both the British and New York sections of Art & Language may have been motivated by critiques that these groups leveled against *Artforum* and *October*, publications with which he was closely affiliated. The New York group questioned the former in *The Fox*; and as for the latter, see the article "On the Material Necessity that the Editors of *October*, its Contributors, Supporters and Relatives, and Particularly, the Arch Fool, the Illiterate Liar Jeremy G. Rolfe, be Sought Out, Their Hands Smashed, Their Eyes Put Out, Their Offices, Ateliers Destroyed, Burned and Portions of the Bloodstained Ashes Sent to the Towering Wretches of French Structuralism" published in *Art-Language* (1977a).

6. While Alberro and Stimson's inclusion of "On Practice" in their anthology does justice to Ramsden, it can't make up for the decades-long marginalization of ALNY. Recently, a new generation of art historians started revaluat-

ing, and to some extent destigmatizing, its legacy. See, for example, Bailey 2016 and Charnley 2016.

7. Michael Corris uses these phrases for ALUK ([1996] 1999:470, 471).

8. Ian Burn, Michael Corris, Preston Heller, Joseph Kosuth, Michael Krugman, Andrew Menard, and Mel Ramsden.

9. Michael Corris, email to the author, 12 December 2020.

10. Michael Corris, email to the author, 12 December 2020.

11. See the introduction by Michael Baldwin and Thomas Dreher to the ZKM internet presentation of *Blurting in Art & Language*: container.zkm.de/blurting/introduction.html. Gilbert qualifies "→" as "the strong connector" and "&" as the "weaker" one (2007:84).

12. For example, blurt 169, "Ideology," reads: "If the ideological milieu of a theory is in some way uniquely determined in that theory, then the use of that theory outside of its native domain can be a bit problematic." Taken as an entry point, this blurt offers the reader a number of further blurt options under the "→" and "&" operations. One of the seven blurts indicated by the → leads to blurt 282, "Problematic": "Louis Althusser uses problématique to mean a theoretical and ideological framework. That is, a word or concept cannot be considered in isolation; it only exists in the theoretical/ideological framework in which it is used: its problematic." As mentioned in the previous note, the Center for Art and Media in Karlsruhe, Germany, digitized the *Annotations*. They are available at http://container.zkm.de/blurting/annotations.html

13. While the members ALNY had known all along that Ramsden stood behind "Peter Benchley," the first public acknowledgment of the true identity of the author of the introduction came in Gilbert 2004. The identity of the "Dramatis Personae" stamper remains unknown.

14. Harrison: "The individualist basis of Kosuth's actions tended to undermine attempts to maintain some form of community on the basis of a critique of individualism" (1991:123); Corris: "Since his association with Art & Language in the late 1960s, Kosuth 'independent' practice had always been a contentious issue for many members of the group; but it was probably Kosuth's alleged opportunism with respect to *The Fox* that provided the straw that broke the camel's back" ([1996] 1999:478).

15. For an early draft of the AICU principles of unity, see Corris 1999:477. After *The Fox* folded, Carole Condé, Karl Beveridge, Jill Breakstone, Preston Heller, Andrew Menard, and Michael Corries started the journal *Red-Herring*, which had only two issues. It was succeeded by *Main Trend*.

16. J. Byrron is the artist Jerry Kearns's pseudonym. Here the reasons for pseudonymity are completely different than in "The Lumpen-Headache."

17. In her recognition that "the institution of art" is "internalized in and embodied in people" Fraser approaches the boundary that separates institutional critique and the critique of the apparatus ([2005] 2009:414). However, her "institution of critique" keeps very much alive the idea that artist as subject constitutes the unimpeachable kernel of art institutions.

18. *Who Comes after the Subject?*, an excellent volume edited by Eduardo Cadava, Peter Connor, and Jean-Luc Nancy (1991), offers a number of responses from different philosophical perspectives.

19. Rastko Močnik, a member of Ljubljana Lacanian group, opposes strongly the assumption of the passivity of the subject in Althusser's theory of interpellation. He anchors his argument in the process of double identification that he recognizes in the instance of interpellation: "At some point, the demand for meaning initiates an unconscious desire, which leads to the identification with 'the subject supposed to believe'; the process rebounds from that point and returns to the interpreter *as interpellation*. The interpreter whom we are addressing, the addressee, is, according to this schema, an *active participant* in the process of interpellation; his (individual, idiosyncratic, uniquely particular) unconscious desire is a decisive axis in the process of interpellation, and the demand for meaning is the starting impulse that simply thrusts the individual into the trap of interpellation" (2003:48). The author's translation from Serbian.

20. Certain instances of post-revolutionary art in Soviet Union evidenced this radical reimagining of the subject. Consider, for example, Daniil Kharms's birth narrative in Leonid Lipavskii's "Conversations:" "I was born from caviar. . . . I was in a state of unconsciousness. I only know that for a long time my parents avoided putting me in the corner because I used to adhere to the wall," etc. (2005:331). Although farcical in form, it evidences an intuition of the change of subjectivity necessitated by the revolution. The sequence that was initiated by the political revolution and was supposed to continue with social revolution experienced a hard stop with the revolution of subjectivity. The increased violence in the 1930s was designed to suppress the proliferation of new subjectivities as much, if not even more than, the opposing the old, "bourgeois," subjects, which was one of the main justifications of Stalinist terror. In the end, this and other twentieth-century revolutions left the bourgeois subject intact, while repositioning it within a different set of power relations.

CHAPTER 6

1. Occasional Papers published the script in 2014 as part of *Marginalia*, a display that accompanied *Plastic Words*, a series of talks and presentations exploring "the contested space between contemporary literature and art," which took place in Raven Row exhibition center in London from 13 December 2014 to 30 January 2015 (http://www.ravenrow.org/exhibition/plastic_words).

2. For a discussion and documentation of Antin's alternative personae, see Liebert 2013; for Hershman Leeson's Breitmore project, see Hershman 1978; and for Adrian Piper, see Bowles 2011.

3. During the ensuing decades, this artistic strategy was surveyed in several art exhibits. For useful information about artists who created alternative identities, see the catalogs for exhibitions *Persona*, curated by Lynn Gumpert

and Ned Rifkin (New Museum, New York, 1981), and *Altered Egos*, curated by Karen Moss (Santa Monica Museum of Art, 1994).

4. Carol Duncan included Bernstein's writings in her book *The Aesthetics of Power: Essays in Critical Art History* (1993), and O'Doherty collected Josephson's writings in *A Mental Masquerade: When Brian O'Doherty was a Female Art Critic* (2019).

5. Nor was he the last to sign his works with another person's name: In 2007, three Slovenian artists, Emil Hrvatin, Davide Grassi, and Žiga Kariž, legally changed their names into Janez Janša, which happened to be the name of the conservative prime minister of Slovenia at that time. While Thomas's strategy of ceding authorial signature amounts to a surrogation, the Janez Janša project can be seen as an act of usurpation. For more on this art project, see Lukan 2008.

6. The name of the internet domain of the company that caters to art investors masterworks.art/warhol indicates that Warhol's "business art" was no less successful than his "art art." On its website, Masterworks promotes itself as the company that represents "an exclusive community investing in blue-chip art" (masterworks.art, 2021).

7. This didn't work out as planned. After his premature death from AIDS in 1995, there were several attempts to present his works as a coherent oeuvre, even if it appeared under the names of different collectors. First, in 1999 Alexis Valliant published a compendium of texts *Sur un lieu commun et autres textes*, and the following year Corrine Disernes curated a survey exhibition *Metti la tua firma nella storia dell'arte* at Museu d'Art Contemporani de Barcelona, Spain. In 2021, Musée d'art moderne et contemporain in Geneva published *The Agency* (Bernard et al. 2021), which consists of extensive interviews Thomas did with Stéphane Wargnier. This book came out just in time for my work on revising this chapter, and it has been invaluable in that process.

8. While working on *Philippe Thomas Declines His Identity*, Thomas submitted a proposal to the New Museum in New York for a project that would involve setting up an art agency installed in the museum. One of the main points of this project would be to take the business aspects of this important element of the art industry, hitherto untouched by institutional critique, for what they really are: evidence that the art agency is a merchant not only of artworks, but of artists: "The notion of a subject, author, or artist [that] is nothing more than a position or role, may be subjected to the sole economic law of generalized exchange . . . in short, the veritable status of the artist then has become A COMMODITY" (in Lebovici 2018:18). The proposal was, as it were, declined and Thomas set up his agency readymades belong to everyone® (*les ready-made appartiennent à tout le monde*®) at the Cable Gallery, located at 611 Broadway in New York, from 3 December 1987 to 16 January 1988. He continued working on this project until the end of his life.

9. Antony Hudek, the English translator of the script, provides in a note

the French version of the epigraph, together with his explanation that because the author "specifies *'moderne ou moderniste'* as a translation of Benjamin Buchloh's 'modernist,'" he had decided to render *moderne* as "modern(ist) in order to capture the author's intended ambiguity" (in Bosser 2014:12).

10. Kosuth's comments on the Duchampian legacy of readymades is referenced in *Frage der Präsentation* (1999:24).

11. In 2011, when this issue of *Texte zur Kunst* was published, the findings of the sociologist Ulf Wuggenig suggested that the majority of high-end collectors in the West came from the banking and financial industry (2011:68). By the time of this writing, a decade later, digital capitalists such as Jeff Bezos were close to the top of *ARTnews'* annual list of "Top 200 Collectors." That certainly reflects the impact of surveillance capitalism on global soft power. However, some tendencies remained unchanged: from inside the list, Zhukova advanced to the cover of *ARTnews* that featured the top collectors in 2021.

12. Predictably, this work was perceived as scandalous in the art world and beyond. For a very useful discussion of this piece, see Susan E. Cahan's article "Regarding Andrea Fraser's *Untitled*" (2006:7–15).

13. More recently, pursuing this avenue of research, Fraser produced an impressive 943-page report: *2016 in Museums, Money, and Politics* (2018).

14. Benjamin's attention to ideological dimensions of institutions of (art) history and collecting antedates Althusser's critique of ideology. I couldn't find any reference in Althusser's writings to this text by Benjamin, or to him in general. For an illuminating reading of Althusser and Benjamin, see Butler 2015.

15. Translation from French by Jasminka Jakovljević and the author

16. Thomas is in general agreement with his interviewer, who uses his two projects, *Fictionalism* and the agency readymades belong to everyone®, as identifiers of two distinct parts of his artistic career: the first one falls in the 1980s (and has been also referred to as *Art of the Society*), and the second in the 1990s (2021:45).

17. In the modern bourgeois state, there is no "real" that has not been appropriated and transformed into property. Moly Nesbit explains that when France passed its first copyright law in 1793, it did not "designate a particular profession, like poet" or painter, but only distinguished "a particular kind of labor from another, the cultural from industrial" (1987:234). And what distinguished the former from the latter was that it "reflected" the personality of the author. So paintings, yes, but technical drawings of advertising posters, no.

18. This issue was guest-edited by Brian O'Doherty.

19. This interview was conducted by Alain Grosrichard, Gérard Wajeman, Jacques-Alain Miller, Guy Le Gaufey, Dominique Celas, Gérard Miller, Catherine Millot, Jocelyne Livi, and Judith Miller.

20. https://www.worldcat.org/title/recent-writings/oclc/881316698&referer=brief_results (accessed 20 December 2021).

CHAPTER 7

1. For an excellent and detailed discussion of *La Mamelle,* see Tacata unpublished dissertation (2015). I am grateful to Clive Robertson for clarifying for me details about his performance.

2. Beuys explained his choice for facial covering in this action in the following way: "Gold and honey indicate a transformation of the head, and therefore, naturally and logically, the brain and our understanding of thought, consciousness and all the other levels necessary to explain pictures to a hare" (in Tisdall 1979:105).

3. Over the next few years, Robertson realized two more projects in which he returned to Beuys: the photo-performance *Fetish T-Shirt Pedagogy Special Issue,* published in the art magazine *FILE* (1977); and the tele-performance *Explaining Pictures to Dead Air* on 8 September 1978 at the Concert Hall in Toronto.

4. In the book *Museums by Artists,* Bronson explains that "image bank" was a project on which artists Michael Morris, Vincent Trasov, and Gary Lee-Nova collaborated from 1970 until 1975 (Bronson 1983).

5. In addition to Beuys's piece, the show included Bruce Nauman's *Body Pressure* (1974), Vito Acconci's *Seedbed* (1972), Valie Export's *Action Pants: Genital Panic* (1969), Gina Pane's *The Conditioning, First Action of Self-Portrait(s)* (1973), and Abramović's own *Lips of Thomas* (1975), as well as her new performance created specifically for this occasion, *Entering the Other Side* (2005).

6. On 1 May Abramović had the table removed, so that for the final month of the exhibit there was no object separating her from the person sitting across from her.

7. For an informative account of the dynamics that developed in the line, see Fisher 2012.

8. Online consent forms have been the subject of extensive debate among legal scholars, activists, and lawmakers. Big tech has been trying to avoid and circumscribe consumers' consent as much as legally possible. Zuboff writes that legal wrangling over online consent forms reached a dead end when in March 2017, "a newly elected Republican Congress voted in favor of a resolution to overturn the broadband privacy regulations over which the FCC [Federal Communications Commission] had struggled just months earlier. The rules had required cable and phone companies to obtain meaningful consent before using personal information for ads and profiling. The companies understood, and they persuaded Republican senators, that the principle of *consent* would strike a serious blow to the foundational mechanisms of the new capitalism: the legitimacy of unilateral surplus dispossession, ownership rights to surplus, decision rights over surplus, and the right to lawless space for the prose-

cution of these activities. To this end the resolution also prevented the FCC from seeking to establish similar protections in the future" (2019:172).

9. Foucault's lectures were first published in 2004, some fifteen years after Deleuze's articles on *dispositif* and the societies of control, and almost a decade after his death.

10. The compendium *Workscoreport* contains several examples of "identity transfer," including a document that details the authors' understanding of this method. This document, which includes a very useful diagram of the range of phenomena covered by "identity transfer," seems to have been first published in the journal *Contact* on 18 April 1973. See Robertson and Woodrow 1975.

11. At the time of this writing, Cassils lived and worked in Los Angeles. They subsequently relocated to New York, and then back to Toronto.

12. In the late 1990s, Antin confirmed to the art historian Lisa E. Bloom that she used Clark's book in preparation for this piece (Bloom 1999:168, 189 n. 24).

13. *Anarchitecture* was the name of collaborative exhibition held in March 1974 at 112 Greene Street in New York. Over the year leading up to the exhibition, a group of artists held regular meetings. The members of this loosely organized group were Laurie Anderson, Tina Girouard, Suzanne Harris, Jene Highstein, Bernard Kirschenbaum, Richard Landry, Gordon Matta-Clark, and Richard Nonas. For more on the Anarchitecture exhibition and group, see Brentano and Savitt 1981.

14. In November 2023, Cassils underwent a gender-affirming top surgery. As they explained to me in an email, "I am tired of being mis gendered constantly. You know that my general opinion has been that society is the problem, not my body. . . . But it takes a toll to be constantly mis gendered your whole life. . . . I have to say it has made in my life more comfortable" (16 February 2024).

15. This semi-mythical status that *Five Car Stud* occupied for decades in the art world and beyond is evidenced in Jean-François Lyotard's short book *Pacific Wall* about his years at UC San Diego: "Then there's the Kienholz story, told me by a girl studying at UCSD when I was there an Associate Prof. Her mother told it to her, a Mrs. Greenstone, a New York widow who'd just visited the Documenta 5 exhibition at Kassel in Germany. . . . Ms. Greenstone recounted how her mother was struck with Kienholz's refusal to show his piece in a hall, instead getting organizers to set up a huge tent in an area away from the Fridericianum, where the Documenta was housed." Lyotard then adds in a note that he checked on this information, and it turned out to be incorrect. He adds: "The only explanation for this error seems to be a choice made by the Greenstones or one made by the narrator or else one made by both" (Lyotard [1979] 1990:11).

16. See the essays by Roberto Ohrt and Thomas McEvilley in Holm 2011.

17. For more on eighteenth-century school of Ideologists (Idéologues) and its founder, Antoine Destutt de Tracy, see Kennedy 1978.

18. In his attempt to update Foucault's and Deleuze's theory of the appara-

tus, Agamben confuses it with machines of everyday use, from axes to cellular phones. Lazzarato makes a similar mistake (2014:91–94).

19. See the cover page of this book.

POSTSCRIPT

1. We have seen these two mechanisms at work in different approaches to Covid-19 pandemic by different governments, where China and Sweden represented the polar opposites of disciplinary and security regimes; the others deployed different combinations of these apparatuses.

Bibliography

Abramović, Marina. 2007. *7 Easy Pieces*. Milan: Edizioni Charta.

Abramović, Marina and Iwona Blaswick. 2011. "The Artist Is Present." *Art Monthly*, no. 349: 1–8.

Abramović, Marina and Amelia Jones. 2012. "The Live Artist as Archaeologist." In *Perform Repeat Record: Live Art in History*, edited by Amelia Jones and Adrian Heathfield, 543–566. Bristol: Intellect.

Advanced Workers, The. 1977. "Amiri Baraka and the Advance Workers Berlin Jazztage 2. Konzert. Berlin, Germany." https://www.youtube.com/watch?v=4DqLDnp1AFo, last accessed 21 August 2020.

Advanced Workers with the Anti-Imperialist Singers, The. 1976a. "Better Red Let Others Be Dead." https://www.youtube.com/watch?v=xPn0x_UzfvU, last accessed 21 August 2020.

Advanced Workers with the Anti-Imperialist Singers, The. 1976a. "You Was Dancin' Need to Be Marchin'." https://www.youtube.com/watch?v=x5RAvDZZyCI, last accessed 21 August 2020.

Agamben, Giorgio. 2009. *What Is an Apparatus? And Other Essays*. Translated by David Kishik and Stefan Pedatella. Stanford, CA: Stanford University Press.

Alberro, Alexander. 2009. "Institutions, Critique, and Institutional Critique." In *Institutional Critique: An Anthology of Artists' Writings*, edited by Alexander Alberro and Blake Stimson, 2–19. Cambridge, MA: MIT Press.

Allen, Richard. 1995. *Projecting Illusion: Film Spectatorship and the Impression of Reality*. Cambridge: Cambridge University Press.

Alliez, Éric and Maurizio Lazzarato. 2018. *Wars and Capital*. Translated by Ames Hodges South Pasadena, CA: Semiotext(e).

Althusser, Louis. [1965] 1969. *For Marx*. Translated by Ben Brewster. New York: Pantheon.

Althusser, Louis. [1966] 2010. "On the Cultural Revolution." *Décalages* 1, no. 1: 1–18.

Althusser, Louis. 1971. *Lenin and Philosophy and Other Essays*. Translated by Ben Brewster. New York: Monthly Review Books.

Althusser, Louis. [1975] 1976. *Essays in Self-Criticism*. Translated by Grahame Lock. London: New Left Books.

Althusser, Luis. 1990. *Philosophy and the Spontaneous Philosophy of the Scientists and Other Essays*. Edited by Gregory Elliot. London: Verso.

Althusser, Louis. 2003. "On Brecht and Marx." In *Louis Althusser*, by Warren Montag, 136–149. Basingstoke: Palgrave Macmillan.

Anti-Imperialist Cultural Union. 1978. "Principles of Unity." *Main Trend*, no. 1: 31.

Antin, Eleanor and Cindy Nemser. 1975. "Eleanor Antin." In *Art Talk: Conversations with 12 Women Artists*, 267–295. New York: Charles Scribner.

Apter, Emily. 2005. "Dan Graham Inc. and the Fetish of Self-Property." In *The Lure of the Object*, edited by Stephen Melville, 15–38. Williamstown, MA: Sterling and Francine Clark Art Institute.

Apter, Emily. 2008. "What Is Yours, Ours, and Mine: Authorial Ownership and the Creative Commons." *October* 126 (Fall): 91–114.

Art & Language. 1977a. "On the Material Necessity That the Editors of *October*, Its Contributors, Supporters and Relatives, and Particularly, the Arch Fool, the Illiterate Liar Jeremy G. Rolfe, Be Sought Out, Their Hands Smashed, Their Eyes Put Out, Their Offices, Ateliers Destroyed, Burned and Portions of the Bloodstained Ashes Sent to the Towering Wretches of French Structuralism." *Art-Language* 4, no. 2: 7–9.

Art & Language. 1977b. "'Artists Meeting for Cultural Change' and 'Anti-Imperialist Cultural Union': A History of Two Cultural Institutions, as Illustration." *Art-Language* 4, no. 2: 66–81.

"'Artists Meeting for Cultural Change' and 'Anti-Imperialist Cultural Union': A History of Two Cultural Organizations, as illustration." *Art-Language* 4, no. 2: 66–81.

Austin, J. L. [1962] 1975. *How to Do Things with Words*. Cambridge, MA: Harvard University Press.

Bailey, Robert. 2016. *Art & Language International: Conceptual Art between Art Worlds*. Durham, NC: Duke University Press.

Balibar, Étienne. 1978. "From Bachelard to Althusser: The Concept of 'Epistemological Break.'" *Economy and Society* 7, no. 3: 207–237.

Balibar, Étienne. 2009. "Althusser and the Rue d'Ulm." Translated by David Fernbach. *New Left Review*, no. 58: 91–107.

Balibar, Étienne. 2015. "Althusser's Dramaturgy and the Critique of Ideology." *differences: A Journal of Feminist Cultural Studies* 26, no. 3: 1–22.

Ball, James R., III. 2020. *Theater of State: A Dramaturgy of the United Nations*. Evanston, IL: Northwestern University Press.

Baraka, Amiri. [1963] 1999. *Blues People: Negro Music in White America*. New York: Harper.

Baraka, Amiri. [1968] 2010. *Black Music*. Brooklyn: Akashic Books.

Baraka, Amiri. 1971a. "The Pan-African Party and the Black Nation." *Black Scholar* 2, no. 7: 24–32.

Baraka, Amiri. 1971b. *Raise, Race, Rays, Raze*. New York: Random House.

Baraka, Amiri. 1974a. *Revolutionary Party: Revolutionary Ideology*. Newark: Jihad Productions.

Baraka, Amiri. 1974b. "Some Questions about the Sixth Pan-African Congress." *Black Scholar* 6, no. 2: 42–46.

Baraka, Amiri. 1974c. "Toward Ideological Clarity: Nationalism, Pan Africanism, Socialism." *Black World* 24, no. 1: 24–33, 84–95.

Baraka, Amiri. 1976. *PRRWO & RWL: Not a "Revolutionary Wing," but a Dangerous Duo!* Newark: Revolutionary Communist League (M-L-M).

Baraka, Amiri. 1979. *Selected Poetry of Amiri Baraka / LeRoi Jones*. New York: William Morrow.

Baraka, Amiri. 1984. *The Autobiography of LeRoi Jones*. Chicago: Lawrence Hill Books.

Baraka, Amiri. 1996. *Funk Lore: New Poems (1984–1995)*. Los Angeles: Littoral Books.

Barilli, Renato. [1972] 2017. *Comportamento: Biennale di Venezia 1972, Padiglione Italia*. Milan: Silvana Editoriale.

Barilli, Renato. 1979. "Ponašanje." *Ideje* 10, no. 6, 135–142.

Barthes, Roland [1957] 1972. *Mythologies*. Translated by Annette Lavers. New York: Hill and Wang.

Barthes, Roland. 1972. *Critical Essays*. Translated by Richard Howard. Evanston, IL: Northwestern University Press.

Barthes, Roland. 1977. *Image-Music-Text*. Translated by Stephen Heath. New York: Noonday Press.

Baudry, Jean-Louis. 1967. "Écriture, fiction, idéologie." *Tel Quel* 31 (Fall): 15–30.

Baudry, Jean-Louis. 1970. "Cinéma: Effets idéologiques produits par l'appareil de base." *Cinéthique*, nos. 7–8: 1–8.

Baudry, Jean-Louis. [1970] 1980. "Ideological Effects of the Basic Cinematographic Apparatus." In *Apparatus, Cinematographic Apparatus: Selected Writings*, edited by Theresa Hak Kyung Cha, 25–37. New York: Tanam Press.

Baudry, Jean-Louis. 1975. "Le dispositif." *Communications*, no. 23: 56–72.

Baudry, Jean-Louis. 1976. "The Apparatus." Translated by Jean Andrews and Bertrand Augst. *Camera Obscura*, no. 1: 104–126.

Beard, Dena and Constance Lewallen. 2019. *Terry Fox Resonance: Gallery Guide*. San Francisco: The Lab.

Beckstette, Sven, Beatrice von Bismarck, and Isabelle Graw. 2011. "Preface." *Texte zur Kunst* 21, no. 83: 6–7.

Bell, Daniel. 1960. *The End of Ideology: On the Exhaustion of Political Ideas in the Fifties*. New York: Free Press.

Bell, Daniel, ed. [1967] 1969. *Toward the Year 2000: Work in Progress*. Boston: Beacon Press.

Benchley, Peter. 1976. "The Lumpen-Headache." *The Fox*, no. 3: 1–37.

Benjamin, Walter. 2002. *Selected Writings*. Vol. 3: *1935–1938*. Translated by Edmund Jephcott et al. Cambridge, MA: Harvard University Press.

Benjamin, Walter. 2003. *Selected Writings*. Vol. 4: *1938–1940*. Translated by Edmund Jephcott et al. Cambridge, MA: Harvard University Press.

Benjamin, Walter. 2013. *Recent Writings*. Vancouver: New Documents.

Bernard, Paul, Emeline Jaret, Philippe Thomas, and Stéphane Wargnier. 2021. *The Agency*. Geneva: MAMCO.

Blau, Herbert. 1983. "Ideology and Performance." *Theatre Journal* 35, no. 4: 441–460.

Blau, Herbert. 1992. *To All Appearances: Ideology and Performance*. London: Routledge.

Bloom, Lisa E. 1999. "Rewriting the Script: Eleanor Antin's Feminist Art." In *Eleanor Antin*, edited by Howard N. Fox, 159–190. Los Angeles: Los Angeles County Museum of Art.

Bolden, Tony. 2013. "Groove Theory: A Vamp on the Epistemology of Funk." *American Studies* 52, no. 4: 9–34.

Boltanski, Luc and Ève Chiapello. 2005. *The New Spirit of Capitalism*. Translated by Gregory Elliott. London: Verso.

Bosser, Daniel. 2014. *Philippe Thomas Declines His Identity*. Translated by Anthony Hudek. London: Occasional Papers.

Bottoms, Stephen J. 2003. "The Efficacy/Effeminacy Braid: Unpicking the Performance Studies / Theatre Studies Dichotomy." *Theatre Topics* 13, no. 2: 173–187.

Bottoms, Stephen J. and Matthew Goulish, eds. 2007. *Small Acts of Repair: Performance, Ecology and Goat Island*. London: Routledge.

Bourdieu, Pierre. [1980] 1990. *The Logic of Practice*. Translated by Richard Nice. Stanford, CA: Stanford University Press.

Bourriaud, Nicolas. [1998] 2002. *Relational Aesthetics*. Translated by Simon Pleasance and Fronza Woods. Paris: Les presses du reel.

Bowles, John P. 2011. *Adrian Piper: Race, Gender, and Embodiment*. Durham, NC: Duke University Press.

Brecht, Bertolt. 1977. *Collected Plays*. Vol. 2. Edited by Ralph Manheim and John Willet. New York: Random House.

Brecht, Bertolt. 2015. *Brecht on Theatre*. Edited by Marc Silberman, Steve Giles, and Tom Kuhn. London: Bloomsbury.

Breitwieser, Sabine. 2016. "Kinetic Painting: Carolee Schneemann's Media." In *Caroleee Schneemann: Kinetic Painting*, edited by Sabine Breitwieser, 13–25. Munich: Orestel.

Brentano, Robyn, and Mark Savitt. 1981. *112 Workshop, 112 Greene Street: History, Artists & Artworks*. New York: New York University Press.

Bronson, A. A. 1983. "Image Bank." In *Museums by Artists*, edited by Peggy Gale and A. A. Bronson, 193–194. Toronto: Art Metropole.

Brook, Peter. 1968. *The Empty Space*. New York: Atheneum.

Brooks, Daphne. 2021. *Liner Notes for the Revolution: The Intellectual Life of Black Feminist Sound*. Cambridge, MA: Harvard University Press.

Buchloh, Benjamin. 1982. "Allegorical Procedures: Appropriation and Montage in Contemporary Art." *Artforum* 21, no. 1: 43–56.

Buchloh, Benjamin. 1984. "Since Realism There Was . . . (On the Current Conditions of Factografic Art)." In *Art & Ideology*, edited by Marcia Tucker, 5–11. New York: New Museum of Contemporary Art.

Buchloh, Benjamin. 1990. "Conceptual Art 1962–1969: From the Aesthetic of Administration to the Critique of Institutions." *October* 55: 105–143.

Buchloh, Benjamin. 2008. "Darcy Lange: Paco Campana." In *Darcy Lange: Study of an Artist at Work*, edited by Mercedes Vicente, 49–64. New Plymouth: Govett-Brewster Art Gallery.

Buchloh, Benjamin. 2012. "Farewell to an Identity." *Artforum* 51, no. 4: 253–261.

Burn, Ian, Mel Ramsden, and Terry Smith. 1974. *Draft for an Anti-textbook. Art-Language* 3, no. 1.

Butler, Judith. [1990] 2006. *Gender Trouble: Feminism and the Subversion of Identity*. London: Routledge.

Butler, Judith. 1993. *Bodies That Matter: On the Discursive Limits of "Sex"*. London: Routledge.

Butler, Judith. 1997a. *Excitable Speech: A Politics of the Performative*. New York: Routledge.

Butler, Judith. 1997b. *The Psychic Life of Power: Theories in Subjection*. Stanford, CA: Stanford University Press.

Butler, Judith. 2015. "Theatrical Machines." *differences: A Journal of Feminist Cultural Studies* 26, no. 3: 23–42.

Cadava, Eduardo, Peter Connor, and Jean-Luc Nancy, eds. 1991. *Who Comes after the Subject?* London: Routledge.

Cahan, Susan. 2006. "Regarding Andrea Fraser's *Untitled*." *Social Semiotics* 16, no. 1: 7–15.

Carriger, Michelle Liu. 2021. "Of Affects, Effects, and X." *Journal of Dramatic Theory and Criticism* 35, no. 2: 9–11.

Carroll, Noël. 1986. "Performance." *Formations* 3, no. 1: 63–81.

Casser, Anja and Philipp Ziegler, eds. 2010. *Stephen Willats: Art Society Feedback*. Nuremberg: Verlag für moderne Kunst.

Cassils. 2019. *Solutions*. Houston: Station Museum of Contemporary Art.

Cassils and E. Cram. 2019. "Cassils: On Violence, Witnessing, and the Making of Trans Worlds." *QED: A Journal in GLBTQ Worldmaking* 6, no. 1: 117–130.

Cassils and David Getsy. 2015. *Cassils*. [City not identified] Netherlands: MU.

Cha, Theresa Hak Kyung, ed. 1980. *Apparatus, Cinematographic Apparatus: Selected Writings* New York: Tanam Press.

Charnley, Kim. 2016. "Failure, Revolution and Institutional Critique." *Art & the Public Sphere* 5, no. 1: 35–52.

Chaudhuri, Una. 1995. *Staging Place: The Geography of Modern Drama*. Ann Arbor: University of Michigan Press.

Chomsky, Noam. 1973. *For Reasons of State*. New York: Pantheon.

Cockroft, Eva. 1974. "Abstract Expressionism: Weapon of the Cold War." *Artforum* 12, no. 10: 39–41.

Corris, Michael. 1973. "Introduction." In *Blurting in Art & Language*. http://blurting-in.zkm.de, last accessed 15 July 2024.

Corris, Michael [1996] 1999. "Inside a New York Art Gang: Selected Documents of Art & Language, New York." In *Conceptual Art: A Critical Anthology*, edited by Alexander Alebrro and Blake Stimson, 470–485. Cambridge, MA: MIT Press.

Corris, Michael and Sezgin Boynik. 2017. "In the Belly of the Beast." *Rab-Rab*, no. 4.2: 10–57.

Cotter, Holland. 2010. "700-Hour Silent Opera Reaches Finale at MoMA." *New York Times*, 31 May 2010, C1.

Cras, Sophie. [2018] 2019. *The Artist as Economist: Art and Capitalism in the 1960s*. Translated by Malcolm DeBevoise. New Haven: Yale University Press.

Cvejić, Bojana. 2015. *Choreographing Problems: Expressive Concepts in European Contemporary Dance and Performance*. Basingstoke: Palgrave Macmillan.

Daddario, Will, Matthew Goulish, and Lin Hixson. 2020. "In the Making: An Incomplete Consideration of the First Decade of *Every House Has a Door* 2008–2018 as Performance Philosophy." In *The Routledge Companion to Performance Philosophy*, edited by Laura Cull Ó Maoilearca and Alice Lagaay, 424–436. London: Routledge.

Debord, Guy. [1957] 1980. "Report on the Construction of Situations and on the International Situationist Tendency's Conditions of Organization and Action," in Ken Knabb, ed. *Situationist International Anthology*: 17–25. Berkeley: Bureau of Public Secrets.

De Duve, Tierry. 2014. "The Invention of Non-art: A History." *Artforum* 52, no. 6: 192–199, 238.

Deleuze, Gilles. [1986] 1988. *Foucault*. Translated by Seán Hand. Minneapolis: University of Minnesota Press.

Deleuze, Gilles. [1988] 2006. "What Is a *Dispositif*?" In *Two Regimes of Madness: Texts and Interviews, 1975–1995*, translated by Ames Hodges and Mike Taormina, 338–348. Los Angeles: Semiotext(e).

Deleuze, Gilles. [1990] 1992. "Postscript on the Societies of Control." *October* 59 (Winter): 3–7.

Deleuze, Gilles and Félix Guattari. [1972] 1983. *Anti-Oedipus: Capitalism and Schizophrenia*. Translated by Robert Hurley, Mark Seem, and Helen R. Lane. Minneapolis: University of Minnesota Press.

Deleuze, Gilles and Félix Guattari. [1980] 1987. *A Thousand Plateaus*. Translated by Brian Massumi. Minneapolis: University of Minnesota Press.

Demos, T. J. 2017. *Against the Anthropocene: Visual Culture and Environment Today*. Berlin: Stenberg Press.

Denegri, Ješa. [1978] 2024. "Some Problems of the Art Practices of the Past Decade: General Characteristics of the New Art Practices." In *The Yugoslav*

Art Space: Ješa Denegri in the First Person, Branislav Dimitrijević and Jelena Vesić, 322–351. Vienna: Kontakt Collection.

Déotte, Jean-Louis. 2007. "Alberti, Vasari, Léonard, du *disegno* comme dessin au *disegno* comme milieu projectif." In *Appareil et Intermédialité*, edited by Jean-Louis Déotte, Marion Froger, and Silvestra Mariniello, 51–62. Paris: L'Harmattan.

Déotte, Jean-Louis. 2019. "Théâtre, appareil(s), medias: Notes à propos de l'article de Sophie-Aurore Roussel, 'Le théâtre, un appareil originaire?'" *Appareil*, no. 19. https://journals-openedition-org.stanford.idm.oclc.org/appareil/3252, last accessed 1 December 2021.

Derrida, Jacques. 1978. *Writing and Difference*. Translated by Alan Bass. Chicago: University of Chicago Press.

Derrida, Jacques. [1977] 1988. *Limited Inc*. Translated by Samuel Weber and Jeffrey Mehlman. Evanston, IL: Northwestern University Press.

Derrida, Jacques. 2004. "Countersignature." *Paragraph* 27, no. 2: 7–42.

Dittmer, Lowell. 1973. "The Structural Evolution of 'Criticism and Self-Criticism.'" *China Quarterly*, no. 73: 708–729.

Dolan, Jill. 1988. *The Feminist Spectator as Critic*. Ann Arbor: UMI Research Press.

Dort, Bernard. 1967. *Théâtre public, 1953–1966*. Paris: Éditions du Seuil.

Duncan, Carol. 1993. *The Aesthetics of Power: Essays in Critical Art History*. Cambridge: Cambridge University Press.

Dreyblatt, Arnold and Angela Lammert, eds. 2015. *Terry Fox: Elemental Gestures*. Dortmund: Verlag Kettler.

Dutton, John M. and William H. Starbuck. 1971. *Computer Simulation of Human Behavior*. New York: Wiley.

Eagleton, Terry. 1990. *The Ideology of the Aesthetic*. Oxford: Blackwell.

Eagleton, Terry. 1991. *Ideology: An Introduction*. London: Verso.

Eagleton, Terry, ed. 1994. *Ideology*. London: Longman.

Eckersall, Peter. 2018. "On Dramaturgy to Make Visible." *Performance Research* 23, nos. 4–5: 241–243.

Edelman, Bernard. [1973] 1979. *Ownership of the Image: Elements for a Marxist Theory of Law*. Translated by Elizabeth Kingdom. London: Routledge & Kegan Paul.

Elam, Harry Justin. 1997. *Taking It to the Streets: The Social Protest Theater of Luis Valdez and Amiri Baraka*. Ann Arbor: University of Michigan Press.

Elsaesser, Thomas, ed. 2004. *Harun Farocki: Working on the Sight-Lines*. Amsterdam: Amsterdam University Press.

Elsaesser, Thomas. 2011. "What Is Left of Cinematic Apparatus, and Why We Should Retain (or Return to) It." *Cinéma & Technologie / Cinema & Technology* 31, 1-2-3,: 33–44.

Elsaesser, Thomas. 2016. *Film History as Media Archaeology: Tracking Digital Cinema*. Amsterdam: Amsterdam University Press.

Eshun, Kodwo. 1998. *More Brilliant Than the Sun: Adventures in Sonic Fiction.* London: Quartet Books.

Fairfield, Joy Brooke. 2016. "Fugitive Intimacies: The Unsettling Vows of Queer Wedlock Performance." PhD dissertation, Stanford University.

Falguières, Patricia. 2000. "Codicil." In *Metti la tua firma: nella storia dell'arte,* Diserens, Corinne, 45–52. Barcelona: Museu d'Art Contemporani de Barcelona.

Fanon, Franz. [1952] 2008. *Black Skin, White Masks.* Translated by Richard Philcox. New York: Grove Press.

Felman, Shoshana. [1983] 2003. *The Scandal of the Speaking Body: Don Juan with J.L. Austin, or Seduction in Two Languages.* Stanford, CA: Stanford University Press.

Fischer-Lichte, Erika. [2004] 2008. *The Transformative Power of Performance: A New Aesthetics.* Translated by Saskya Iris Jain. London: Routledge.

Fischer-Lichte, Erika. 2009. "Culture as Performance." *Modern Austrian Literature* 42, no. 3: 1–10.

Fisher, Jennifer. 2012. "Proprioceptive Friction: Waiting in Line to Sit with Marina Abramović." *Senses and Society* 7, no. 2: 153–172.

Flaubert, Gustave. [1857] 1997. *Selected Letters.* Translated by Geoffrey Wall. Harmondsworth: Penguin.

Foucault, Michel. [1966] 1990. "Maurice Blanchot: The Thought from Outside." In *Foucault/Blanchot,* translated by Brian Massumi, 7–58. New York: Zone Books.

Foucault, Michel, ed. 1968. *Théorie d'ensemble.* Paris: Éditions du Seuil.

Foucault, Michel. [1969] 1972. *The Archeology of Knowledge & The Discourse on Language,* translated by A. M. Sheridan Smith. New York: Barnes & Noble.

Foucault, Michel. [1969] 1998. "What Is an Author?" In *Aesthetics, Method, and Epistemology,* edited by James D. Faubion, translated by Robert Hurley et al., 205–222. New York: New Press.

Foucault Michel. [1973] 1983. *This Is Not a Pipe.* Translated by James Harkness. Berkeley: University of California Press.

Foucault, Michel. [1976] 1978. *The History of Sexuality.* Vol. 1: *An Introduction.* Translated by Robert Hurley. New York: Random House.

Foucault, Michel. [1977] 1980. "The Confession of the Flesh." In *Power/Knowledge: Selected Interviews & Other Writings, 1972–1977,* edited by Colin Gordon, translated by Colin Gordin et al., 194–228. New York: Pantheon.

Foucault, Michel. 1997. *The Politics of Truth.* Translated by Lysa Hochroth and Catherine Porter. Los Angeles: Semiotext(e).

Foucault, Michel. 1998. *Essential Works of Michel Foucault 1954–1984.* Vol. 2: *Aesthetics, Method and Epistemology.* Edited by James D. Faubion. New York: New Press.

Foucault, Michel. [2004] 2007. *Security, Territory, Population: Lectures at the Collège de France, 1977–1978.* Translated by Graham Burchell. Basingstoke: Palgrave Macmillan.

Foucault, Michel. [2013] 2015. *The Punitive Society: Lectures at the Collège de France, 1972–1973*. Translated by Graham Burchell. New York: Picador.

Fox, Terry. 1971. ". . . I Wanted to Have My Mood Affect Their Looks." Interview by Willoughby Sharp. *Avalanche*, no. 2: 70–81.

Fox, Terry. 1979. "The Impetus Might Have Been Similar to Dada . . ." Interview by Robin White. In *View* 2, no. 3. Oakland: Crown Point Press.

Fox, Terry, and Zdenek Felix. 1982. *Terry Fox—Metaphorical Instruments*. Essen: Museum Folkwang.

"Frage der Präsentation." 1999. In *Sur un lieu commun et autres textes*, edited by Alexis Vaillant, 11–42. Geneva: MAMCO and Presses Universitaires de Rennes.

Franke, Anselm, Nida Ghouse, Paz Guevara, and Antonia Majaca. 2021. *Parapolitics: Cultural Freedom and the Cold War*. Berlin: Sternberg Press.

Fraser, Andrea. [2005] 2009. "From the Critique of Institutions to an Institution of Critique." In *Institutional Critique: An Anthology of Artists' Writings*, edited by Alexander Alberro and Blake Stimson, 408–417. Cambridge, MA: MIT Press.

Fraser, Andrea. 2011. "L'1%, c'est moi." *Texte zur Kunst* 21, no. 83: 114–127.

Fraser, Andrea. 2018. *2016 in Museums, Money, and Politics*. Cambridge, MA: MIT Press..

Frazier, Robeson Taj. 2006. "The Congress of African People: Baraka, Brother Mao, and the Year of '74'." *Souls* 8, no. 3: 142–159.

Frieze, James. 2016. *Reframing Immersive Theatre: The Politics and Pragmatics of Participatory Performance*. London: Palgrave Macmillan.

Frueh, Joanna. 1994. "The Body through Women's Eyes." In *The Power of Feminist Art: The American Movement of the 1970s. History and Impact*, edited by Norma Broude and Mary Garland, 190–297. New York: Harry Abrams.

Fuchs, Elinor. 1996. *The Death of Character: Perspectives on Theater after Modernism*. Bloomington: Indiana University Press.

Fuegi, John. 1994. *Brecht and Company: Sex, Politics, and the Making of the Modern Drama*. New York: Grove Press.

Gale, Peggy. 1979. "Explaining Pictures to Dead Air. The Robertson/Beuys Admixture." *Parachute: revue d'art contemporain*. No14 (Spring):4–8.

Gilbert, Christopher. 2004. "Art & Language, New York, Discusses Its Social Relations in 'The Lumpen-Headache.'" In *Conceptual Art: Theory, Myth, and Practice*, edited by Michael Corris, 326–341. Cambridge: Cambridge University Press.

Gilbert, Christopher. 2007. "Art & Language and the Institutional Form in Anglo-American Collectivism." In *Collectivism after Modernism: The Art of Social Imagination after 1945*, edited by Blake Stimson and Gregory Sholette, 77–93. Minneapolis: University of Minnesota Press.

Goat Island. 1997. *Schoolbook*. Chicago: Goat Island.

Gollner, Adam Leith. 2014. "An Investigation into the Reappearance of Walter

Benjamin." Hazlitt blog, 11 September. https://hazlitt.net/longreads/investigation-reappearance-walter-benjamin, last accessed 20 December 2021.

Goodman, Nelson. 1981. "Twisted Tales; or, Story, Study, and Symphony." In *On Narrative*, edited by W. J. T. Mitchell, 99–115. Chicago: University of Chicago Press.

Goulish, Matthew. 2000. *39 Microlectures: In Proximity of Performance*. London: Routledge.

Goulish, Matthew. 2014. "Performance and the Limits of Fiction." Lecture by Matthew Goulish. San Francisco Art Institute. Vimeo, 26 September. https://vimeo.com/107651809, last accessed 15 November 2021.

Goulish, Matthew and Lin Hixson. 2015a. "From One Meaning to Another." Unpublished keynote lecture at Performance Philosophy Conference, Chicago 11 April 2015.

Goulish, Matthew and Lin Hixson. 2015b. "A Poetics of the Thing Outlived." Unpublished lecture at the symposium Afterlives: The Persistence of Performance, Museum of Modern Art, New York, 26 September 2015.

Grotowski, Jerzy. 1968. *Towards a Poor Theatre*. New York: Simon and Schuster.

Gržinić, Marina. 2000. *Fiction Reconstructed: Eastern Europe, Post-socialism & the Retro-Avant-Garde*. Vienna: Edition Selene.

Guattari, Félix. [1972] 2015. *Psychoanalysis and Transversality: Texts and Interviews, 1955–1971*. Translated by Ames Hodges. Los Angeles: Semiotext(e).

Guattari, Félix. [2011] 2016. *Lines of Flight: For Another World of Possibilities*. Translated by Andrew Goffey. London: Bloomsbury.

Gumpert, Lynn and Ned Rifkin, eds. 1981. *Persona*. New York: New Museum.

Habermas, Jürgen. [1968] 1970. *Toward a Rational Society: Student Protest, Science, and Politics*. Translated by Jeremy J. Shapiro. Boston: Beacon Press.

Habermas, Jürgen. [1968] 1971. *Knowledge and Human Interests*. Translated by Jeremy J. Shapiro. Boston: Beacon Press.

Halberstam, Jack. 2018. "Unbuilding Gender: Trans*Anarchitectures in and beyond the Work of Gordon Matta-Clark." *Places*, October. https://placesjournal.org/article/unbuilding-gender, last accessed 9 September 2021.

Harding, James Martin and Cindy Rosenthal. 2011. *The Rise of Performance Studies: Rethinking Richard Schechner's Broad Spectrum*. Basingstoke: Palgrave Macmillan.

Harris, William, ed. 1991. *The LeRoi Jones / Amiri Baraka Reader*. New York: Basic Books.

Harrison, Charles. 1991. *Essays on Art & Language*. Cambridge, MA: MIT Press.

Heath, Stephen. 1976. "On Screen, in Frame: Film and Ideology." *Quarterly Review of Film Studies* 1, no. 3: 251–265.

Heims, Steve Joshua. 1991. *The Cybernetics Group*. Cambridge, MA: MIT Press.

Hershman, Lynn. 1978. *Lynn Hershman Is Not Roberta Breitmore / Roberta Breitmore Is Not Lynn Hershman: An Exhibition April 1–May 14, 1978, M.H. DeYoung Memorial Museum, Golden State Park, San Francisco*. San Francisco: DeYoung Museum.

Hewitt, Andrew. 2005. *Social Choreography: Ideology as Performance in Dance and Everyday Movement*. Durham, NC: Duke University Press.

Heylighen, Francis and Cliff Joslyn. 2001. "Cybernetics and Second-Order Cybernetics." In *Encyclopedia of Physical Science & Technology*, 3rd ed., edited by R. A. Meyers, 1–24. San Diego: Academic Press.

Holm, Michael Juul, ed. 2011. *Kienholz / Five Car Stud*. Humlebaek, Denmark: Louisiana Museum of Modern Art.

Hudek, Antony. 2018. "A Porous Entity: The Centre for Behavioural Art at Gallery House, 1972–1973." In *London Art Worlds: Mobile, Contingent, and Ephemeral Networks, 1960–1980*, edited by Jo Applin, Catherine Spencer, and Amy Tobin, 39–54. University Park: Pennsylvania State University Press.

"In Response to the General Criticism Self-Criticism Put Out by the Steering Committee." 1978. Unpublished typescript. Getty Archive.

Irish, Sharon. 2020. *Concerning Stephen Willats and the Social Function of Art: Experiments in Cybernetics and Society*. London: Bloomsbury Visual Arts.

Jackson, Shannon. 2004. *Professing Performance: Theatre in the Academy from Philology to Performativity*. New York: Cambridge University Press.

Jakovljević, Branislav, et al. 2018. "The Voice from the 10th Row: Carl Weber and the Berliner Ensemble." *TDR* 62, no. 3 (T239): 55–108.

Jameson, Fredric. 1981. *The Political Unconscious: Narrative as a Socially Symbolic Act*. Ithaca, NY: Cornell University Press.

Jaret, Émeline. 2014. "Philippe Thomas: For an Art of Society." In Bosser, *Philippe Thomas Declines His Identity*, n.p. London: Occasional Papers.

Jaret, Émeline. 2015. "Le dispositif à l'œuvre chez Philippe Thomas: L'exemple d'AB (1978–1980)." *Marges*, no. 20: 44–59.

Jaret, Émeline. 2016. "Thoughts on the Place of Publications in Philippe Thomas's Oeuvre." *Shelf Journal*, no. 4: 46–61.

Johnson, Barbara. 1977. "Poetry and Performative Language." *Yale French Studies* 54: 140–158.

Jones, Amelia. 2011. "'The Artist Is Present': Artistic Re-enactments and the Impossibility of Presence." *TDR* 55, no. 1 (T209): 16–45.

Jones, Amelia. 2015. "Material Traces: Performativity, Artistic 'Work', and New Concepts of Agency." *TDR* 59, no. 4 (T228): 18–35.

Kelley, Robin D. G. 2002. *Freedom Dreams: The Black Radical Imagination*. Boston: Beacon Press.

Kelley, Robin D. G. and Betsy Esch. 1999. "Black Like Mao: Red China and Black Revolution." *Souls: Critical Journal of Black Politics and Culture* 1, no. 4: 6–41.

Kennedy, Emmet. 1978. *A Philosophe in the Age of Revolution: Destutt de Tracy and the Origins of "Ideology."* Philadelphia: American Philosophical Society.

Kirby, Michael, ed. 1965. "New Theater." Special issue of *Tulane Drama Review* 10, no. 2.

Kirby, Michael. 1987. *A Formalist Theatre*. Philadelphia: University of Pennsylvania Press.

Knabb, Ken. 1981. *Situationist International Anthology*. Berkeley, CA: Bureau of Public Secrets.

Krauss, Rosalind. 1986. *The Originality of the Avant-Garde and Other Modernist Myths*. Cambridge, MA: MIT Press.

Lauretis, Teresa de. 1984. *Alice Doesn't: Feminism, Semiotics, Cinema*. Bloomington: Indiana University Press.

Lauretis, Teresa de. 1987. *Technologies of Gender: Essays on Theory, Film, and Fiction*. Bloomington: Indiana University Press.

Lauretis, Teresa de and Stephen Heath. 1980. *The Cinematic Apparatus*. New York: St. Martin's Press.

Lazzarato, Maurizio. [2009] 2017. *Experimental Politics: Work, Welfare, and Creativity in the Neoliberal Age*. Translated by Arianna Bove, Jeremy Gilbert, Andrew Goffey, Mark Hayward, Jason Reed, and Alberto Toscano. Cambridge, MA: MIT Press.

Lazzarato, Maurizio. 2014. *Signs and Machines: Capitalism and the Production of Subjectivity*. Translated by Joshua David Jordan. Los Angeles: Semiotext(e).

Lebovici, Elisabeth. 2018. *The Name of Philippe Thomas*. Berlin: Sternberg Press.

Lefebvre, Henri. 1971. *Au delà du structuralisme*. Paris: Editions Anthropos.

Lenin, Vladimir Illich. (1902) 1977. "What Is to Be done?" In *Selected Works*, vol. 1. Moscow: Progress Publishers.

Leroi-Gourhan, André. [1964] 1993. *Gesture and Speech*. Translated by Anna Bostock Berger. Cambridge, MA: MIT Press.

Lessing, Gotthold Ephraim. 1962. *Hamburg Dramaturgy*. Translated by Helen Zimmern. New York: Dover.

Lessing, Gotthold Ephraim. 2019. *The Hamburg Dramaturgy by G. E. Lessing*. Edited by Natalya Baldyga, translated by Wendy Arons and Sara Figal. London: Routledge.

Levine Beckman, Britanny. 2020. "How Performative Became the Most Searing Callout in 2020." Mashable.com. https://mashable.com/article/performative-activism, last accessed 13 December 2022.

Liebert, Emily et al. 2013. *Multiple Occupancy: Eleanor Antin's "Selves."* New York: Wallach Art Gallery.

Lipavskii, Leonid. 2005. *Issledovanie uzhasa*. Edited by Valerii Sazhin. Moscow: Ad Marginem.

Lippard, Lucy and John Chandler. (1968) 2000. "The Dematerialization of Art." In *The Artist's Body*, edited by Amelia Jones and Tracey Warr, 203–205. London: Phaidon.

Lotringer, Sylvère, ed. 1989. *Foucault Live: Collected Interviews, 1961–1984*. New York: Semiotext(e).

Lowen, Rebecca. 1997. *Creating the Cold War University: The Transformation of Stanford*. Berkeley: University of California Press.

Lukan, Blaž, ed. 2008. *NAME Readymade*. Ljubljana: Moderna Galerija.

Lütticken, Sven. 2005. *Secret Publicity: Essays on Contemporary Art*. Rotterdam: NAi Publishers.

Lyotard, Jean-François. [1979] 1990. *Pacific Wall*. Translated by Bruce Boone. Venice, CA: Lapis Press.

Maak, Niklas. 2011. "Between Pinault and Pinchuk: The Network and Rituals of a New Transnational System of Collectors." *Texte zur Kunst* 21, no. 83: 38–55.

MacDonald, Scott. 1988. *A Critical Cinema: Interviews with Independent Filmmakers*. Vol. 1. Berkeley: University of California Press.

Mao Zedong. 1965. *Selected Works*. Vol. 3. Peking: Foreign Languages Press.

Martel, James R. 2017. *The Misinterpellated Subject*. Durham, NC: Duke University Press.

Marx, Karl and Friedrich Engels [1932] 1998. *The German Ideology*. Translated by C. J. Arthur. New York: Prometheus Books.

Mauss, Marcel. 2006. *Technologies, Technology and Civilization*. New York: Durkheim Press and Berghahn Books.

Mazzucato, Mariana. 2015. *The Entrepreneurial State: Debunking Public vs. Private Sector Myths*. New York: Public Affairs.

McKenzie, Jon. 2001. *Perform or Else: From Discipline to Performance*. London: Routledge.

McKenzie, Jon. 2006. "Is Performance Studies Imperialist?" *TDR* 50, no. 4 (T192): 5–8.

McKenzie, Jon, Heike Roms, and C. J. Wan-ling Wee, eds. 2010. *Contesting Performance: Global Sites of Research*. London: Palgrave Macmillan.

Močnik, Rastko. 2003. *3 teorije: Ideologija, nacija, institucija*. Belgrade: Centar za savremenu umetnost.

Montag, Warren. 1995. "'The Soul Is the Prison of the Body': Althusser and Foucault, 1970–1975." *Yale French Studies* 88: 53–77.

Moore, Jason W. 2015. *Capitalism in the Web of Life: Ecology and the Accumulation of Capital*. London: Verso.

Morbio, Vittoria Crespi. 2018. *Strehler e i suoi scenografi / and His Scenographers*. Milan: Amici della Scala.

Moten, Fred. 2003. *In the Break: The Aesthetics of the Black Radical Tradition*. Minneapolis: University of Minnesota Press.

Munder, Heike, ed. 2019. *Stephen Willats: Languages of Dissent*. Zurich: Migros Museum für Gegenwartskunst.

Muñoz, José Esteban. 1999. *Disidentifications: Queers of Color and the Performance of Politics*. Minneapolis: University of Minnesota Press.

Nesbit, Molly. 1987. "What Was an Author?" *Yale French Studies* 73: 229–257.

O'Doherty, Brian. 2019. *A Mental Masquerade: When Brian O'Doherty Was a Female Art Critic: Mary Josephson's Collected Writings*. Leipzig: Spector Books.

Olson, Charles. 1959. *Projective Verse*. New York: Totem Press.

Peach, Filiz. 2008. *Death, "Deathlessness" and Existenz in Karl Jaspers' Philosophy*. Edinburgh: Edinburgh University Press.

Pêcheux, Michel. [1978] 1982. *Language, Semantics, and Ideology*. Translated by Harbans Nagpal. New York: St. Martin's Press.

Phay-Vakalis, Soko. 2008. *Miroir, appareils et autres dispositifs*. Paris: L'Harmattan.

Phelan, Peggy. 1993. *Unmarked: The Politics of Performance*. New York: Routledge.

Phelan, Peggy. 1997. *Mourning Sex: Performing Public Memories*. London: Routledge.

Pickering, Andrew. 2010. *The Cybernetic Brain: Sketches of Another Future*. Chicago: University of Chicago Press.

Piketty, Thomas. 2020. *Capital and Ideology*. Translated by Arthur Goldhammer. Cambridge, MA: Harvard University Press.

Piper, Adrian. 1996. *Out of Order, Out of Sight. v. 1. Selected Writings in Meta-Art 1968–1992. v. 2. Selected Writings in Art Criticism 1967–1992*. Cambridge, MA: MIT Press.

Piscator, Erwin. [1963] 1978. *The Political Theater : A History 1914–1929*. Translated by Hugh Rorrison. New York: Avon Books.

Pollock, Della. 1998. "Performing Writing." In *The Ends of Performance*, edited by Peggy Phelan and Jill Lane, 73–103. New York: New York University Press.

Ramsden, Mel. 1975a. "'City Arts Workshop—People's Art in New York City' by Eva Cockcroft and James D. Cockcroft (Left-Curve, Summer, 1975)." *The Fox*, no. 2: 39–48.

Ramsden, Mel. 1975b. "On Practice." *The Fox* no. 1: 66–83.

Rancière, Jacques. [1974] 2011. *Althusser's Lesson*. Translated by Emiliano Battista. London: Bloomsbury.

Reed, Anthony. 2021. *Soundworks: Race, Sound, and Poetry in Production*. Durham, NC: Duke University Press.

Reilly, Charlie, ed. 1994. *Conversations with Amiri Baraka*. Jackson: University Press of Mississippi.

Revolutionary Communist League (M-L-M). 1976a. "Revolutionary Communist League (M-L-M)." *Unity and Struggle* 5, no. 6: 1, 6–9.

Revolutionary Communist League (M-L-M). 1976b. "RLC's Position on Party Building." *Unity and Struggle* 5, nos. 7–10: 1, 3–14, 16.

Revolutionary Communist League (M-L-M). 1977. "RLC's Position on Party Building, Part 2." *Unity and Struggle* 6, nos. 1–6: 1, 6–8.

Ricoeur, Paul. 1986. *Lectures on Ideology and Utopia*. New York: Columbia University Press.

Roberts, John. 2007. *The Intangibilities of Form: Skill and Deskilling in Art after the Readymade*. London: Verso.

Robertson, Clive. 1976. "An Identity Transfer with Joseph Beuys." Performance issue of *La Mamelle*, Spring: n.p.

Robertson, Clive. 1977. "Fetish T-Shirt Pedagogy Special Issue." *FILE* 3, no. 3.

Robertson, Clive. 1978. "A Beuys-Shaped Frame." *Centerfold*, December, 23–28.

Robertson, Clive. 1979. "The Sculptured Politics of Joseph Beuys." In *Performance by Artists*, edited by Peggy Gale, 133. Toronto: Art Metropole.

Robertson, Clive and Paul Woodrow. 1975. *Workscoreport*. Calgary, Alberta: W.O.R.K.S.; Cullompton, Devon: Beau Geste Press.

Robinson, Cedric J. [1983] 2000. *Black Marxism: The Making of the Black Radical Tradition*. Chapel Hill: University of North Carolina Press.

Robinson, Cedric J. 2019. *On Racial Capitalism, Black Internationalism, and Cultures of Resistance*. London: Pluto Press.

Robinson, Kim Stanley. 2020. *The Ministry for the Future*. New York: Orbit.

Rosen, Philip, ed. 1986. *Narrative, Apparatus, Ideology: A Film Theory Reader*. New York: Columbia University Press.

Rosenberg, Harold. [1959] 1965. *Tradition of the New*. New York: McGraw-Hill.

Rosenblueth, Arturo, Norbert Wiener, and Julian Bigelow. 1943. "Behavior, Purpose, and Teleology." *Philosophy of Science* 10: 1–5.

Roussel, Sophie-Aurore. 2016. "Le théâtre, un 'appareil originaire'?" *Appareil*, no. 17. https://journals-openedition-org.stanford.idm.oclc.org/appareil/, last accessed 1 November 2021.

Russell, Charlie L. 1971. "Barbara Ann Teer: We Are Liberators Not Actors." *Essence* 1, no. 11: 56–59.

Sartre, Jean-Paul. 1976. *Sartre on Theater*. Edited by Michel Contat and Michel Rybalka, translated by Frank Jellinek. New York: Pantheon.

Saunders, Frances Stonor. 1999. *Who Paid the Piper: The CIA and the Cultural Cold War*. London: Granta Books.

Saunders, Frances Stonor. 2000. *The Cultural Cold War: The CIA and the World of Arts and Letters*. New York: New Press.

Schechner, Richard. 1969. *Public Domain: Essays on the Theatre*. Indianapolis: Bobbs-Merrill.

Schechner, Richard. 1973a. "Drama, Script, Theater, Performance." *TDR* 17, no. 3: 5–36.

Schechner, Richard. 1973b. "Performance & the Social Sciences: Introduction." *TDR* 17, no. 3: 3–4.

Schechner, Richard. [1973] 1994. *Environmental Theater*. New York: Applause.

Schechner, Richard. 1974. "From Ritual to Theatre and Back: The Structure/Process of the Efficacy-Entertainment Dyad." *Educational Theatre Journal* 26, no. 4: 455–481.

Schechner, Richard. [1977] 1988. *Performance Theory*. New York: Routledge.

Schechner, Richard. 1981. "Restoration of Behavior." *Studies in Visual Communication* 7, no. 3: 2–45.

Schechner, Richard. 1985. *Between Theater and Anthropology*. Philadelphia: University of Pennsylvania Press.

Schechner, Richard and Mady Schuman. 1976. *Ritual, Play, and Performance: Readings in the Social Sciences/Theater*. New York: The Seabury Press.

Schechner, Richard. 1988. "Performance Studies: The Broad Spectrum Approach." *TDR* 32, no. 3: 4–6.

Searle, John. 1969. *Speech Acts: An Essay in the Philosophy of Language*. London: Cambridge University Press.

Searle, John. 2005. "What Is an Institution?" *Journal of Institutional Economics* 1, no. 1: 1–22.

Sedgwick, Eve Kosofsky. 2003. *Touching Feeling: Affect, Pedagogy, Performativity*. Durham, NC: Duke University Press.

Serra, Richard. 1973. *Television Delivers People*. https://www.youtube.com/watch?v=LvZYwaQlJsg&t=287s, last accessed 22 December 2022.

Shanken, Edward A. 2003. "From Cybernetics to Telematics: The Art, Pedagogy, and Theory of Roy Ascott." In *Telematic Embrace: Visionary Theories of Art, Technology, and Consciousness*, by Roy Ascott, 1–95. Berkeley: University of California Press.

Shatz, Adam. 2024. *The Rebel's Clinic: The Revolutionary Lives of Frantz Fanon*. New York: Farrar, Strauss and Giroux.

Simanga, Michael. 2015. *Amiri Baraka and the Congress of African People: History and Memory*. New York: Palgrave Macmillan.

"Some Proposals and Etc. for AICU." 1978. Unpublished typescript. Getty Archive.

Somaini, Antonio. 2016. "Walter Benjamin's Media Theory: The *Medium* and the *Apparat*." *Grey Room* 62 (Winter): 6–41.

Souriau, Étienne. 1928. "L'arabesque." *Revue des cours et des conferences* 30, no. 2: 113–127.

Souriau, Étienne. [1943] 2015. *The Different Modes of Existence*. Translated by Erik Beranek and Tim Howles. Minneapolis: Univocal.

Souriau, Étienne. 1950. *Les deux cent mille situations dramatiques*. Paris: Flammarion.

Souriau, Étienne. [1956] 2015. "Of the Mode of Existence of the Work to-Be-Made." In *The Different Modes of Existence*, translated by Erik Beranek and Tim Howles, 219–240. Minneapolis: Univocal.

Stimson, Blake. 2009. "What Was Institutional Critique?" In *Institutional Critique: An Anthology of Artists' Writings*, edited by Alexander Alberro and Blake Stimson, 20–42. Cambridge, MA: MIT Press.

Tacata, Ryan David. 2015. "*La Mamelle*: Early Bay Area Conceptual Performance Art and the Alternative Art Archive." PhD dissertation, Stanford University. http://purl.stanford.edu/qn935ty7877

Thomas, Aaron C. 2021. "Infelicities." *Journal of Dramatic Theory and Criticism* 35, no. 2: 13–25.

Tisdall, Caroline. 1979. *Joseph Beuys*. New York: Solomon R. Guggenheim Museum.

Todosijević, Raša. 1983. "Nova umetnička praksa: performans." *Treći program* 56: 57–61.

Tournereau, Michel. 1999. "Philippe Thomas: Sujet à discrétion." In *Sur un lieu commun et autres textes*, edited by Alexis Vaillant, 49–65. Geneva: MAMCO and Presses Universitaires de Rennes.

Tsaconas, Hella E. 2016. "Bad Math: Calculating Bodily Capacity in Cassils's *Cuts: A Traditional Sculpture*." *Women & Performance* 26, nos. 2–3: 197–207.

Turner, Fred. 2013. *The Democratic Surround: Multimedia & American Liberalism from World War II to the Psychedelic Sixties*. Chicago: University of Chicago Press.

Ursprung, Philip. 2011. "Anarchitecture: Gordon Matta-Clark and the Legacy of the 1970s." In *Laurie Anderson Trisha Brown Gordon Matta-Clark: Pioneers of the Downtown Scene. New York 1970s*, edited by Lydia Yee, 133–142. New York: Prestel.

Vaillant, Alexis, ed. 1999. *Sur un lieu commun et autres textes*. Geneva: Presses Universitaires de Rennes.

Varney-Carron, Georges. 2000. "Sur un lieu commun / On a Commonplace." Interview by Éric Duyckaerts. In *Metti la tua forma: Nella storia dell'arte*, Diserens, Corrine, 63–70. Barcelona: Museum d'Art Contemporani de Barcelona.

Vincent, Rickey. 1996. *Funk: The Music, the People, and the Rhythm of the One*. New York: St. Martin's Griffin.

Vincente, Mercedes, ed. 2008. *Darcy Lange: Study of an Artist at Work*. New Plymouth, New Zealand: Govett-Brewster Art Gallery.

Wetzler, Rachel. 2014. "Walter Benjamin: Writings after Death." *Los Angeles Review of Books*, 21 April. https://lareviewofbooks.org/article/walter-benjamin-writings-death/, last accessed 20 December 2021.

Watts, Jerry Gafio. 2001. *Amiri Baraka: The Politics and Art of a Black Intellectual*. New York: New York University Press.

Weheliye, Alexander. 2014. *Habeas Viscus: Racializing Assemblages, Biopolitics, and Black Feminist Theories of the Human*. Durham, NC: Duke University Press.

Willats, Stephen. 1969. "The Artist as a Structurist of Behaviour." *Control*, no. 5.

Willats, Stephen. 1973. "International Science-Art News." *Leonardo*, no. 6: 166.

Willats, Stephen. [1973] 2010. *The Artist as an Instigator of Changes in Social Cognition and Behaviour*. London: Occasional Papers.

Willats, Stephen. 1974a. "Edinburgh Project: Stephen Willats Discusses His Social Model Construction Project." *Art and Artists*, January, 6–9.

Willats, Stephen. 1974b. "The Externalisation of Models in Art Practice." *Control*, no. 8: 10–14.

Willats, Stephen. 1976. *Life Codes and Behaviour Parameters: Related Works and Texts*. Nottingham: Midland Group Gallery.

Woodard, Komozi. 1999. *A Nation within a Nation: Amiri Baraka (LeRoi Jones) and Black Power Politics*. Chapel Hill: University of North Carolina Press.

Worringer, Wilhelm. [1908] 1997. *Abstraction and Empathy: A Contribution to the Psychology of Style*. Translated by Michael Bullock. Chicago: Ivan R. Dee.

Wright, Amy Nathan. "A Philosophy of Funk: The Politics and Pleasure of a Parliafunkadelicment Thang!" In *The Funk Era and Beyond: New Perspectives on Black Popular Culture*, edited by Tony Bolden, 33–50. New York: Palgrave Macmillan.

Wuggenig, Ulf. 2011. "An der goldenen Nabelschnur." *Texte zur Kunst* 21, no. 83: 56–75.

Young, T. R. and Garth Massey. 1978. "The Dramaturgical Society: A Macroanalytic Approach to Dramaturgical Analysis." *Qualitative Sociology* 1: 78–98.

Žižek, Slavoj. 1989. *The Sublime Object of Ideology*. London: Verso.

Žižek, Slavoj. 1993. *Tarrying with the Negative: Kant, Hegel, and the Critique of Ideology*. Durham, NC: Duke University Press.

Žižek, Slavoj, ed. 1994. *Mapping Ideology*. London: Verso.

Zuboff, Shoshana. 2019. *The Age of Surveillance Capitalism: The Fight for a Human Future at the New Frontier of Power*. New York: Public Affairs.

Index

Note: Page numbers are given in Roman type, illustration numbers in italic type.